# ŽIŽEK ON RACE

## ALSO AVAILABLE AT BLOOMSBURY

*Continental Philosophy and the Palestinian Question: Beyond the Jew and the Greek*, Zahi Zalloua

*Sex and the Failed Absolute*, Slavoj Žižek

*Disparities*, Slavoj Žižek

*Antigone*, Slavoj Žižek

# ŽIŽEK ON RACE

Toward an Anti-Racist Future

## Zahi Zalloua

**Foreword by Slavoj Žižek**

BLOOMSBURY ACADEMIC
LONDON • NEW YORK • OXFORD • NEW DELHI • SYDNEY

BLOOMSBURY ACADEMIC
Bloomsbury Publishing Plc
50 Bedford Square, London, WC1B 3DP, UK
1385 Broadway, New York, NY 10018, USA

BLOOMSBURY, BLOOMSBURY ACADEMIC and the Diana logo are trademarks
of Bloomsbury Publishing Plc

First published in Great Britain 2020

Cover design by Egbert Clement

A catalogue record for this book is available from the British Library.

A catalog record for this book is available from the Library of Congress.

ISBN: HB: 978-1-3500-9421-5
PB: 978-1-3500-9420-8
ePDF: 978-1-3500-9422-2
eBook: 978-1-3500-9423-9

Typeset by Newgen KnowledgeWorks Pvt. Ltd., Chennai, India
Printed and bound in Great Britain

To find out more about our authors and books visit www.bloomsbury.com
and sign up for our newsletters.

To Nicole

# CONTENTS

# ACKNOWLEDGMENTS

In many ways this current project grew out of my work on *Continental Philosophy and the Palestinian Question* (Bloomsbury, 2017). In that book I traced how the Palestinian question had historically been silenced by Continental philosophy and how it is now emerging as a concern for contemporary philosophers, including Judith Butler, Etienne Balibar, and Alain Badiou, as well as Slavoj Žižek. Going beyond the Jew and the Greek was my attempt to record and assess the ethical and political dilemmas involved in talking about Palestinians without falling into the classical opposition between Universalism and Particularism. To raise the question productively required first abandoning the ploy of folding the Palestinian cause under the umbrella of a humanist vision that downplays difference and power, and second, abandoning the reading of the Palestinian question as a reactive defense of a particular difference. This reading of difference always risks becoming fetishized—my difference is more important than yours, and so on. While writing the book, my sympathies clearly aligned with the partisans of difference—Derrida, Said, and Butler—but I was also becoming increasingly intrigued by Žižek's universalist intervention. His work offered a creative alternative to the abstract universalism championed by traditional humanism. My challenge in writing a book on Žižek was obvious from the start: how can I articulate a Žižekian position on race and racism when Žižek himself seems so disparagingly dismissive of identity politics and anything that smells of particularism?

*Žižek on Race* struggles with this question. But it wagers on the hermeneutic benefits of a Žižekian vantage point when it comes to tackling today's global challenges of race and racism in the "post-political" age of neoliberalism. It invites the reader to move beyond the fashionable dismissal of Žižek as too Eurocentric—too indebted to European philosophy and psychoanalysis—to truly understand and intervene on behalf of the victims of racism. *Žižek on Race* makes the case for the need to read Žižek, to carefully engage his provocative thoughts, even to read

Žižek as an anti-racist theorist in his own right—not only for what Žižek says about race and racism but also for what his ideas inspire and enable the rest of us engaged in the labor of critique to say about them.

Two particular events at Whitman College played an important role in shaping this book. In the spring of 2016, my colleague Shampa Biswas invited me to participate in a teach-in on Islamophobia and the racialization of US politics, and in the fall of 2017, shortly after Charlottesville, I joined colleagues at a similar event engaging the community in a dialogue about this tragedy. In preparing for both of these discussions, Žižek was constantly on my mind, pushing me to contest the liberal script of anti-racism and seek out an anti-racist critique that goes beyond the comfort of blaming the Islamophobe or neo-Nazi racist over there for all of our racial ills. Subsequently, in the classroom, I greatly benefited from my discussions with my Race and Ethnic Studies students. Their hunger for more—more theory, more nuance, more explanation, more critique—helped me fine-tune many of my ideas. At Whitman, I'm grateful for my conversations with Shampa Biswas, Aaron Bobrow-Strain, Matt Bost, Chetna Chopra, Arash Davari, Tarik Elseewi, Heather Hayes, Bruce Magnusson, Gaurav Majumdar, Lydia McDermott, and Lisa Uddin. Leah Koyle and Marlene Anderson contributed valuable research assistance. Outside of Whitman, I'm thankful to my brother Mounir's steadfast support of my work. I had the chance to share and test my ideas at numerous conferences and symposia. For the many fruitful encounters, I want to thank Jake Blevins, Andrew Cole, Jeffrey Di Leo, Peter Hitchcock, Christopher Langlois, Sophia McClennen, Paul Allen Miller, Christian Moraru, Brian O'Keeffe, Herman Rapaport, Robert Tally, and Harold Veeser. Particular thanks go to Peter Hitchcock, Ilan Kapoor, Randy LeBlanc, Brian O'Keeffe, and Robert Tally for diligently reading earlier versions of the manuscript. I'm grateful to Liza Thompson at Bloomsbury for her encouragement to pursue this project. I'm also deeply appreciative of Slavoj Žižek's willingness to write the Foreword to this book. As always, my greatest debt of gratitude belongs to Nicole Simek: her acumen is only matched by her generosity.

Portions of Chapter 1 appeared elsewhere in a revised form: "The Politics of Undeserved Happiness," *symplokē* 26, 1–2 (2018): 373–85. This project was supported in part by a Louis B. Perry Summer Research Grant.

# FOREWORD: THE IMPORTANCE OF THEORY

*Slavoj Žižek*

While I am immensely proud to be the topic of Zalloua's book, this same fact also fills me with a strange fear, a fear that prohibits me from directly engaging with its lines of argumentation, as if this would involve either patronizing arrogance or its mirror-image, false self-humiliation. All I am able to do here is to restate some general principles—and, in order to escape the deadlock I find myself in, I will begin with a joke.

Jews are gathered in a synagogue to publicly declare their failures. First, a mighty rabbi says: "Forgive me, god, I am nothing, not worthy of your attention!" After him, a rich merchant says: "Forgive me, god, I am a worthless nothing!" Then a poor ordinary Jew steps forward and says: "Forgive me, god, I am also nothing . . ." The rich merchant whispers to the rabbi: "Who does he think he is, this miserable guy, that he can also say he is nothing?" There is a deep insight in this joke: to "become nothing" requires the supreme effort of negativity, of tearing oneself off from the immersion into a cobweb of particular determinations. Such a Sartrean elevation of the subject into a void, a nothingness, is not a true Lacanian (or Hegelian) position: Lacan explains how, to do this, one has to find a support in a particular element that functions as a "less than nothing"—Lacan's name for it is *objet a*. Let's take a political example. The Politically Correct prohibition of asserting the particular identity of White Men (as the model of oppression of others), although it presents itself as the admission of their guilt, confers on them a central position: this very prohibition to assert their particular identity makes them into the universal–neutral medium, the place from which the truth about the others' oppression is accessible. And this is why white liberals so gladly indulge in self-flagellation: the true aim of their activity is not really to help the others but the *Lustgewinn* brought about by their self-accusations, the feeling of their own moral superiority over others. The problem with the self-denial of white identity is not that it goes too far but that it does not go far enough: while its enunciated content seems radical, its position of enunciation remains that of a privileged universality. So yes, they declare themselves to be "nothing," but this very renunciation to a (particular) something is sustained by the surplus enjoyment of their moral superiority, and we can easily imagine the scene from the quoted Jewish joke repeated here: when, say, a black guy says "I am also nothing!," a white guy whispers to his (white) neighbor: "Who does this guy think he is to be able to claim that he is also nothing?" But we can easily move from imagination to reality here. A decade or so ago, at a round table in New York where the Politically Correct Leftists predominated, I remember a couple of big names among "critical thinkers" one after the other engaging in self-flagellation, blaming Judeo-Christian tradition for our evils, pronouncing scathing verdicts on "Eurocentrism," and so on. Then, unexpectedly, a black activist joined the debate and also made some critical remarks about the limitations of black Muslim movement; hearing this, the white "critical thinkers" exchanged annoyed glances whose message was something like "Who does this guy think he is that he can also claim he is a worthless nothing?"

This anecdote makes it clear what the problem is with fake Left-liberal "antiracists." In their zeal for identity politics, they all support the effort of the black communities to retain and strengthen their cultural identity; they worry that black communities will lose their specific identity and get drowned in the global universe defined by white categories, a world in which they are a priori in a subordinated position. However, the reason white liberal "anti-racists" support black identity is a much more murky affair: what they really fear is that the blacks will leave behind their particular identity, assume "being nothing" and formulate *their own universality* different from the universality imposed by the hegemonic white culture and politics.

This, of course, does not mean that, in order to reach universality, blacks have to erase their particular identity: we are dealing here with the Hegelian "determinate negation" where the negation (of a particular identity) bears the mark of what it negates. This is the paradox of what Hegel called "concrete universality," and the topic of Black Lives Matter (dealt with admirably at the end of Zalloua's book) exemplifies it perfectly. The common-sense liberal reproach to "Black Lives Matter" is: do not all lives, independently of the color of the skin, matter? Why should black lives matter more than others? The Hegelian answer is that while this is in principle true, in today's concrete constellation, the violence to which blacks are exposed is not just a neutral case of social violence but its privileged, exemplary case—to reduce it to a particular case of violence means to ignore the true nature of violence in our society. This is the Hegelian "concrete universality": we can formulate the universal dimension only if we focus on a particular case which exemplifies it.

The same goes for the authentic Leftist critique of some tendencies in MeToo and LGBT+ movement. Many liberal commentators who like to distance themselves from the "excesses" of Political Correctness miss the point. These (often ridiculous) excesses are not indications that the revolutionary zeal went too far—on the contrary, they clearly indicate that the revolution was redirected and lost its radical edge. A black woman, Tarana Burke, who created the MeToo campaign more than a decade ago, observed in a recent critical note that in the years since the movement began, it deployed an unwavering obsession with the perpetrators—a cyclical circus of accusations, culpability, and indiscretions: "We are working diligently so that the popular narrative about MeToo shifts from what it is. We have to shift the narrative that it's a gender war, that it's anti-male, that it's men against women, that it's only for a certain type of person—that it's for white, cisgender, heterosexual, famous women."[1] In short, one should struggle to refocus MeToo onto the daily suffering of millions of ordinary working women and housewives. This emphatically can be done—for example, in South Korea, MeToo exploded in tens of thousands of ordinary women demonstrating against their sexual exploitation. Only through the link between the two "contradictions," sexual exploitation and economic exploitation, can we mobilize the majority: men should not be portrayed only as potential rapists, they should be made aware that their violent domination over women is mediated by their experience of economic impotence. The truly radical MeToo is not about women against men but also about the prospect of their solidarity.

Furthermore, the antagonism that cuts across MeToo and LGBT+ movements is not to be reduced to an external pressure of "class struggle" and economic exploitation on the sphere of sexual relations. An antagonism also operates at the very heart of the LGBT+ movement— suffice it to recall *The Girl* (Lucas Dhont, 2018), a Belgian film about a 15-year-old girl, born in the body of a boy, who dreams of becoming a ballerina.[2] Why did this film trigger such ferocious reactions in some powerful post-modern post-gender circles? The predominant LGBT+ doctrine encourages the rejection of biologically and/or socially given gender identities and advocates the individual's self-acquaintance and politicization of its identities: "You are free to define yourself as how you feel yourself! And everybody shall accept you as how you define yourself." This, exactly, is what happens in the film: the teenage protagonist is fully encouraged to adopt "the way she feels," her identity; she is encouraged to improve "point" in ballet (despite very strict and difficult classical ballet training standards), her doctor prescribes hormones, the ballet instructor gives private lessons to her, the father continuously asks her about her problems to encourage her to talk, she is even encouraged to elucidate her fantasies to her psychologist and to her father . . . and we see things getting worse . . . Many LGBT+ activists attacked the film ferociously for its focus on the traumatic aspects of gender transition, for its depiction of the painful details of gender change, claiming that it functions as a pornographic horror show—although the ballerina on whose life the movie is based defended it staunchly, insisting that it portrays perfectly her troubles. In these critiques, we are obviously dealing with a conflict between the painful reality of gender transitions and its official sanitized version, which puts all the blame on social pressure.

The point of these short introductory remarks is the importance of general philosophical ideas and distinctions even for concrete critical and political work. And this is why I sincerely admire Zalloua's book: it is a living and practical book of how conceptual analysis is a *sine qua non* of correct political interventions.

# INTRODUCTION: THE POST-POLITICAL IS THE POST-RACIAL

*Race is the child of racism, not the father.*

**TA-NEHISI COATES[1]**

*The political (the space of litigation in which the excluded can protest the wrong or injustice done to them) foreclosed from the Symbolic then returns in the Real in the guise of new forms of racism.*

**SLAVOJ ŽIŽEK[2]**

The events of Charlottesville, Virginia, August 12, 2017, serve as a tragic reminder that we are not living in an age of postraciality. A color-blind, raceless society remains at best a distant future, at worst an ideological idea that dangerously distorts how we understand race and racism. At one level, what Charlottesville revealed has been well documented: the persistence of racism in the United States, spurred today by the Alt-Right. The neo-Nazi rally in Charlottesville showed the obstinacy of racism in its unabashed display of anti-Semitism, Islamophobia, antiblackness, and anti-immigrant sentiment. We heard from the protesters that "Jews will not replace us."[3] This chant sends us back to Nazi Germany: it recycles and reactivates the myth of the Jewish plot (the notion that Jews are running society), as well as Aryan supremacist tropes. Transported to contemporary American society, this white supremacist racism targets Jews and other figures deemed too powerful, too threatening, and, most importantly, responsible for society's ills: blacks, so-called "illegals," and Muslims.

We might think of this hatred as a racist cocktail of old anti-Jewish conspiracy theories mixed with fantasies of threats from nonwhites along with backlashes against the civil rights movement and ongoing globalization. The chant "Jews will not replace us" smacks of the kind of racial thinking we can also hear in assertions that blacks and "illegals" will not take "our" (white) jobs and that Sharia law will not replace the US constitution. In their painful familiarity, the events of Charlottesville feel on the one hand like a dangerous resurgence, a return of a racism easily named and described—though, clearly, not so easily combatted—and on the other hand, for those more optimistic about different futures, like a remnant, a remainder or final gasp of a long-discredited and socially condemned pseudo-biologism. Viewed from either of these positions, Charlottesville, for anti-racism activists, primarily raises questions of tactics—how can separatist thinking be shifted? Why has racial division persisted? In what ways have previous tactics succeeded and failed?

Yet, attuned to the workings of ideology in a putatively post-ideological world, Slavoj Žižek warns us not to take the culprits of Charlottesville as a paradigm for today's racism—as the vulgar exception to our post-racial, post-ideological reality—since to do so is to run the risk of limiting how we imagine the face and challenge of racism. The familiarity of white separatism and the arguments against it could give white liberal America a false sense of enlightened security: a false belief that mainstream Americans are not like these extremists. Even if this mainstream spoke with one voice denouncing the open racism of white supremacists, it would not be enough. We should not too quickly pat ourselves on the back, turning our disgust into pleasure ("a paradoxical pleasure procured by displeasure"[4]), into an index or proof of our postraciality. We must instead ask critically, as David Theo Goldberg does, "What racial work is the postracial doing, what racist expression is it enabling, legitimating, rationalizing?"[5] Seeing racism exclusively or primarily as an anomaly, a problem with bad apples (white extremists and fringe groups), at best distorts the ordinary social reality of racism and, at worst, makes us complicit with everyday racism, with what Žižek, following Sara Ahmed, calls "civil racism."[6] Civil racism is racism with a smile. It is racism in the age of the postracial. It does not spit in your face or argue that you are biologically inferior. Rather, today's Western liberal society pays lip service to tolerance, diversity, and alternative ways of living. It shuns fundamentalism, dogmatism, and hate speech. It promotes democracy and inclusivity, and purports to accommodate, respect, and even celebrate cultural difference (the civil racist loves ethnic foods, samples global music and cinema, etc.). But what this society really wants from others—that is, from nonwhites—is measured exposure, docility, and conformity, a taste of difference from a comfortable distance. What it desires, in short, is *decaffeinated* alterity.[7]

Because Žižek has not carried out a systematic study of race to date, his repeated engagements with the question, dispersed throughout his work, risk going unseen. Yet Žižek's perspicacious comments on racism in its myriad contemporary expressions—anti-Semitism, Islamophobia, scapegoating, popular nationalism, anti-refugee sentiment, Eurocentrism, the War on Terror, neocolonialism, and rioting, for example—create productive friction and pathways for engaging with the problematic of race in a global and globalizing world.[8] This study sets off down these paths, putting Žižek's work in critical dialogue with multiculturalism, deconstruction, postcolonial theory, Critical Race Theory, and Afro-Pessimism. It interrogates a number of problematics and case studies prevalent in critical race and anti-colonial studies that serve both to highlight the singular contribution of Žižek's thought to the analysis of the perplexities of race and racism within the United States and abroad, and also to extend his direct comments on the topic, developing more fully the unrealized potential of his thought.

From this critical dialogue emerge two central arguments this book advances: that enjoyment or *jouissance* is a key but often overlooked dimension of racism's affective appeal and that confronting and altering racism's violence requires infusing a philosophy of race with a negative dialectics[9] and a universalist or cosmopolitan sensibility.

## Race, Class, Violence

Like many leftist theorists concerned with race and racism, Žižek rejects the narrative of racial progress. He does so however without treating race "as an addendum,"[10] or racial tension as an epiphenomenon of ruthless capitalism. Žižek's distinctive Lacanian–Marxist framework rejects the interpretation of racism as "a secondary appendix to the 'real' economic struggle," as a mere symptom of material conditions; he thus nuances the priority of class over race, and economics over culture found in classic Marxist arguments. Žižek does not fetishize class (a frequent but mistaken objection to his argument).[11] Quite the opposite, Žižek explicitly warns against it: "Class difference itself can be the fetish which obfuscates class struggle."[12] What Žižek foregrounds is not class essentialism but class struggle in all its dynamism and complexities. The point is not to displace race with class but to enlarge the former's explanatory force by accounting for the dynamics of power in the latter.[13] What is needed is a recognition of the fundamental antagonism and shared struggle that cuts across capitalist societies:

> The formula of revolutionary solidarity is not "let us tolerate our differences," it is not a pact of civilizations, but a pact of struggles which cut across civilizations, a pact between what, in each civilization, undermines its identity from within, fights against its oppressive kernel. What unites us is the same struggle. A better formula would thus be: in spite of our differences, we can identify the basic antagonism or antagonistic struggle, in which we are both caught; so let us share our intolerance, and join forces in the same struggle.[14]

Žižek cautions against committing too quickly to what he views as pseudo-conflicts (such as the Brexit vote, or debates in France over the Yellow Vests[15] and economic insecurity), urging us instead to focus on the world's inherent antagonisms:

> In all these cases, although one might slightly prefer one side to the other, the ultimate stance should be one of indifference, best rendered by Stalin who, when asked in the late 1920s which deviation is worse, the Right one or the Leftist one, snapped back: "They are both worse!" Is there still the potential for true change beneath these pseudo-struggles? There is, since the function of these pseudo-struggles is precisely to block the explosion of the true ones.[16]

The struggle for anti-racism avoids becoming a pseudo-struggle when it effectively politicizes its claim, when it refuses the neoliberal framework of the post-political and actively works to destabilize and eliminate the naturalized violence of global capitalism.

That violence and racism go hand in hand hardly seems to require elaboration. We all know that racism is violent and that violence is at times racist in nature. And yet, as Žižek points out, how we imagine violence today is often mystified and overdetermined by cultural discourses. What is typically perceived as violence in our cultural imaginary is what Žižek calls "subjective violence": it is the violence that is "performed by a clearly identifiable agent . . . [and] . . . is seen as a perturbation of the 'normal,' peaceful state of things."[17] As a necessary conceptual supplement to our understanding of violence, Žižek adds "objective violence," which he then divides into, first, "symbolic violence" (the violence of language as the hegemonic imposition of a given universe of meaning) and second, "systemic violence" (such as the violence done by capitalism, which becomes a naturalized, smooth-functioning background force, masking its oppressive exacerbation of inequalities). "Objective violence is invisible," Žižek maintains, "since it sustains the very zero-level standard against which we perceive something as subjectively violent."[18] As Peter Hitchcock notes, objective violence "overdetermines normalcy," against which any framed act of subjective violence can then "be posed as extraordinary, spectacular, crazy and out of joint."[19] An effective account of violence would thus not simply complement a critique of subjective violence but demonstrate how a concern for subjective violence, in effect, helps *to sustain* the existence of this more subtle and insidious type.

Where does racism fit in Žižek's conceptual mapping of violence? Subjective violence can easily be invoked to explain racism. The events of Charlottesville exemplify subjective violence, as well as the manipulative lure of its explanatory power. The victims and the perpetrators are clearly discernable. The mediatized events came to function as a spectacle, an object of fascination, a source of moral outrage *and* obscene enjoyment, authorizing, as it were, their liberal viewers to hate the haters. Most importantly, the events register racism as a disturbance of our postracial peaceful state of things, identifying the agents of racism exclusively with the individual neo-Nazi attackers and their sympathizers.

If in media culture, racism as a problem of subjective violence is by far the dominant script, Žižek for his part tends to align racism with objective violence in both its symbolic and systemic forms. The impact of symbolic violence on racialized minorities was made starkly clear by Frantz Fanon in *Black Skin, White Masks*. Living in an enclosed racist universe of meaning, being habitually exposed to the violence of hegemonic language affects your ontology, your "socio-symbolic being."[20] Fanon describes the devastating effects of being hailed in a racist world ("'Dirty nigger!' or simply, 'Look! a Negro!'"), an experience that hollowed out his being, evacuating his consciousness and reducing him to the status of an inert object: "I came into this world anxious to uncover the meaning of things, my soul desirous to be at the origin of the world, and here I am an object among other objects."[21] As Achille Mbembe also pointedly observes, "the act of violation [*le viol*] often begins with language."[22]

It is for this reason that Simone de Beauvoir described the condition of blacks in the American South as one of inferiority, for symbolic violence degrades one's own ontology. Defending Beauvoir from a recent liberal detractor who objected to her comments,[23] Žižek takes issue with this critique, viewing the solution proposed as inadequate: "[The critic's] solution, propelled by the care to avoid racist claims on the factual inferiority of blacks, is to relativise their inferiority into a matter of interpretation and judgement by white racists, and distance it from the question of their very being."[24] The claim—that blacks *are* inferior to whites—can appear quite shocking, coming from a leftist thinker who is so attentive to the processes of marginalization and othering. But Beauvoir's interpretation of blacks' inferiority cuts much deeper. Beauvoir's interpretation paradoxically warns against the limits of interpretation, of the danger of remaining at the level of ideas when one tries to refute racism. The label of inferiority is not merely a subjective judgment on the part of the racist that liberals can dismiss simply by claiming it is not true, that blacks, in reality, are equal to whites. By insisting that blacks *are* inferior, Beauvoir is also claiming that representation and reality cannot be so easily separated from one another. The antidote to symbolic violence is not a liberal anti-racism at the level of ideas. An anti-racist struggle cannot limit itself to demystifying ideas, to claiming that blacks are equal (ontologically) and inferiorized (ontically) and that people just fail to see that they are.[25] This, for Beauvoir, Fanon, and Žižek, is to underappreciate the "performative efficiency"[26] of racist interpellation and rhetoric.

Racism is also an expression of "systemic violence" when it takes the form of exclusion and silence whereby only the beneficiaries of global capitalism can freely and expectedly register their pain as pain. Developed Western countries experience violence (via, for example, terrorist attacks) as "a momentary disturbance"—as manageable eruptions of subjective violence—whereas Third World countries endure violence as "a permanent fact of life."[27] Systemic violence epitomizes the daily life of the globally discounted and neglected. In this racial capitalism, globalization's constitutive others experience "uninterrupted terror and brutality," absent any ready international expression of solidarity (as contrasted, for example, with the slogan *Je suis Paris* after the November 13, 2015 Paris attacks).[28] Judith Butler has also commented on this absence in mainstream media discourse: "Mourning seems fully restricted within the national frame. The nearly 50 dead in Beirut from the day before are barely mentioned, and neither are the 111 in Palestine killed in the last weeks alone, or the scores in Ankara."[29] But whereas Butler articulates her political critique primarily in ethical terms, lamenting the West's inability to perform what she dubs "transversal grief,"[30] its failure to relate to others as vulnerable and grievable beings, Žižek formulates his ethical critique in squarely political terms, faulting the ever-expanding logic of capital: global capitalism's unprecedented reach introduces "a radical class division across the entire globe, separating those protected by the sphere from those outside its cover."[31] A sense of urgency, of the pressing need for true alternatives to the false choice between different forms of capitalism that we are presented with, guides Žižek's thoughts: "I think today the world is asking for a real alternative. Would you like to live in a world where the only alternative is either Anglo-Saxon neoliberalism or Chinese-Singaporean capitalism with Asian values? What I'm afraid of is that with this capitalism with Asian values, we get a capitalism that is much more efficient and dynamic than our Western capitalism. But I don't share the hope of my liberal friends. The marriage between capitalism and democracy is over."[32] Today's anti-democratic capitalism gives the lie to the notion that capitalism and liberalism necessarily go hand in hand and propagate together the conditions for (formal) equality. "Capitalism with Asian values" is "productive and it functions even better. But it doesn't generate a long-term demand for democracy."[33]

An anti-racist critique must unflinchingly interrogate this "totalitarian capitalism."[34] Toward that end, Žižek moves to politicize the global economy: Why are some more susceptible than others to systemic violence or the traumatic Real of capital? What legitimizes our current socio-economic barrier? Žižek contests this separation of the "Inside from the Outside,"[35] the elevated from the devalued, not by invoking an ethics of vulnerability but by fully avowing our complicity in this global catastrophe[36] and by challenging racialized social narratives of antagonism (Westerners versus refugees, white blue-collar workers versus illegal immigrants, etc.) that de-politicize struggle. Such narratives remove this catastrophe from "public scrutiny and debate"[37]—construing it too narrowly as a problem of tolerance or dialogue (we *ought* to be more open to cultural others and their ways of life; isn't "an enemy someone whose story [we] have not heard"[38]?), while neglecting questions of inequality, exploitation, and justice. As a result, what goes unheeded are ideology and its insidious workings, the "true wall"[39] separating "us" and "them."

A political intervention that would adequately confront this wall must cultivate a universalist or cosmopolitan sensibility. Žižek endorses, after Immanuel Kant, the "constitutive 'homelessness'" of philosophy,[40] its perpetual state of out-of-jointness, its unwillingness to conform to the popular beliefs and suppositions of the day. In "What is Enlightenment?" Kant argued that while individuals in an official capacity have to obey orders (in the domain of the "private use of reason"), individuals (as would-be-philosophers) must not compromise on their "public use of reason," that is, they must not relinquish their right to address their views, to speak as "*a scholar . . . before the entire public of the reading world*."[41] As Žižek notes, the public use of reason, "in a kind of short-circuit, by-passing the mediation of the particular, directly participates in the universal," enabling the individual to be cosmopolitan, to break with the "communal-institutional order of one's particular identification."[42] Žižek's universality is a universality grounded in the "part of no-part," a notion he freely borrows from Jacques Rancière.[43] The "part of no-part" stands for the others who are systematically excluded, disprivileged, and racialized by society's laws and norms, falling outside the liberal and humanist umbrella. As a given order's constitutive outsiders, they stand for "true universality"; since their interests are not pre-determined by their subject positions, when they seek to remedy wrongs, they speak to universal concerns (the feminist chant "women rights are human rights" captures this sentiment). Not attached to the status quo in the same libidinal and ideological way, they hold the promise of transformative change—of enacting politics as such. They articulate and affirm what Étienne Balibar calls *égaliberté*, equality-freedom, as an unconditional demand.[44]

If race is the child, and not the father, of racism—as Ta-Nehisi Coates poetically notes—then race *is* the product of racist ideology. Race does not exist as a biological given but is posited retrospectively as the condition of possibility for racism. Any anti-racist discourse, then, must strive not to naturalize/ontologize race or race-thinking[45] and thereby perpetuate that which it seeks to contest.[46] Negativity in the form of interpretive skepticism—Žižek's propensity to introduce an infectious, "fundamental doubt" about what passes for common sense in one's social reality[47]—dovetails with the public use of reason and attests to this need to keep the category of "race" out of joint, open, less fixed, and away from identitarian investments. This need underpins Žižek's general suspicion of identity politics and his turn to Pauline universalism, a universalism which is, in Alain Badiou's bold formulation, "*indifferent to differences.*"[48] "The task of philosophy," as Žižek defines it, "is not to solve problems but to redefine them; not to answer questions, but to raise the proper question."[49] Žižek's philosophical inventiveness in dealing with race lies in this critical negativity, in his indefatigable will to raise the *proper question*, in the ways he makes us realize that how we perceive or conceptualize the problem of racism may in fact be part of the problem.

## Ideology, Fantasy, Enjoyment

In conceptualizing racism (old and new) from a Žižekian vantage point, this study highlights the manipulative role of fantasy in the functioning of ideology. It contests liberal society's (aspirational claim to) postraciality, its belief in the post-political (and the former as a sign of the latter), while urgently endeavoring to find ways to traverse the fantasy of postraciality by taking up anti-racism as a universal cause.

While insisting on the presence and relevance of ideology, Žižek redefines this key Marxist concept as signifying more than falsification or distortion. Critically assessing racist ideology or racial projects cannot follow the exclusive path of cognitive reasoning. Ideology critique or anti-racist thinking is not simply about determining the truth or falsity of a given matter but also about evaluating its framing, packaging, or staging for comprehension. Ideology critique must not settle for discerning the truth or falsehood of facts. Even in the "post-truth"[50] age of Trump, insisting on facts is not in and of itself a *sufficient* antidote to ideology. Rather, this critique must dwell on their interpretation:

> If you don't change the ideological background, facts alone don't do the job.[51]

> The starting point of the critique of ideology has to be full acknowledgement of the fact that it is easily possible to *lie in the guise of truth.*[52]

That is to say, ideology critique should not limit its object to the conscious beliefs of individuals (*ideology as false consciousness*). Ideology operates most frequently at the level of the unconscious, soliciting and securing our libidinal investment: "the fundamental level of ideology . . . is not of an illusion masking the real state of things but that of an (unconscious) fantasy structuring our social reality itself."[53] Racist fantasies teach us to see the social world as always already racially classified, nurturing implicit bias—locking individuals (would-be racists) into their unconscious patterns of judgment and behavior, encouraging and ensuring, in short, toxic relationality with racialized others. They teach us what's wrong (why we aren't enjoying) so as to keep alive "the possibility of enjoyment."[54] To paraphrase Beauvoir, you're not born racist, you unconsciously learn/desire to become one.

At the macro-level, ideology naturalizes and legitimizes as it conceals processes of racialization and capitalist relations of power and domination. Nearly three decades ago, Fredric Jameson alerted us to the dangerous and alarming ways neoliberal ideology infiltrates not only how we conceptualize the economic field but also how we understand our place within that field: "'The market is in human nature' is the proposition that cannot be allowed to stand unchallenged; in my opinion, it is the most crucial terrain of ideological struggle in our time."[55] More recently, echoing Jameson, Žižek has expressed a sense of urgency mixed with dismay at the cognitive state of the public at large, noting how "it seems easier to imagine the 'end of the world' than a far more modest change in the mode of production."[56] Accepting capitalism is taken as a sign of our maturity and realism: "*Today's predominant form of ideological 'closure' takes the precise form of a mental block which prevents us from imagining a fundamental social change, in the interests of a 'realistic' and 'mature' attitude.*"[57] Neoliberal ideology has thus thoroughly naturalized itself—appearing to its defenders and dissenters alike as the only game in town. As the argument goes, global capitalism may not be perfect—*but what else is really out there as an alternative?*[58]

The naturalization of meaning—when a contingent meaning passes for common sense, when it is presented as inevitable, beyond contestation—is thus more or less synonymous with the scene of ideology.[59] But as Žižek argues, we cannot conclude "that the only non-ideological position is to renounce the very notion of extra-ideological reality and accept that all we are dealing with are symbolic fictions, the plurality of discursive universes, never 'reality'—*such a quick, slick 'postmodern' solution . . . is ideology par excellence.*"[60] Countering the complacent constructivist position (there is no extra-discursive, no extra-ideological reality) does not mean moving toward the "post-political," which would be the pinnacle of "ideological misconception,"[61] but rather recalling that ideology *does* falter, that the field of ideology cannot be totalized: "ideology is not all,"[62] no ideological system is ever foolproof.

Moreover, what is deemed ideological is not restricted to the thoughts that a subject might entertain, but applies to the category of the subject itself. This foundational and cherished category of all liberals and humanists turns out to be an ideological construction, the effect of what Louis Althusser calls interpellation. You are first an individual, then you become a subject endowed with agency: "*all ideology hails or interpellates concrete individuals as concrete subjects.*"[63] Your emergence as a subject is predicated on your recognizing yourself as a subject when you are hailed by another (Althusser's paradigmatic example is the police officer who calls out to you, *demanding* your response/confirmation). Shaping how people understand their relationship to society, ideology through interpellation humanizes the social world. Ideology discloses a meaningful world, in which there is a place for you, where you count, where you have rights, and where your voice matters.

An eye attuned to racism might of course point out that the target of this interpellation is the privileged, white male individual of liberal discourse. The excluded, often racialized others can only experience this interpellation as an intensification of their alienation—a reminder that they do not matter, that they are disposable, and so forth. But this is where Žižek's investment in universalism proves critically resourceful for addressing and redressing the violence of racist ideology. He turns to the example of Haitian revolutionaries who "misread" the Declaration of the Rights of Man as meant for them. Their *misreading*, as Žižek stresses, "had explosive emancipatory consequences," radically democratizing and expanding the meaning of "human rights": "Human rights were 'really meant' to be accepted only by white men of property, but their universal form was their truth. It was thus the first interpellation which was wrong, but the true interpellation could only actualize itself through the false one, as its secondary misreading."[64] In *politicizing* human rights the Haitian revolutionaries found and brought forth the universal within their particular plight—their revolution "came to stand for something more than itself,"[65] and also proved emphatically that *racist ideology is not all*.

In pursuit of effective modes of resistance—of inventive ways to energize the engine of critique in our post-political and post-racial world—Žižek opts to rewrite Marx's saying from *Das Kapital,* "They do not know it, but they are doing it,"[66] reconfiguring its psychoanalytic bases and implications by highlighting the problem of disavowal: "They know that, in their activity, they are following an illusion, but still they are doing it."[67] We are "fetishists in practice, not in theory."[68] Belief supersedes knowledge.[69] For example, we know that race is a social construct, but nonetheless we act as if it were a biological given. As Derek Hook avers,

> This understanding of fetishistic disavowal reminds us again of the limitations of the myth of racism as mere ignorance: one can repeatedly challenge racists with the proof of (biological/genetic) racial non-difference in all the ways that matter, without making the slightest dent in their racist perceptions, because, after all, they have already acknowledged that race makes no difference; they just opt anyway to act as if it does.[70]

We are thus constructivists in theory but ontologists in practice when it comes to blackness. Philosophers such as Kwame Anthony Appiah and Robert Gooding-Williams who simply dismiss race as an illusion or myth not supported by science do not appreciate the fetishist allure of race.[71] Žižek's critical task consists of exposing such a disavowal on the part of the allegedly post-ideological subject of late capitalism.

Žižek's critique of ideology takes its inspiration from Virgil's saying, "Dare to disturb the underground of the unspoken underpinnings of our everyday lives."[72] What must be disturbed is fantasy—fantasy understood not as a flight from reality, but as a support for reality. As Lacan explains: "Everything we are allowed to approach by way of reality remains rooted in fantasy."[73] Ideology's grip on its subjects lies in its ability to colonize our fantasies. A critique of ideology (racist or otherwise) must begin by disturbing such fantasies, that is, by critically reframing the relation of fantasy to reality: "If we subtract fantasy from reality, then reality itself loses its consistency and disintegrates. To choose between 'either accepting reality or choosing fantasy' is wrong: if we really want to change or escape our social reality, *the first thing to do is change our fantasies that make us fit this reality.*"[74] Moving the underground of our fantasies is a necessary prerequisite for the transformation of reality.[75]

Racist ideological fantasies operate most frequently at the level of the unconscious, soliciting and securing our libidinal investment and passionate attachments. For this crucial reason, Žižek's observations help to reorient our critical attention to racism's affective pull and fantasies, to the desires and enjoyment that it effectively provides, (re)produces, and satisfies in its believers (the enjoyment of racializing others, of scapegoating the defenseless or blaming others for the theft of one's own enjoyment) and critics (the enjoyment of believing that one is not racist—the libidinal satisfaction of hating racists!—of believing that one is postracial, tolerant, kind, and so on).

## Anti-Racism and the Logic of the "Non-All"

To truly intervene in the symbolic order, Žižek frequently turns to the Lacanian notion of the act. Unlike a *passage à l'acte*—which is not a genuine political act, but more often than not a sign of frustration and impotence (which thus poses no threat to the existing order of things)—the act succeeds in changing the coordinates of one's social being: "An act does not occur within the given horizon of what appears to be 'possible'—it redefines the very contours of what is possible (an act accomplishes what, within the given symbolic universe, appears to be 'impossible,' yet it changes its conditions so that it creates retroactively the conditions of its own possibility)."[76] An act seeks nothing less than to traverse the fantasy of the post-political: "because *the depoliticized economy is the disavowed 'fundamental fantasy' of postmodern politics*—a properly political *act* would necessarily entail the repoliticization of the economy: within a given situation, a gesture counts as an act only in so far as it disturbs ('traverses') its fundamental fantasy."[77] As an intervention, however, the act comes with no guarantee of success. A would-be act can always miss its target: "This lack of guarantee is what the critics cannot tolerate; they want an Act without risk—not without empirical risks, but without the much more radical 'transcendental risk' that the Act will not only simply fail, but radically misfire."[78] Without the possibility of radical failure, then, no act could ever take place. When a true act does happen, when the impossible is rendered possible, the subject of the act undergoes an ontological transformation; "you" are no longer the same as before, as you were prior to the act:

> The act differs from an active intervention (action) in that it radically transforms its bearer (agent): the act is not simply something

I "accomplish"—after the act, I'm literally "not the same as before."
In this sense, we could say that the subject "undergoes" the act
("passes through" it) rather than "accomplishes" it: in it, the subject is
annihilated and subsequently reborn (or not); i.e., the act involves a
kind of temporary eclipse, *aphanisis,* of the subject.[79]

As a locus of negativity, the act subverts the Symbolic and touches the
Real. It reconfigures the realm of possibilities; it creates a lack in social
reality, disclosing that the Symbolic is "non-all" (*pas-tout*).

In his use of the "non-all," Žižek is creatively drawing from Lacan's
"formulae of sexuation." Lacan defines sexuation in Seminar XX, *Encore,*
in terms of a fundamental difference in the structure of enjoyment.
"Masculine" and "feminine" do not refer to anatomical differences, but
to a subject's relation to the phallus. On the masculine side, we find
two formulae: (1) there is at least one x that says "no" to the phallic
function, and (2) all x are subject to the phallic function. Together
these state the masculine logic of exception—of law and its necessary
transgression. While all men are symbolically castrated (they are all
subject to the phallic function, the law, the big Other) due to their entry
into the symbolic order, into the realm of the signifier (the substitution
of things—including oneself—by words), there is always one "Man" who
does not sacrifice his *jouissance*, one Man who must remain immune to
the law of castration, holding on to the promise of a phantasmatic return
to the full plenitude of a pre-symbolic *jouissance*. For Lacan, the mythical
primal father of Freud's *Totem and Taboo* exemplifies such a figure. While
the primal father—who enjoyed all women at will, "achieving complete
satisfaction"[80]—had to be killed for the symbolic order to emerge, his
exceptional subject position persists in the cultural imaginary.

Žižek devalues the biological overtones of sexual difference,
underscoring the *logic* of Lacan's formulae of sexuation, so that any body
might very well occupy the position of the primal father. Lacan makes
this point explicit: the "relation between the subject and the phallus . . .
forms without regard to the anatomical distinction between the sexes."[81]
"Woman as exception"—that is, a biological woman with a male structure
of enjoyment—is precisely, Žižek proposes, the case of the merciless Lady
of courtly love:

As the exemplary case of the exception constitutive of the phallic
function, one usually mentions the fantasmatic, obscene figure of

the primordial father-*jouisseur* who was not encumbered by any prohibition and was as such able fully to enjoy all women. Does, however, the figure of the Lady in courtly love not fully fit these determinations of the primordial father? Is she not also a capricious Master who wants it all, i.e., who, herself not bound by any Law, charges her knight-servant with arbitrary and outrageous ordeals?[82]

This Lady—in comparison to all other women—operates or rather is *imagined* operating, outside social norms, whimsically transgressing society's moral codes.

Much of Žižek's innovative reading of the formulae of sexuation emerges in his commentary on the feminine side of Lacan's formulation. Here too we are confronted with two formulae: (1) there is no x that says "no" to the phallic function, and (2) not all x are subject to the phallic function. Unlike the masculine side, there is no claim of universality rooted in exception here, suggesting that woman (unlike Man) does not constitute a totality. If there is no exception that stands outside the system, then the system *as such* is never whole or complete. And because there is nothing of woman *outside* the Law (no constitutive exception), woman is also "non-all" *inside* of the symbolic order. Or, as Lacan glosses his own formulae, "Woman does not exist [*la femme n'existe pas*]."[83]

Harnessing the feminine logic of the "non-all" for a leftist politics, Žižek makes the case for an understanding of materialism (ontology, more generally) through Lacan's formulae of sexuation. Žižek points out that there are two ways of negating the statement that "material reality is all there is." Drawing on Kant's distinction between "negative judgment" and "infinite judgment," we could say that "material reality is not all there is" and "material reality is non-all." The former is a negative judgment in that it negates the predicate (implying some transcendent spiritual reality), whereas the latter is an infinite judgment that expresses the *non-all* of reality without suggesting any exception. We can see how Žižek aligns the Kantian infinite judgment with the feminine side of the formulae of sexuation. The feminine logic of the "non-all" reframes materialism, troubles its transparent, if not crude, metaphysics, captured by the simple slogan "material reality is all there is." Using the feminine formulae of sexuation, we get a less transparent, a less complete materialism: there is nothing which is not material reality *and* material reality is "non-all."[84] Materiality does not reflect the inert density of matter but is always traversed by an immanent antagonism, a fundamental disunity. Materiality needs consciousness or the symbolic to realize itself as materiality.[85] It is itself posited or generated retroactively. "For the materialist," Žižek adds, "the 'openness' goes all the way down, that is, necessity is not the underlying universal law that secretly regulates the chaotic interplay of appearances—it is the 'All' itself which is non-All, inconsistent, marked by an irreducible contingency."[86] Žižek characterizes his materialism as "dialectical," alerting us that "we should read the term 'dialectics' in the Greek sense of *dialektika* . . . not as a universal notion, but as 'dialectical [semiotic, political] matters,' as an inconsistent (non-All) mixture."[87]

Adopting and adapting it further, Žižek deploys the logic of the "non-all" in the context of ethics and politics to rethink the Real of subjectivity and otherness beyond the tired debate over essentialism versus constructivism. The "non-all" orients us not only to the harshness of being (the reality of the Real) but also compels us to take an interpretive stance appropriate to a being understood as *a becoming* (a being that lacks—"*there is no ontology of the real*"[88]), to a social reality that never coincides with the Real. Whereas the masculine logic does the work of ideology, projecting the racist fantasies of national unity, of personal and social wholeness—a plenitude of enjoyment, an original harmony, always seemingly under threat by some undeserving, racialized others (such as undocumented immigrants[89])—and thus suturing the symbolic order's inherent instability and discord, the feminine logic of the "non-all" delights in refuting society's phantasmatic and ideological pretentions, tirelessly registering society's immanent gap, incompleteness, and inconsistency, avowing reality's lack of inner peace,[90] the failure of symbolic identification (a reality that the masculine logic subsequently distorts).

Without the Real, with pure symbolic enclosure, no political act would thus ever be possible. There is politics as such only when there is a recognition of "the inconsistency and/or non-existence of the big Other—of the fact that there is no Other of the Other, no ultimate guarantee of the field of meaning."[91] Indeed, politics begins by insisting on the *gap* between the existing administered social order and the ontological lack that bolsters it. The political for Žižek is a contestation of the established order's positivity. It is "the space of litigation in which the excluded can protest the wrong or injustice done to them."[92] But when this space is eliminated in the Symbolic (as in the era of the post-political and its foreclosure of class struggle), it reemerges in the Real "in the guise of new forms of racism."[93] In combatting these "new forms of racism," Žižek's brand of anti-racism does not foster a Manichean reality of "blacks" versus "whites," producing race as an ontological category—it does not read white privilege, for example, as *the* cause for global injustice and inequalities. Rather, it engages in the *historical* struggle to (re)open the political within the Symbolic, focusing on what Paul Gilroy has described as the "complex machinery of inequality."[94]

Žižek constantly repeats Walter Benjamin's observation that "every fascism is a sign of failed revolution."[95] For Žižek, the blame for this failure lies with the Left and its "palliative damage-control measures within the global capitalist framework,"[96] with the Left's failure to argue for and insist on egalitarian justice and economic equality. Again the point here is not that xenophobia and racism, as manifestations of a burgeoning fascism, are secondary concerns but that the staging of the antagonism takes on a distorted face, when the real antagonism is externalized, for example, as a struggle between white blue-collar workers and illegal immigrants, as "a struggle for *domination* between *us* and *them*, those who cause antagonistic imbalance,"[97] those who are stealing our enjoyment, jeopardizing our pursuit of the American Dream. Similarly, liberals who see racism only as happening "over there," as a problem of an extremist fringe, eschew struggle in fetishizing Fascism; the figure of the neo-Nazi becomes for liberals the "new political fetish . . . in the simple Freudian sense of a fascinating image whose function is to obfuscate the true antagonism."[98] As we saw above with the reactions to the events of Charlottesville, an acknowledgement of racism in no way unsettled liberal America's commitment to global capitalism, to its aspirational ideal of "capitalism with a human face": a capitalism with more tolerance, more rights, more charity, and so forth—*but not a capitalism with less systemic violence.*

For this reason, to retain its purchase on social reality an anti-racist critique must take the form of a political act, break the spell of the post-political, and refuse the current democratic–liberal horizon as its destiny. Žižek argues against "abandon[ing] the horizon of radical change in favor of the prospect of multiple local 'practices of resistance.'"[99] A leftist critique cannot suspend or dilute its questioning of "the very foundations of capitalism as a global system," and must continue "to clearly articulate the limitation of the democratic political project."[100] It cannot be something that contents itself simply with working within the confines of the existing order. Such a critique will be effective only if it *"changes the very framework that determines how things work."*[101] Toward that end and such a future, Žižek submits the struggle against racism to an immanent critique, pushing the anti-racist fight beyond itself so that it can realize and live up to its emancipatory potential.[102] A Žižekian anti-racist critique "tarries with the negative" by practicing a skeptical hermeneutics that resists both the traps of postraciality and the lures of identity politics—which in their own ways fill the void in the self and the social, displacing or covering up the problem of economic exploitation (the Real of social antagonism). The chapters that follow approach Žižek and his interlocutors through such a hermeneutics, dwelling on the sparks struck up by this dialogue and the differences, gaps, and absences it points up.

Chapter 1, "Liberal Multiculturalism: From 'Checking Your Privilege' to 'Checking Our Fantasy,'" examines liberal multiculturalism's enthusiastic adoption of privilege theory as an interpretive framework correcting society's racial shortcomings, as an antidote to the plague of white privilege. While privilege theory offers liberal multiculturalism the tools to name society's racists and calls on its practitioners to curtail the unearned pleasures of their own privilege, liberal multiculturalism's faithful subjects are compensated with an enjoyment-in-sacrifice, an enjoyment-in-confession. At its base level, privilege theory provides you with the fantasy of intervention and action; it offers you criticism (attention to subjective violence) without critique (occluding objective violence). What is needed is to rethink the object of checking: to substitute "check our fantasy" for "check your privilege." An inquiry into fantasy foregrounds the logic of desire, which marks from the start my exposure to the racial order of things.

Chapter 2, "Deconstruction: Hospitality, Hostility, and the 'Real' Neighbor," takes up the question of the other—emblematized in the figure of the refugee—as a source of ethical and political demands. Against widespread European "autoimmune" responses to the threat of racial and racialized refugees—refugees who look different (based on their phenotypic characteristics or cultural habits) and who are as a result considered subhuman—Žižek turns to the biblical injunction, "Love thy neighbor." When (re)politicized and redefined, this command stands as a locus of resistance to the immune disorders that are currently plaguing Western communities. Moreover, it takes the form of an invaluable corrective to today's reigning ethics of difference, to a depoliticized ethical sentimentalism emanating from the deconstructive camp, which objects to the racist and hostile logic of the Same, idealistically (and ideologically) preaching open borders and pure hospitality to the other—without confronting the *causes* behind the refugee crisis.

Chapter 3, "Postcolonialism: From the Culturalization of Politics to the Politicization of Culture," tackles postcolonialism's conflation of culture with politics, or its "culturalization of politics." As with deconstruction, postcolonial theory is critical of liberal multiculturalism's co-optation and defanging of difference. But unlike with deconstruction, its objections tend to be more political and historical than ethical and speculative in nature. Postcolonial theory, and even more so its offshoot or rebellious variant, decoloniality, proceed through a rejection of Western modernity, seeing it as inseparable from the spread and legacy of colonialism. Žižek concedes that postcolonial critics are fully justified in denouncing the false ideological universality that masks, naturalizes, and legitimizes a racist and neocolonial condition and agenda. Next, however, Žižek insists on the need to go further, seeing these competing progressive movements as limiting themselves to resisting only false universality, to resisting abstractions such as "Man" as the bearer of human rights. At best, their intervention constitutes only half of the Marxist critique (its moment of demystification: revealing Man as white, male, and bourgeois); at worst, it succumbs to an easy and hasty anti-Eurocentrism—unequivocal and one-dimensional—manifested as a depoliticized call to respect authentic difference, an indulgence in a cult of victimhood, a retreat behind communitarian boundaries, or a nostalgic desire for a return to authentic precolonial or indigenous realities.

In Chapter 4, "Critical Race Theory: The Subject Supposed to Loot, Rape, and Terrorize," I explore Critical Race Theory's (CRT) emphasis on racial dominance, structural racism, and the fragility of racial progress. With its notion of "racial realism" CRT warns that any gain is always tainted with white interest along with the ever-threatening possibility of backlash and reversal. CRT's interest-convergence thesis argues that for the interests of domestic minorities to be addressed they must first align with the self-interest of elite whites. This thesis helps to explain how a racial order sustains itself, preserving its hierarchical stability and reproducing its social structures, while satisfying the liberal fantasy of postraciality or at least the feeling of racial progress. CRT's skeptical view of racial progress and Žižek's discussion of racist fantasies, scapegoating, and the logic of dehumanization at work globally complement one another well. But Žižek's approach to racism also diverges from the deterministic overtones of CRT. Racial realism is not destiny. Whiteness desires immunity and purity; it yearns to be walled off, safeguarded from the barbarians who dwell on the other side, in another world, serving as a phantasmatic screen onto which whites project their innermost fears and desires. The *subject supposed to loot, rape, and terrorize* is thought to be on the other side of the wall, waiting to break through and contaminate our prosperous way of life. But again, the remedy for this cultural apartheid, for overcoming endemic racism is not better multiculturalism and more tolerance. What gets covered up in these idealist solutions is the "true wall" protecting white interests: the social-economic wall, the reality of class division.

Chapter 5, "Afro-Pessimism: Traversing the Fantasy of the Human, or Rewriting the Grammar of Suffering," considers Afro-Pessimism's bold claim that it is antiblackness rather than white supremacy that governs the production of meaning and value in white civil society. The operative antagonism is between the Human (nonblack) and black. While Afro-Pessimism follows CRT in rejecting the myth of racial progress, it views with suspicion the coalitional impulse in nonwhite anti-racist movements. The drive to gather racial and ethnic minorities around the idea of "people of color" fails to account for the historical specificity of the black experience—the grammar of black suffering. But Afro-Pessimists, in depicting antiblackness as an unavoidable feature of white civil society, also tend to ontologize blackness and totalize the Symbolic. Žižek follows the Afro-Pessimists in seeing no hope for change within the current configuration of civil society, but he does not rule out the possibility of a different model of solidarity. Without solidarity, traversing the fantasy of the Human remains a comfortable impossibility that only solidifies the status quo, civil society as we know it. A more viable approach attends to what the fundamental fantasy obfuscates: my virtual disposability in the era of global capitalism.

# 1 LIBERAL MULTICULTURALISM: FROM "CHECKING YOUR PRIVILEGE" TO "CHECKING OUR FANTASY"

*Whiteness is not really a color at all, but a set of power relations.*
**CHARLES W. MILLS[1]**

*Multiculturalism is a racism which empties its own position of all positive content (the multiculturalist is not a direct racist, he doesn't oppose to the Other the particular values of his own culture), but nonetheless retains this position as the privileged empty point of universality from which one is able to appreciate (and depreciate) properly other particular cultures—the multiculturalist respect for the Other's specificity is the very form of asserting one's own superiority.*
**SLAVOJ ŽIŽEK[2]**

Liberal multiculturalism is a sympathetic response to the ills of global capitalism. It counters the malaise and nativist violence provoked by capitalism with a dose of diversity, infusing an appreciation of relativism and the plurality of cultures within its economic matrix. It conceives of its enemy as the intolerant white male subject threatened by globalization and the mixing of cultures. On Žižek's account, however, liberal multiculturalism's pedagogical model misses the target; it fails to properly conceptualize capitalism's globally devastating reach. Its commitment to reforming capitalism—to "capitalism with a human face"—blinds it to the latter's systemic violence, and, more importantly, proposes an answer to racism that only compounds the problem by mystifying the situation. Žižek insists on "*this* global dimension of capitalism," exposing the fakeness of liberal multiculturalism's "anti-capitalism"[3] since it still fantasizes about a progressive capitalism, a capitalism more tolerant of differing ways of life. Žižek even folds Michel Foucault's anti-normative practices—"these Foucauldian practices of inventing new strategies, new identities, are ways of playing the late capitalist game of subjectivity"—into a liberal multicultural framework.[4] Liberal multiculturalism's valorization of diversity "bears witness to the unprecedented homogenization of the contemporary world. It is effectively as if . . . everybody silently accepts that *capitalism is here to stay*—critical energy has found a substitute outlet in fighting for cultural differences which leave the basic homogeneity of the capitalist world-system intact."[5]

What we are left with, then, are competing tribes whose "politics"/wrongs are articulated almost exclusively at the cultural register.[6] Identity politics becomes a defense of certain ways of life and their inclusion in the social fabric, a defense that excludes the economy and class relations from serious critical analysis.[7] In its desire to give voice to society's marginalized voices, liberal multiculturalism de-emphasizes or flattens society's "antagonistic gap,"[8] and, consequently, the true enemy is eclipsed.[9] To be clear, Žižek does not reject "multiculturalism as such," which he views as a necessary counter to the fetishization of one's heritage or culture (a problem that is not caused solely by capitalism); what he objects to is "the idea that it constitutes the fundamental struggle of today."[10] Preaching tolerance and respect for alterity while ignoring capitalism's systemic violence produces a toothless anti-racism, an anti-racism only comfortable with blaming the type of behavior witnessed in the events of Charlottesville.[11] This type of anti-racism is never sufficient to produce meaningful change. Against liberal multiculturalism's bland program of cultural tolerance, Žižek argues refreshingly for *intolerance*, for the need to refocus on global, economic antagonisms and to politicize them:

> One should thoroughly reject the standard multiculturalist idea that, against ethnic intolerance, one should learn to respect and live

with the Otherness of the Other, to develop a tolerance for different lifestyles, and so on—the way to fight ethnic *hatred* effectively is not through its immediate counterpart, ethnic *tolerance*; on the contrary, what we need is *even more hatred*, but proper *political* hatred: hatred directed at the common political enemy.[12]

Attentiveness to this "common political enemy" marks Žižek's difference from Sara Ahmed's own perceptive critique of liberal multiculturalism. Ahmed contests Žižek's claim that multiculturalism's hegemonic reign is an empirical fact. What we have, according to Ahmed, is not multiculturalism as a reality but as a fantasy: "Multiculturalism is a fantasy which conceals forms of racism, violence and inequality as if the organisation/nation can now say: how can you experience racism when we are committed to diversity?"[13] Liberals would like to be multiculturalists, but in reality they have never stopped being monoculturalists:

> The best description of today's hegemony is "liberal monoculturalism" in which common values are read as under threat by the support for the other's difference, as a form of support that supports the fantasy of the nation as being respectful at the same time as it allows the withdrawal of this so-called respect. The speech act that declares liberal multiculturalism as hegemonic is the hegemonic position.[14]

In his response to Ahmed, Žižek agrees that liberal multiculturalism is through and through ideological in nature but disagrees that it hides a liberal monoculturalism.[15] Liberal multiculturalism is not about sameness—adherence to the (impossible and cruel) injunction: be Western like us!—but about reified and manageable differences.[16] It takes up "the privileged *empty point of universality* from which one is able to appreciate (and depreciate) properly other particular cultures,"[17] a false universality that is really only the truly racist assumption of one's own culture as the norm, a norm from which others are excluded: "multiculturalism is a disavowed, inverted, self-referential form of racism, a 'racism with a distance'—it 'respects' the Other's identity, conceiving the Other as a self-enclosed 'authentic' community towards which he, the multiculturalist, maintains a distance rendered possible by his privileged universal position."[18] This respect for the other is not the respect one shows an equal (with whom you might freely and openly disagree) but rather the patronizing deference one shows a child so as not to upset them. "When multiculturalists tell you to respect the others," Žižek observes, "I always have this uncanny association that this is dangerously close to how we treat our children: the idea that we should respect them, even when we know that what they believe is not true."[19]

Liberal multiculturalism engages, as Ahmed puts it, in "non-performatives," that is, "speech acts that do not do what they say, and that *do not bring into effect what they name.*"[20] It pays lip service to cultural difference when what it really wants is "cultural apartheid": as Žižek puts it, paraphrasing this line of thought, "others should not come too close to us, we should protect our 'way of life.'"[21] Of course the latter concern for protecting our "way of life" is couched ethically as a concern for the other: don't lose your authentic (natural, innocent, organic, exotic, etc.) "way of life" and become too modern like us. Žižek reminds us that this line of argument was deployed by South Africa's Afrikaners whose "official regime's ideology was multiculturalist"; they shamelessly argued that "apartheid was needed so that all the diverse African tribes would not get drowned in white civilization."[22]

Does this make liberal multiculturalism irremediable? After all, doesn't a fake multiculturalism at least suggest the possibility of a "true" multiculturalism, one that overcomes or exorcizes its monoculturalism? We can see this type of self-critical work being done by liberal multiculturalists who have turned to privilege theory as a corrective to these shortcomings. Liberal multiculturalism 2.0 takes "whiteness," the undeserved privileges accumulated by whites, as today's most challenging social problem. The true enemy, then, turns out to be the liberal multicultural subject itself. But from a Žižekian vantage point, privilege theory can only exacerbate the limitations of liberal multiculturalism, repeating the latter's flight from universality. In this chapter, I want to critically engage with privilege theory and the now widespread liberal activist slogan "check your privilege" so prevalent on US college campuses. Feminists were the first to criticize unearned privilege, and in particular male privilege, as well as resistance on the part of the privileged to recognizing that privilege, as exclusionary. Feminists also sought in their critique to draw out the structural dimensions of such privilege. But what does it mean today to "check" privilege? What is privilege theory's critical force? Is it adequate as a strategy for social change? Does privilege-checking transform the racial polity? Simply stated, what is privilege theory questioning and what is it leaving intact and reproducing? We might indeed ask whether it is really privilege that needs checking. Does this prevailing conception of anti-racism require instead a psychoanalytic supplement? A Žižekian response to the challenges of liberal multiculturalism might be formulated as an injunction to shift from privilege to fantasy: from the imperative to "check your privilege" to the psychoanalytic injunction to "check *our* fantasy."

# Privilege and its Limits

In discovering her own white privilege, American feminist Peggy McIntosh comments, "I have come to see white privilege as an invisible package of unearned assets that I can count on cashing in each day, but about which I was 'meant' to remain oblivious."[23] To correct such shortcomings, privilege theory teaches that there is no privilege without the unprivileged. Privilege is entrenched and difficult even to acknowledge as such. Some men react negatively to the critique of male privilege, McIntosh notes for example, illustrating their reluctance to give up their power.[24] Even when men acknowledge historical discrimination against women, according to McIntosh, they often fail to see privilege as divisive: they fail to see, that is, how the notion of privilege is governed by a logic of exclusion. What comes out of the analysis of McIntosh and others, then, is the imperative to self-analyze, to check one's privilege.

The critique of privilege theory has emanated from two main camps: the Right condemns privilege theory for creating a victim industry and helping to legitimize a stifling atmosphere of political correctness (one in which marginalized groups—the unprivileged—are seen as exempt from criticism while white, Christian, heterosexual males are fair game), while the Left questions privilege theory's approach for its failure to truly get at oppression, seeing it as reformist rather than revolutionary.[25] Žižek gestures toward a third line of critique. His objections to privilege theory share much with the Left's verdict that this approach does not go far enough—as well as the Right's suspicion of political correctness, of tolerant liberal multiculturalism more generally—but, as we shall see, these lines of thought converge here for significantly different reasons.

Again, in its best forms, privilege theory makes important observations about social inequality and the normalization of power, about the ways privilege infiltrates all aspects of social existence. As Barbara Applebaum puts it, "privilege is not *only* a matter of receiving benefits but also consists in ways of being in the world."[26] The call to check one's privilege, as I've already mentioned, is an invitation for self-critique, for knowing yourself, for scrutinizing your "being in the world," your perspective of the world and others. Some of the more leftist advocates of privilege theory underscore that privilege is a structural and relational problem, and that self-critique does not merely entail looking inward into one's character but is rather about developing awareness of one's position and vantage point in relation to others. As the editors of *Privilege: A Reader* point out, "Refusing to be male, white, or straight does neither the privileged nor the unprivileged much good. One can no more renounce privilege than one can stop breathing."[27] This makes the imperative "check your privilege" more of a rhetorical gesture, and a performative doing: by checking my privilege I'm actually producing a certain kind of subjectivity, a more tolerant and vigilant subject. This self-critical subject is, more often than not, today's liberal subject, the subject who is attentive to the marginalization of others (especially those of different cultures), who prides itself on its multiculturalism (its reformed, liberal, less Eurocentric sensibility) and its respect for diversity, and who stands apart precisely from those individuals who fail to check their implicit biases: whites who benefit from the system without knowing it—or rather who actively produce and sustain their racialized ignorance, their ignorance of racial matters[28]—who blissfully dwell in existential comfort, and whose happiness is fundamentally procured at the expense of the unprivileged members of society.

This tolerant multicultural subject is often highly invested in policing verbal and visual representations, to the exclusion of a deeper engagement with socioeconomic structures as well as the productive potential of those representations deemed politically incorrect. We can see this type of policing at work in the reception of Barry Blitt's cover for the July 2008 *New Yorker*, caricaturing Michelle and Barack Obama as Black Panthers and terrorists. The image was published when Obama was the presumptive nominee of the Democratic Party. The response to the cartoon was almost unanimously negative. It seemed that everybody objected to it: from the self-styled progressive news channel MSNBC to the opposing McCain camp, the charge was that the *New Yorker* had crossed the line, that it had behaved irresponsibly in helping to circulate such a willful and racist distortion of the Obamas. The strongest endorsement of this position came from the Obama camp, which expressed outrage at the image on moral grounds, considering it "tasteless and offensive." This in turn foreclosed any serious discussion of the parody's critique.

Revisiting this caricature more than a decade later, we can see how the image illustrates the problem of humor, the interpretive dilemmas of parody, and the limitations of "checking" political incorrectness.[29] To read something as parodic, to see this image not as a representation of the Obamas, but as a representation and critique of the stereotypes circulating about the Obamas, one needs to be able to identify critical distance between the representation and its object—one needs to recognize, in other words, that the visual language is functioning in a double sense, referring to one thing but meaning another. Who gets the joke of the *New Yorker* is the one who is able to look beyond the surface of the image and see it as a parody of fringe discourse on the Right. And here is the paradox: if the parody is too subtle, the joke will be missed, and what you're left with is the racist stereotype, the distorted representation of Obama.

While it might be true that some naïve observers were unable to spot the joke, if anything the image—especially with its title "The Politics of Fear"—was overdetermined to be read as parody. But it nevertheless failed to be read as such, or, at the very least, the benefits of the image's parodic effects were negated by its potential to offend. So, on the one hand, you had the absurdity of right-wing fantasies about Obama's secret identity (mocked by the image) and, on the other hand, you had a surface reading (recognized as such by the media) but deemed too dangerous to discuss in depth. One can only wonder if the media's coverage would have been different, or better, if Obama had laughed (publically) at the caricature and taken its critique seriously? It is hard to tell. At the very least, such a response could have created a moment of pause and reflection. We might interpret this moment as a missed opportunity (especially on the part of the media, the Left, and the Obama campaign itself) to think differently about racism and visual representation, and more pointedly, to think about the fantasy of race. It was easier to dismiss the image than to engage it than to see how the image functions as a fantasy screen, projecting as well as helping to organize and manage people's anxieties about a supposedly unknown Obama.

Why was this the case? Was there simply an unwillingness to probe the image, to work through its ridicule of racist fantasies of Obama's otherness? While the image was denounced because it misrepresented Obama as a Muslim, it left for the most part unquestioned the hidden logic behind the racist accusation: that being a Muslim means being a terrorist, a bad, violent, or even evil actor (or at the very least politically disastrous). The editor of the *New Yorker*, David Remnick, defended Blitt's cover pointing out that it

> combines a number of fantastical images about the Obamas and shows them for the obvious distortions they are. The burning flag, the nationalist-radical and Islamic outfits, the fist-bump, the portrait on the wall—all of them echo one attack or another. Satire is part of what we do, and it is meant to bring things out into the open, to hold up a mirror to prejudice, the hateful, and the absurd. And that's the spirit of this cover.[30]

This reasonable explanation did not assuage the liberal pundits—for them, "merely to acknowledge racism . . . is to be racist."[31] The *New Yorker* was berated by the liberal Left: how can you be so irresponsible as to circulate this racist image of Obama? Why are you, wittingly or unwittingly, doing the dirty work of the Right?

Against this debilitating form of political correctness we might risk a Žižekian rereading of the cover, rereading Remnick's statement perversely or against the grain. We can follow Remnick's mirror analogy but also build on its ironies by introducing fantasy into the analysis, by reframing its relation to reality—recalling Žižek's observation that "if we really want to change or escape our social reality, *the first thing to do is change our fantasies that make us fit this reality*."[32] In many ways, the cover's caricature reveals the fantasies that structure American reality. The cover dramatizes American fears of becoming what they already are but refuse to avow: undemocratic and war-mongering, on the one hand, but also capable of radical resistance on the other. These fears are displaced onto the Obamas, but the real causes lie elsewhere. The framed picture of Osama Bin Laden hanging inside the Oval Office, read ironically, reminds us that the enemy is already within: it was the CIA who, in an attempt to drive the Soviets out of Afghanistan, gave Bin Laden and the Taliban the support required to increase their influence.[33] Portraying Obama as Muslim reminds us that America is not simply Christian, but Muslim and multiple. To be Muslim here is not to return to Obama's imaginary Kenyan roots (the racist fantasy of the Alt-right) but to identify with "the part of no-part," today's racialized and marginalized others, who are shunned or unrecognized by society's laws and norms.

Unlike the liberal multiculturalist who is too eager to indulge in the games of identity politics, identifying the other narrowly with his or her ethnic roots, this gesture interrogates "the concrete existing universal order on behalf of its symptom, of the part which, although inherent to the existing universal order, has no 'proper place' within it."[34] Similarly, the Black Panther movement, excised from the dominant American narrative of racial progress that focuses exclusively on nonviolent resistance—a liberal privilege if there ever was one—is brought back into visibility here as that which liberal white Americans most fear: the radical rejection of business as usual and the militant affirmation of the need to upend the racial order of things.[35]

# Victimization and the Theft of Happiness

Fear of change in the fundamental status quo—capitalism masquerading as a meritocracy in which effort is rewarded and progress from within is possible—also characterizes the fantasies that support liberal multicultural concerns about privilege. From the perspective of privilege theory, it is as if the undeservedly privileged are stealing the happiness of those who are more deserving, or at least no less deserving, than they. We can see this as reversing Žižek's notion of "the theft of enjoyment."[36] As Žižek initially put it, the theft of enjoyment reflects the ideological belief that some undeserving, excluded others—such as undocumented immigrants—are robbing me of my enjoyment, derailing, as it were, my pursuit of happiness, my pursuit of the American dream and so forth. Privilege theory seems to flip this scenario around, highlighting its ideological quality but also unwittingly reproducing, in reverse, its structure. If the so-called victim in the theft of enjoyment scenario is a phantasmatic projection of the racist who blames his misfortunes on the wrong target (unjustly scapegoating, for example, the undocumented immigrant rather than blaming an economic system that divides and exploits its labor force), the victim of others' unearned privilege appears far less ideological. The assumption of privilege theory is that if the unprivileged only had the same privileges, they would be happy too. But the question is, *how do we get there?* Recording and documenting the privilege of others, compelling others to confess their *undeserved* privilege, does little to change racial inequality, to dismantle institutional structures of oppression, and to weaken lingering psychic attachments to privilege.

Marxist critique often overlooks this question of psychic attachment, yet it is paramount. Taking a Žižekian-psychoanalytic approach to the problem leads us to conclude that in dealing with the question of happiness for all, we must move away from the question of who has really earned their privilege and who has not, an obsessive question that privilege theory has difficulty breaking with. Peggy McIntosh has herself registered her uneasiness with this framework, and with the idea of privilege itself. Distinguishing between privileges that "we can work to spread" and those that "unless rejected will always reinforce our present hierarchies," she observes:

> The word "privilege" . . . seems to me misleading. Its connotations are too positive to fit the conditions and behaviors which "privilege systems" produce. We usually think of privilege as being a favored state, whether earned, or conferred by birth or luck. School graduates are reminded they are privileged and urged to use their (enviable) assets well. The word "privilege" carries the connotation of being something everyone must want. Yet some of the conditions I have described here work to systemically over-empower certain groups. Such privilege simply *confers dominance*, gives permission to control, because of one's race or sex. The kind of privilege that gives license to some people to be, at best, thoughtless and, at worst, murderous should not continue to be referred to as a desirable attribute. Such "privilege" may be widely desired without being in any way beneficial to the whole society.[37]

A notion of "earned privilege"—a privilege that we ought to desire without guilt—haunts privilege theory, limiting its critical potential as it focuses exclusively on *unearned* privileges, negative advantages, immunizing privilege from deeper and sustained interpretive scrutiny.

We might first counter here what could be described as privilege theory's liberal critique of unearned privilege by considering one alternative Marcuse describes as "the need for 'undeserved' happiness." As if preempting privilege theory's task of "democratizing" privilege— the liberal ideological fantasy of a restored democracy, a just and fair meritocracy à la John Rawls (as opposed to a "callous" one[38]) where everyone's privilege is in fact earned—Marcuse's insistence on "'undeserved' happiness" changes the terms of the discussion themselves. Marcuse helps to reframe the issue as one of need rather than privilege but also shifts the debate to the terrain of the universal and to the question of the fundamental structures required for human fulfillment, while retaining the capacity to identify and critique inequality, to distinguish between those whose needs are met and those whose needs are not. The "happiness" in "'undeserved' happiness" here should not be conflated with complacent satisfaction, with the attainment of a happy "state"—a form of happiness that psychoanalysis consistently questions and denounces as a "betrayal of desire" ("the subject's inability or unreadiness fully to confront the consequences of its desire"[39]), as a submission to the pleasure principle, which minimizes the subject's eternal struggle, its death drive or self-sabotaging ways.[40] Rather, it should be understood as referring to modes of enjoyment, to unruly acts of libidinal gratification and self-cultivation incongruous with the capitalist maxim, *happiness as the deserved fruits of social productivity*. Moreover, Marcuse's formulation throws a wrench in the logic of reward and punishment that often informs the contemporary discourse of privilege, a logic that unwittingly transforms the critique of structural inequalities into a matter of individual conscience: you should be verbally punished for assuming your unearned privilege (as attested by the act of calling out someone's privilege in the accusatory charge, "your privilege is showing"), and rewarded for confessing your given privilege (whether or not that confession leads to a deeper engagement with the structural problems at work). Marcuse's formulation enables a more decisive break with the economic and racial status quo, a definite rupture with these founding assumptions. The need for undeserved happiness withdraws "happiness" from a preexisting normative framework. It discredits from the start the application of any criterion when it comes to the need for happiness. Because it is acknowledged as unearned, undeserved, the need for happiness can only be boldly affirmed, not "objectively" measured or assessed. This means that the need is not something that can be taken away or discounted. We might say that happiness functions not as a privilege but as a right, an ontological entitlement.

The need for undeserved happiness can be understood as akin to the need for grievability and mournability, a need that is *undeserved* or *unearned* in that it preexists any contingent determination of merit. The discourse of privilege can only go so far to help us make sense of grievability. Mournability can certainly come under the definition of privilege given by "Check Your Privilege 101,"[41] a text authored by the activist group Transformative Justice Law Project of Illinois Justice that circulated among the Occupy Wall Street protestors. This group defines privilege as "any right, immunity, or benefit enjoyed only by a person or group beyond the advantages of most"; the authors list a number of undeserved privileges that meet this definition—including sexuality and ableism—while also making clear that it is not exhaustive.

Mournability is also clearly not a right enjoyed equally by everyone. At its best, privilege theory might compel individuals to question how their lives are experienced and seen as more valuable than those of others. This is a point that Judith Butler repeatedly makes in her analysis of the War on Terror and critique of Zionism.[42] For ungrievable bodies— the *homines sacri* of the world, who lack a sense of belonging—it is a "privilege" to be mourned and an even greater privilege to be protected and perceived as liveable/grievable. To take Israel's mistreatment of Palestinians as a case in point (a case that we will return to throughout this book), the framework that reads Palestinians as less than fully mournable simultaneously racializes the Palestinian, the non-Jewish other inhabiting the same contested land. As David Theo Goldberg observes, "Israelis occupy the structural position of whiteness in the racial hierarchy of the Middle East. Arabs, accordingly—most notably in the person of Palestinians—are the antithesis."[43] White privilege translates smoothly into Zionist privilege and Palestinian *dis*privilege. Yet countering the logic of disprivilege should not involve a simple negation of the situation: a negation that would claim Palestinian privilege. Wouldn't it be somewhat obscene to argue that Palestinians deserve to be mourned, that they have earned mournability? Such a formulation would in effect confirm and make their mournability conditional, contingent on the will of the other/Other: a favorable Israeli government, a benevolent West, and so on. "Earned" mournability is also inseparable, as Žižek points out, from a certain performance of victimhood. Palestinian privilege is a way of saying my culture merits recognition and safeguarding: the Palestinian people as an indigenous group needs protection from the international community (I will return to these issues in more detail in Chapter 3). The need for undeserved happiness, like that for mournability and grievability, expresses a non-negotiable thesis, a refusal to couch one's value in culturalist terms, to subject life to a dubious calculus, to a cost/benefit analysis in which merits can be totaled up, added, or subtracted.

# The Subject of Privilege (Theory) and the Postmodern Superego

Marcuse locates the need for undeserved happiness in a society to come; it belongs to a host of new needs that a truly revolutionary subversive utopia would embody. He writes:

> The new needs, which are really the determinate negation of existing needs, first make their appearance as the negation of the needs that sustain the present system of domination and the negation of the values on which they are based: for example, the negation of the need for the struggle for existence . . .; the negation of the need to earn one's living; the negation of the performance principle, of competition; the negation of the need for wasteful, ruinous productivity, which is inseparably bound up with destruction; and the negation of the vital need for deceitful repression of the instincts. These needs would be negated in the vital biological need for peace, which today is not a vital need of the majority, the need for calm, the need to be alone, with oneself or with others whom one has chosen oneself, the need for the beautiful, the need for "undeserved" happiness.[44]

The need for undeserved happiness cannot be satisfied within the current sociopolitical coordinates; the goal of this critique is precisely *not* reform. In the words of Žižek, a genuine critique "does not wish to stop at merely improving the existing state of affairs."[45] A Marcusian-Žižekian rejoinder to privilege theory is that it is not enough to democratize privilege, to increase access to the system so that others can also reap its benefits. The needs of privilege theory are for the most part consistent with the "performance principle" (the form Freud's "reality principle" takes within late capitalism[46]); they are "needs developed and satisfied in a repressive society."[47] For this reason, the discourse of privilege always risks reproducing the system that it is contesting. In contrast, the need for undeserved happiness reflects an alternative modality of being, or what Marcuse dubs the "scandal of qualitative difference."[48] This introduced "radical alterity"[49] sabotages the "performance principle" according to which "everyone has to earn his living in alienating but socially necessary performances, and one's reward, one's status in society will be determined by this performance (the work-income relation)."[50] This new, utopian complex of needs declines to perpetuate the status quo, to feed the capitalist machine—to desire only that which is efficient, socially useful, and (re)productive.[51]

Marcuse's utopian formulation not only challenges the traditional capitalist work ethic where reward or profit is the result of productive work (no matter how alienating it is, no matter the "surplus-repression" that the "performance principle" induces), but it also clashes with today's consumerist society, where "repressive desublimation," as he puts it, runs supreme. In late capitalism "sexuality is liberated (or rather liberalized) in socially constructive forms."[52] Don't be fooled by today's permissive society, he argues. This is not the age of sexual liberation or gratification but an ideologically freighted freedom that the social order invites and manages. Critical utopia—emblematized in Marcuse's uncompromising call for undeserved happiness—gestures toward an alternative order of things. It opposes what Žižek characterizes as the postmodern superego of late capitalism. Following Lacan, Žižek stresses the dual nature of the superego, complicating its relation to the big Other. He associates the big Other with the Freudian superego, the traditional father of prohibition and censorship, whereas today's superego—modeled after "the 'postmodern' non-authoritarian father"[53]—is a perverse supplement to the traditional Freudian superego. Modeled after Narcissus rather than Oedipus, this superego's injunction is *Enjoy!* The postmodern superego presents itself as a caring and empowering figure; it does not tell us what do but frames the situation as a matter of choice. But this "freedom of choice" that we are presumably afforded is ultimately a fake.[54] Žižek, even more so than Marcuse, sees the superego's promotion of enjoyment as problematic and ideologically laden: it only gives you the illusion of agency.

Enjoyment is experienced now not as a spontaneous transgression of the law, but as a duty, as an imposition. "To enjoy is not a matter of following one's spontaneous tendencies; it is rather something we do as a kind of weird and twisted ethical duty."[55] And far from being a relief from ideology, enjoyment is facilitated and sanctioned by ideology. It seeks to manage and discipline the libido. This other superego installs a new and more insidious model of interpellation. Whereas for Althusser individuals are interpellated into subjects, for Žižek interpellation in today's permissive society functions in reverse: "*The superego-pressure individualizes the subject* . . . . The superego addresses me as a unique individual, confronting me with my guilt and responsibility."[56] The absence of the big Other (a generalized suspicion of all authorities), the demise of symbolic efficiency (the abandonment of master narratives), the weakening of my ego ideal (the failure to assume a symbolic mandate, to fully occupy a place within the symbolic order), all contribute to my anxiety and vulnerability in front of the superego: "In the eyes of the superego, I am alone, there is no big Other behind which I can hide, and I am 'guilty as charged' because the very position of being charged makes me formally guilty."[57]

Now privilege theory, from a Žižekian vantage point, fails to acknowledge the sadistic and manipulative logic of the superego, and unwittingly plays into society's hegemonic order, reinforcing the dominant ideology and concealing, in turn, its own racist tendencies. The liberal superego-agency addresses its citizens as a priori guilty individuals. Did you check your privilege before speaking? Did you dutifully scrutinize and call out the behavior of others? Its compulsory call "to check your privilege" at best provides a limited critical value and, at worst, is hegemonic and complicit with the very racist and sexist ideologies it seeks to eradicate. What the liberal superego-agency obfuscates, what gets lost in this superficial policing of thoughts and endless self-examination is *politics*, and the more global questions about *social* existence, namely, the growing gap between the included and the excluded under late capitalism.[58]

Capitalism's "universal wrong"[59] is depoliticized and privatized: the wrong is framed as an individual shortcoming—whence the neoliberal imperative, "check *your* privilege." But is individual culpabilization really enough to short-circuit society's racist and exploitive machinery? Doesn't the maxim check your privilege conveniently place the problem of white supremacy in the actions of others, fetishizing your self-critique? Doesn't the call only scratch the surface, individualizing your intervention, always risking becoming an end in itself, a narcissistic exercise?

# Surplus-Enjoyment and the Ideology of Self-Critique

Privilege theory offers the liberal multicultural subject a phantasmatic reality. It gives that subject the tools to name society's bad apples: they are easily discernable; they are those who don't check their privilege, blind to the social and cultural power that they undeservedly enjoy.

And if privilege theory calls on you to curtail the pleasures of your own privilege, to willingly renounce your culturally given claims on the world, you are rewarded with "libidinal profit,"[60] with what Lacan calls a "surplus-enjoyment," an enjoyment-in-sacrifice or enjoyment-in-confession. Suffering—the feeling of guilt from realizing that you can never fully eradicate your privilege (again, privilege theory concedes that "one can no more renounce privilege than one can stop breathing"), that you are enjoying the fruits of an impure liberalism, that you're taking up the space of someone more deserving, and so on—and exhaustion—the emotional cost for your unflinching vigilance in naming racism and denouncing prejudice wherever it appears—ironically become signs not of your defeat but of your self-enlightenment, moral righteousness, and true commitment to social justice. There is thus a kind of illicit satisfaction—an unconscious enjoyment—not only in exposing the blind spots of others, in the rhetorical disciplining of others, but in your own self-discipline, in your perceived suffering and exhaustion as well, amounting to an abstract testimony to the heroism of whiteness ("another self-glorification in which whiteness is equated with moral rectitude,"[61] as Butler puts it) and the progress of multicultural liberalism: *it's not perfect, but we're getting there.* Along the way, privilege theory redeems its practitioners: since its biopolitical logic tends to individualize racism—check *your* privilege—your self-check exempts you from the charge of racism. It is fundamentally the problem of *individual* others (typically that of the less educated, white blue collar workers), concealing society's "civil racism," the pervading, naturalized racism of everyday liberal life.

In contrast, psychoanalysis compels the liberal multicultural subject to confront a starker reality. For psychoanalysis, the routinized and ritualized call to check your privilege appears too convenient; it enables the liberal multicultural subject to diminish his or her guilt (*I'm doing something personally about implicit biases*) without needing to take on the sociopolitical framework directly. If privilege theorists are pressed, they will gladly confess that they know that it is not enough to denounce the unearned privileges of others without simultaneously attending to the networks of power relations that sustain such advantages. And yet in their active scholarly activist lives, they act as if it were enough, displaying the psychoanalytic structure of fetishistic *disavowal* (*I know very well, but all the same*). They maintain a split attitude toward anti-racism. They know very well that denouncing white privilege is necessary but not sufficient, yet they don't really believe that this critico-gesture does not accomplish the task at hand. Privilege theory, we might say, "wants social change with no actual change."[62] Rather than addressing the social antagonisms immanent to capitalism, it misapprehends the framework (and its enablement of racism).[63] Privilege theory typically only sees social structures as the sum of their individual parts, their individual consciences.[64] At its base level, it provides you with the fantasy of intervention and action; it offers you *criticism without critique*. For the proponents of privilege theory, social change follows the gradual and predictable path of reform. This makes privilege theory rather than the philosophies of Marcuse and Žižek an instance of utopian idealism. Žižek puts the matter clearly:

> It is my firm conviction, my politico-existential premiss, that the old '68 motto *Soyons réalistes, demandons l'impossible!* still holds: it is the advocates of changes and resignifications within the liberal-democratic horizon who are the true utopians in their belief that their effort will amount to anything more than the cosmetic surgery that will give us capitalism with a human face.[65]

Žižek makes a further qualification to the '68 motto:

> [It] remains fully relevant—on condition that we take note of the shift to which it has to be submitted. First, there is "demanding the impossible" in the sense of bombarding the existing system with demands that it cannot meet: open borders, better healthcare, higher wages . . . . Here we are today, in the midst of a hysterical provocation of our masters (technocratic experts). This provocation has to be followed by a key step further: not demanding the impossible from the system but demanding the "impossible" changes of the system itself.[66]

We could add privilege theory to Žižek's long list of fake leftist "radicals" who bombard the existing system. As with "*Médecins sans frontières*, Greenpeace, feminist and anti-racist campaigns," privilege theory runs the risk of falling prey to what Žižek names "interpassivity": the risk of "doing things not in order to achieve something, but to prevent something from really happening, really changing. All this frenetic humanitarian, Politically Correct, etc. activity fits the formula of 'Let's go on changing something all the time so that, globally, things will remain the same!'"[67] The problem with privilege theory—especially as vulgarized in liberal universities—is that it ends up becoming "an empty gesture which obliges no one to do anything definite."[68] White liberal multiculturalists put on display their "progressive" leanings by calling for inclusivity and tolerance, parading their own self-critique—in a pleasure-ridden act of virtue signaling—as a model for others to follow. Whiteness or white privilege is treated as a reified thing that could be singled out and denounced, and not as "a set of power relations,"[69] as Charles W. Mills insightfully puts it.

Privilege-checking does not necessarily translate into campus radicalism. It remains utopian and impotent when it fails to confront capitalism itself: "The true utopia is the belief that the existing global system can reproduce itself indefinitely; the only way to be truly 'realistic' is to think what, within the coordinates of this system, cannot but appear as impossible."[70] The advocates of privilege theory are today's "true utopians." They muzzle ideology critique, believing that gradualist reform is the key to social transformation. But privilege theory's anti-racist insights are diluted, never really touching the reality of domination and exploitation, never "demanding 'impossible' changes of the system itself."

# Utopia, Desire, and the Problem with/of Envy

Psychoanalysis, for its part, reorients us toward ideology critique by imploring us to substitute "check our fantasy" for "check your privilege." An inquiry into fantasy foregrounds the logic of desire, which marks from the start my exposure to the symbolic order, to the capitalist system. Desire is a desire for the other/Other. The object (and subject) of desire is constitutively doubled. As Žižek puts it, "the problem with human desire is that . . . it is always 'desire for the Other' in all the senses of the term: desire for the Other, desire to be desired by the Other, and especially desire for what the Other desires."[71] Checking my fantasy, checking my desire, can never be solely an individual affair. Whereas privilege theory can all too easily fall into solipsistic if not narcissistic meditations[72] (the problem of racist fantasies are dealt with privately through confessions and the appropriate level of self-scrutiny—spurred of course by the Other's demand to check my privilege), psychoanalysis insists on the irremediably social and ideological framework of desire. Its conceptual apparatus points back to the constitutive role of envy in everyday existence. Privilege theory tacitly accepts the liberal utopia of a democracy free of envy, a world of earned privileges. But privilege theory's demand for equality or social justice—that no one should benefit from unearned privilege—can be critically reread, via Nietzsche and Freud, as a form of privilege envy, an expression of slavish *ressentiment*. I check my privilege—that is, I deny myself privileges—"so that others may have to do without them as well."[73]

Žižek for his part questions the basic assumption of liberalism: that society could legitimize its hierarchies as long as there was a reasonable justification for them. Žižek draws extensively on Jean-Pierre Dupuy's *La Marque du sacré*, in which the author explains how capitalism, through four mechanisms, succeeds in making "the relationship of superiority non-humiliating":

> *Hierarchy* itself (an externally imposed order that allows me to experience my lower social status as independent of my inherent value); *demystification* (the ideological procedure which demonstrates that society is not a meritocracy but the product of objective social struggles, enabling me to avoid the painful conclusion that someone else's superiority is the result of his merit and achievements); *contingency* (a similar mechanism, by which we come to understand that our position on the social scale depends on a natural and social lottery; the lucky ones are those born with the right genes in rich families); and *complexity* (uncontrollable forces have unpredictable consequences; for instance, the invisible hand of the market may lead to my failure and my neighbour's success, even if I work much harder and am much more intelligent).[74]

The work of privilege theory aligns most clearly with the mechanism of "demystification." While privilege theory is unambiguously critical of callous meritocracy and is more concerned with exposing the unearned privileges of those who most benefit from the existing social hierarchies, it does qualify its demystification, implicitly conceding to the possibility of a just meritocracy, a meritocracy grounded in earned privilege. By tacitly upholding the possibility of *earned privilege in capitalism*, privilege theory is not providing an antidote to envy but the condition for its destructive flourishing. Following Dupuy, Žižek thus claims that it is "a great mistake to think that a reasonably just society which also perceives itself as just will be free of resentment: on the contrary, it is in such societies that those who occupy inferior positions will find an outlet for their hurt pride in violent outbursts of resentment."[75] Such theorizations of a "just society" fundamentally misestimate "the power of envy."[76]

The psychoanalytical response to envy is neither to deny/transcend its constitutive presence in human lives (I don't blame you, I blame capitalism and its impersonal, irrational, and objectively unfair ways; but if there were a way to make capitalism just, then we would have a just and *ressentiment*-free society) or to redeem it (to adopt the slogan "envy is good" à la Gordon Gekko). Rather, the political challenge, for psychoanalysis, is how to deal with envy, to resist both a liberal utopian vision where envy is gentrified and a realist attitude where envy, like racism, is treated as an epiphenomenon of ruthless capitalism. Critical utopia—captured so well by the call for the need for undeserved happiness—is an alternative way to relate to envy. It expresses its distaste for the existing social order by de-individualizing the demand for the need for happiness. A sense of collectivity underpins this emancipatory call. The idea of undeserved happiness is not something that I can only claim for myself. By affirming this need, I am not seeking membership in the privileged category of the included. Quite the contrary, I am simultaneously affirming my need *and* the need of others, refusing to perpetuate the production of social and cultural apartheid. As Jameson puts it with regards to enjoyment, happiness itself must be celebrated; "it does not matter who has it inasmuch as no one can really have it in the first place: this is the true overcoming of envy, its elevation into a kind of religion."[77] If there is *ressentiment* in the call for undeserved happiness, it is not of the slavish, reactionary, or racist type but of a life-affirming kind, a *ressentiment* that fuels utopian imagination—the desire for rupture, for an anti-racist future. Rupture here counters the liberal temptation of an anti-racism that would remain at the level of the pure and idealistic. It insists that the pathology of envy and *jouissance* never disappears.

Žižek suggests this unexpected—un-Nietzschean—twist on the meaning of *ressentiment*. Rather than associating *ressentiment* with the reactive and vindictive morality of the weak (Nietzsche had described the men of *ressentiment* as "these cellar rodents full of vengefulness and hatred" in *On the Genealogy of Morals*[78]), Žižek moves to rehabilitate its meaning by introducing the paradoxical notion of "authentic resentment."[79] In its authentic form, *ressentiment* no longer bespeaks spiritual sickness but points to an *active* ethico-political resistance to a given ideological hermeneutics. Žižek's example is that of Holocaust survivor Jean Améry. *Pace* Nietzsche, Améry's *ressentiment* does not reflect a sense of inferiority nor is it the by-product of reactionary envy; rather, it emerges first and foremost as an ethical response to an unacceptable status quo.[80] In his anachronistic stance, writing in the 1960s, when German culture was actively promoting forgiving and forgetting, Améry insisted on the need for justice, for "nailing the criminal to his deed."[81] He stubbornly declined his culture's psychically violent demands for *cheap* and *lazy* forgiveness.[82] Authentic *ressentiment* (the feeling of the wronged subject) stands, then, for "a refusal to 'normalise' the crime, to make it part of the ordinary/explicable/accountable flow of things, to integrate it into a consistent and meaningful life-narrative; after all possible explanations, it returns with its question: 'Yes, I got all this, but nevertheless, *how could you have done it*? Your story about it doesn't make sense!'"[83] Authentic *ressentiment*—or what Žižek now dubs "a Nietzschean heroic resentment"[84]—is in the business of painful exposures and not the neat resolution of problems.

What we might call "Žižekian *ressentiment*" compels you to reject the cruel pragmatism of reform along with its symptomatic enjoyment, to refuse conformity to the "performance principle," and to see today's racial-economic matrix as fundamentally unworkable. The demand for undeserved happiness "clear[s] the terrain for a new beginning."[85] It constitutes a "philosophical Event," announcing "the rise of something New."[86] In this respect, it is also analogous to the logic of the Lacanian act to the extent that "the act proper is the only one which re-structures the very symbolic co-ordinates of the agent's situation."[87] What makes the need for undeserved happiness revolutionary-utopian is not the promise of a perfect society (a liberal, postracial utopia) but the act of reframing the symbolic field, of making the impossible possible, realizing something unthinkable from within the current historical situation, from within the coordinates of late capitalism. The politics of undeserved happiness does not seek to transcend the world but to effectuate a different relation to it—one that is at odds with the neoliberal system's values and economy of enjoyment. It both avoids the traps of liberal individualism (policing happiness as a deserved personal good) and counters the logic of envy (desiring the perceived exclusive happiness of the other). This utopian need—this rupture—manifested as an act is heard as a universal call.[88] It attests to the sheer negativity of the act, "the act as a negative gesture of saying 'No!'"[89]

My refusal to subscribe to the order of power implicates *and* is constituted by its implicit address to others: "I need undeserved happiness" is a demand *open to all, realizable by all*. To paraphrase Lacan, we may reread the call for undeserved happiness as a collective injunction: "Do not compromise on your desire for happiness." This personal and collective desire declines the demands of the liberal superego-agency and refuses to repeat privilege theory's surveillance of happiness that leaves intact the socioeconomic situation, that is, the symbolic structure of global capitalism. Demanding undeserved happiness is a traumatic shock to the social order, throwing everything out of balance, "ruin[ing] the smooth flow of our daily lives."[90] It addresses rather than covers over the antagonism between the included and the excluded, and calls for a different arrangement of the Symbolic: its eventalization "introduc[es] a totally different Universal, that of an antagonistic struggle which, rather than taking place between particular communities, splits each community from within, so that the 'trans-cultural' link between communities is one of a shared struggle."[91] It de-commodifies happiness as a personal good, de-individuates or universalizes desire (and thus restructures and repoliticizes the question of happiness), making the desire for happiness (and enjoyment) both a personal and collective commitment, an attachment to a universalist project, effectively short-circuiting the privatized rewards of privilege—unearned or otherwise.

What is needed today is precisely a collective response rather than an individual one. Or better yet, thinking Kant with Nietzsche, what is required in our struggle against racism is a "public use of *ressentiment*," a life-affirming *ressentiment* in the service of anti-racism. Such *ressentiment*, staged as the uncompromising feeling for racial justice against the backdrop of left-liberal reformists (who promote the fantasy of action), becomes, most importantly, a collective moral feeling and consciousness, based on a shared but unacceptable condition of exclusion. In actively circumventing their particularity, society's marginalized and racialized figures, as the "part of no-part," can come to participate effectively in the collective emancipatory struggle for the universal—for a politics of *ressentiment* is universal or it is not.

# 2 DECONSTRUCTION: HOSPITALITY, HOSTILITY, AND THE "REAL" NEIGHBOR

*Let us say yes to who or what turns up, before any determination, before any anticipation, before any identification, whether or not it has to do with a foreigner, an immigrant, an invited guest, or an unexpected visitor, whether or not the new arrival is the citizen of another country, a human, animal, or divine creature, a living or dead thing, male or female.*

**JACQUES DERRIDA**[1]

*Refugees should be assured of their safety, but it should also be made clear to them that they must accept the destination allocated to them by European authorities, and that they will have to respect the laws and social norms of European states: no tolerance of religious, sexist or ethnic violence; no right to impose on others one's own religion or way of life; respect for every individual's freedom to abandon his or her communal customs, etc. If a woman chooses to cover her face, her choice must be respected; if she chooses not to cover her face, her freedom not to do so must be guaranteed. Such rules privilege the Western European way of life, but that is the price to be paid for European hospitality.*

**SLAVOJ ŽIŽEK**[2]

Like multiculturalism, deconstruction denies race any ontological validity. If white identity is constituted by and predicated on the negation of other racial identities, the goal of anti-racism, commonly understood, is to contest and denaturalize whiteness as the norm and affirm blackness or brownness, for example, as a positive term, as a source of worth and dignity. Whiteness's privilege, power, and its ideological field are historically contingent, and thus subject to unsettling and reconfiguring. Unlike multiculturalism, however, deconstruction (especially as articulated by Jacques Derrida and Emmanuel Levinas) differs in its approach to the other—racialized or not. Against an "insurmountable allergy"[3] to alterity, deconstruction imagines the other in a perpetual state of fragility if not victimization. To think the other is to consider any marginalized figure, any excluded other. Levinas offers his own examples: the stranger, the widow, the orphan, and the Jew.[4] But more generally, we could say that the other *as other* is anyone who resists my identification and domestication. The "face" (*le visage*) of the other "exceed[s] *the idea of the other* in me."[5] This moment of cognitive frustration, which brings into question my autonomy, spontaneity, and self-sufficiency simultaneously, is what Levinas famously names "ethics." Affirming the priority of ethics over ontology, Levinas effectively dethrones the authority of reason and the Kantian ideal of autonomy (rational freedom) in favor of an enduring state of vulnerability and heteronomy where freedom is demoted and made to occupy a secondary role to compassion: "to be exposed to sickness, suffering, death, is to be exposed to compassion."[6]

Pursuing a similar line of inquiry, Derrida emphasizes the ethics of unconditional hospitality, which he contrasts with the conditional hospitality informing the rhetoric of many liberals and anti-immigrant nationalists. Unconditional hospitality posits the exposure to the other as a relation of pure singularity—*tout autre est tout autre*, "every other is wholly other"[7]—where the other as event or singularity punctures my horizon of intelligibility and expectations. In short, there is no relation here, no subject–object split, since a relation would introduce and impose a hermeneutic framework on the other and thus neutralize the other's otherness. Conditional hospitality presupposes instead a calculable relation between subject (host) and object (guest). The other, to whom the ethical subject is responding, may be elusive, but their otherness is always relational to me.

Right-wing European politicians often proffer this model of conditional hospitality. They merely gesture to an openness to immigrants, accepting the latter only insofar as they are able to assimilate. According to Derrida, they tolerate and welcome only "what is homogeneous or homogenizable, what is assimilable or at the very most what is heterogeneous but presumed 'favorable': the appropriable immigrant, the proper immigrant."[8] But this is no hospitality:

> Tolerance is actually the opposite of hospitality. Or at least its limit. If I think I am being hospitable because I am tolerant, it is because I wish to maintain control over the limits of my "home," my sovereignty, my "I can" (my territory, my house, my language, my culture, my religion, and so on).[9]

At the same time, Derrida insists that unconditional hospitality is both indissociable from and heterogeneous to conditional hospitality.[10] And here Derrida diverges significantly from Levinas (a point Žižek does not sufficiently acknowledge). The other for Derrida never comes fully predigested nor totally indigestible; Derrida denies the pure or unmediated alterity of the face—whence deconstruction's skeptical hermeneutics of "eating well."[11] This ethico-interpretive injunction answers the *external* call of the other, my interpellation by the other. It readily confronts the aporetic demands of the singular other, where the other is neither fully subdued nor withdrawn, but unruly and hospitable: to be understood, represented, and engaged with, and yet not be reduced to an object of knowledge, not be reduced to its relations, to any schemes of thought. To insist on this double bind is to insist on my paradoxical relationality, characterized by Derrida as a "relation without relation."[12]

Žižek for his part seems less fascinated with the perplexities of *heterophilia* and appears to give more weight to conditional hospitality, that is, a qualified love for the refugees. Žižek's detractors have been quick to object to what they see as Žižek's Eurocentric and paternalistic, if not xenophobic and hostile remarks concerning the ongoing refugee crisis confronting Europe.[13] Two particular comments stand out. First, Žižek's claim that it is not in itself racist or protofascist for a European host nation to talk of protecting its "way of life"; second, his precondition for "European hospitality": we must "formulate a minimum set of norms that are obligatory for everyone, without fear that they will appear 'Eurocentric': religious freedoms, the protection of individual freedom against group pressure, rights of women, and so on."[14] In comparison with Derrida's call to respect the other in all his or her unruliness and strangeness (his memorable claim that "monsters cannot be announced. One cannot say: 'Here are our monsters,' without immediately turning them into pets"[15]), Žižek seems to uphold national sovereignty, to want to contain and domesticate refugees, subjecting them to European normativity and thus turning them into European pets.

And yet to stop here would be to fail to grasp the complexity and full force of Žižek's position. What Žižek means by "European" is less than self-evident. His deployment of European is in many ways analogous to Derrida's own use of Europe in his late piece "A Europe of Hope," in which Europe becomes a trope for a deconstructive mode of reading, "a Europe that sets the example of what a politics, a thinking, and an ethics could be, inherited from the passed Enlightenment and bearing the Enlightenment to come, which would be capable of non-binary judgments."[16] "European" is a subject position open to all—to Americans, for example, who draw their hope from the civil rights movement, and, as we saw, to the Haitian revolutionaries who inventively misinterpellated human rights discourse. To read like a "European" is to contest what passes for commonsense or moral clarity today. Likewise, Žižek's Europe functions as a trope for universality, a feminine universality, a universality that is "non-all," incomplete and irremediably at odds with the sovereignty and self-transparency of the subject. It is a universality shot through with the unconscious and alterity: "Universality is a universality of 'strangers,' of individuals reduced to the abyss of impenetrability in relation not only to others but also to themselves."[17] Racism arises in no small part from the disavowal of such strangeness: "Racism confronts us with the enigma of the Other, which cannot be reduced to the partner in symbolic communication; it confronts us with the enigma of that which, in ourselves, resists the universal frame of symbolic communication."[18] Racism is one response to this strangeness. Žižek finds in Europe resources for another response.

So it is not a question of crudely applying European universality to the refugees, as if universality were a civilizing measuring stick. Indeed, a European way of life, as Žižek defines it, is antithetical to apartheid logic and sovereign authority; it rejects rather than upholds global capitalism's divide between Us and Them. It is not the refugees but the anti-immigrant Europeans that pose the greatest threat to Europe: "A Europe where Marine Le Pen [in France] or Geert Wilders [in the Netherlands] are in power is no longer Europe. So what is this Europe worth fighting for?"[19] The threat to a "transnational" Europe increasingly appears in what Žižek dubs the "new axis of evil": "countries like Slovenia, Croatia, Hungary, the Czech Republic, now also Austria—these new anti-immigrant racist populists who are taking over there up to Baltic countries."[20] In this light, we might more productively reformulate Žižek's stance toward the refugee crisis as informed by his own double bind, framed as a resistance to today's "double blackmail": the forced choice between humanist identification with refugees or the racist rejection of refugees, between *heterophilia* (pure hospitality) or *heterophobia* (pure hostility).

Against widespread European "'autoimmune' responses"[21] to the threat of racial and racialized refugees—refugees who look different (based on their phenotypic characteristics or cultural habits) and who are as a result considered subhuman—Žižek turns to the biblical injunction "Love thy neighbor." When (re)politicized and redefined, this command takes the form of an invaluable corrective to "today's 'new reign of ethics,'" to a depoliticized ethical sentimentalism or pious ethics of difference emanating from humanist corners and from what Žižek disparagingly calls the "usual *gang of democracy-to-come*-deconstructionist-postsecular-Levinasian-respect-for-Otherness suspects,"[22] who object to the racist logic of the Same, seeking out the recognition of the other. "Love thy neighbor" for Žižek stands as a locus of resistance to the immune disorders that are currently besetting Western communities.[23]

## Žižek *contra* Levinas

As Žižek's critique suggests, Levinas looms large in anti-racist projects, which draw from his account of "astonishing alterity"[24] to explain racism's functioning. A racist economy of the Same fails to see the racial other as worthy of care and respect. What the racial other lacks is precisely a Levinasian face. Meditating on the association of blackness with evil and criminality, George Yancy notes: "In Levinasian terms, my 'face' does not appear in the form of the imperative 'Thou shall not murder.'"[25] Similarly, Achille Mbembe describes antiblack racism in a Levinasian register as an inability to perceive the face of blacks; lacking depth, a "face"—or a face that is systematically disprivileged—the racialized black other can only be read superficially, at the surface level through a regime of visuality, reduced to what Mbembe calls an "image ontology."[26]

Levinas provides Yancy and Mbembe with a by now familiar and generalized Levinasian framework where the face of the racial other fails to be properly encountered. The ethical usefulness of Levinas is not limited to racism but applies as well to efforts at combatting misogyny, homophobia, or phallocentrism. Luce Irigaray, for example, formulates her staunch admonition of masculine philosophical discourse in unmistakably Levinasian terms:

> This domination of the philosophical logos stems in large part from its power to *reduce all others to the economy of the Same*. The teleologically constructive project it takes on is always also a project of diversion, deflection, reduction of the other in the Same. And, in its greatest generality perhaps, from its power to *eradicate the difference* between the sexes in systems that are self-representative of a "masculine subject."[27]

The pertinence of Levinas lies in the philosopher's ability to provide a robust defense of difference. For these thinkers, racism emerges when there is a breakdown in my exposure to the other's face, when I am confronted with a defaced face—a face that is, or has been, structurally ignored, rendered invisible, or assimilated to the order of the Same. Levinas offers anti-racist philosophers, like Yancy and Mbembe, an explanation for the failure of an ethical encounter with the racial other. While neither Yancy nor Mbembe is following Levinas in a strictly orthodox or sustained fashion, their evocation of his work—the latter's obdurate fixation on the face—speaks to the pull of his grammar and its adaptability, as well as his authority in matters of ethics and/as difference. It is on this terrain—the ethics of difference and the primacy of the face—that Žižek confronts Levinas.

Žižek is by no means alone in blaming Levinas for the ethical ideology prevalent today. Alain Badiou argues that the pervasive Levinasian obsession with ethics reduces politics to a series of feel-good platitudes that do little to challenge the status quo:

> Whether they know it or not, it is in the name of this configuration that the proponents of ethics explain to us today that it amounts to "recognition of the other" (against racism, which would deny this other), or to "the ethics of differences" (against substantialist nationalism, which would exclude immigrants, or sexism, which would deny feminine-being), or to "multiculturalism" (against the imposition of an unified model of behaviour and intellectual approach). Or, quite simply, to good old-fashioned "tolerance" which

consists of not being offended by the fact that others think and act differently than you.[28]

If Badiou states unabashedly that "the whole ethical predication based upon recognition of the other should be purely and simply abandoned,"[29] Žižek, though not unsympathetic to Badiou's position, pursues a different approach, exposing Levinasian ethics as politically unproductive and, as we shall see, detrimental to an anti-racist critique. Žižek opposes the historically protean figure of the neighbor to the seemingly timeless Levinasian other.

If Levinas argues that the concept of the "face," as "a being beyond all attributes,"[30] enabled his philosophy to transcend the realm of sociality and the socialization of the other, Žižek, not unlike Derrida, questions this singularization of the face, underscoring instead how Levinas's radical alterity is still subjected to mediation, to the workings of the symbolic order. The face of the other could not be experienced as such, as a face, if it were not always already a discursive product; reading the neighbor as a face thus domesticates the neighbor, making the other's alterity as a resource of infinite responsibility more retrievable. Žižek exposes what he describes as Levinas's "ethical petrification"[31] of otherness, his gentrification of the face (the symbolic neighbor) by juxtaposing it with Primo Levi's account of the *Muselmann*, that living-dead, faceless figure of Auschwitz (the real neighbor). For Žižek, the *Muselmann* discloses the limits of a depoliticizing Levinasian ethics: "When confronted with a Muselmann, one cannot discern in his face the trace of the abyss of the Other in his/her vulnerability, addressing us with the infinite call of our responsibility. What one gets instead is a kind of blind wall, lack of depth."[32] The *Muselmann*, a figure of precarity and bare life, constitutes a disquieting example of the neighbor for whom no relation *as such* is affectively afforded; this "'faceless' face," as Žižek puts it, is a "neighbor with whom no empathetic relationship is possible."[33] Stripped of its symbolic veneer, recalcitrant to one's imaginary projection, denied access to the human realm of intersubjectivity, the *Muselmann* foregrounds the neighbor as real, in which "we encounter the Other's call at its purest and most radical," and "one's responsibility toward the Other at its most traumatic."[34] It is in this context that the ethical injunction to "Love thy neighbor" takes on its full political force.

Setting himself apart from the Levinasian model, Žižek argues that it is not enough to say that I can never account for the other as other, that phenomenologically the other is always in excess of my idea of him or her. Žižek considers the biblical figure of the neighbor the "most precious and revolutionary aspect of the Jewish legacy," stressing how the neighbor "remains an inert, impenetrable, enigmatic presence that hystericizes."[35] Žižek foregrounds the challenge posed by the injunction "Love thy neighbor!" This injunction confounds universalist thinking; it disturbs ethics as such. The biblical injunction might be better characterized as an "anti-ethics"[36] to the extent that it radically deviates from a humanist orientation, where ethics invests itself in a fetishistic ideal of humanity—a gentrified view of Man as the bearer of rights, endowed with a moral sensibility and so forth—disavowing any knowledge of suffering or man-made evil in the world. Jewish law, for its part, de-gentrifies the other, calling us to confront the Real of the other in its figuration of the neighbor. If Greek philosophy neglected the hysterical presence of this other ("Nothing is farther from the message of Socrates than *you shall love your neighbor as yourself, a formula that is remarkably absent* from all that he says," Žižek writes, quoting Lacan[37]), Jewish law avows the Real of the neighbor, that is, the neighbor as the "bearer of a monstrous Otherness, this properly *inhuman* neighbor."[38]

The neighbor is a concretization or embodiment of the Lacanian Real, a reminder and remainder of this Real, an intolerable or traumatic stain which remains untranslatable, irreducible to my interpretive mastery and (humanist) universality. From this vision of the neighbor emerges an ethico-political injunction: "*to love* and respect your neighbor . . . does not refer to your imaginary *semblable*/double, but to the neighbor qua traumatic Thing."[39] The "Real" of the other is impossible but it is an impossibility that paradoxically needs to be sustained:

> The Real is impossible but it is not simply impossible in the sense of a failed encounter. It is also impossible in the sense that it is a traumatic encounter that *does* happen but which we are unable to confront. And one of the strategies used to avoid confronting it is precisely that of positing it as this indefinite ideal which is eternally postponed. One aspect of the real is that it's impossible, but the other aspect is that it happens but is impossible to sustain, impossible to integrate. And this second aspect, I think, is more and more crucial.[40]

The real neighbor is neither assimilable to that which we already know, nor a radical alterity mysteriously exempt from symbolic mediation.

For Fanon, similarly, we must guard against the temptation to think the neighbor's singularity outside mediated relation, the temptation to insist on a radical difference that is tantamount to reified sameness that eschews or denies this encounter this relation. Singularity comes about through history (through history as "non-all," in Žižek's terms), and to forget this is to mistake history for destiny, to reify being and renounce the possibilities of becoming: "If the question once arose for me about showing solidarity with a given past, it was because I was committed to myself and my neighbor, to fight with all my life and all my strength so that never again would people be enslaved on this earth."[41] Fidelity to a "given past" motivates solidarity and action yet also risks arresting this movement. Fanon's neighbor is not *reducible* to a *semblable* (the other with whom I share a colonial past). This neighbor belongs to a different order. The biblical exhortation to love is not grounded in a shared humanity with the other (my imaginary/symbolic counterpart, which always threatens congealing around an identity), but in the acknowledgment of the *inhuman* (the subject's avowed out-of-jointness; the inaccessible, untamable, and anxiety-inducing Real) as the condition of/for universality:

> The most difficult thing for common understanding is to grasp this speculative-dialectical reversal of the singularity of the subject *qua* Neighbor-Thing into universality, not standard "general" universality, but universal singularity, the universality grounded in the subjective singularity extracted from all particular properties, a kind of direct short circuit between the singular and the universal, bypassing the particular.[42]

Conceptualizing the neighbor in this way undermines the opposition between universality and otherness, denying a familiar talking point of the "leftist-multiculturalist liberals who improvise endlessly on the motif of impossible universality."[43] Rather than settling for deference to the other's asepticized particularity, an ethical response to the plight of the real neighbor must pass through universality.[44] Correlatively, we must reconsider who counts as our neighbors, and who has been excluded from that relation.

# Racializing the Other in the Israel–Palestine Conflict

Racialization, as the transformation of others into subhuman inferiors, has been and remains a key social and political mechanism by which neighbors are excluded from "the category of the human as it is performed in the modern west,"[45] persecuted, marginalized, barred from love, and thus made disposable, killable without consequences. The Israel–Palestine conflict throws into particularly stark relief the ethical and political challenges of combatting racialization by appealing to a Levinasian notion of the face—or, conversely, by seeing and treating the racialized other as a neighbor. These challenges come into view, importantly, in a radio interview that Levinas, along with Alain Finkielkraut, gave to Shlomo Malka shortly after the massacre of hundreds of Palestinians between September 16 and September 18, 1982 at the Sabra and Shatila refugee camps in West Beirut, Lebanon, at the hands of Lebanese Christian Phalangist militia in Israeli-occupied Lebanon. In this now infamous interview—which continues to generate much discussion among Levinas's devotees and critics—Levinas makes several comments about the racialized Palestinians that thematize and disclose both the limits and limitations of a philosophy of the face.

The interview starts with a seemingly naïve question by Malka about the relationship between the other, politics, Israel's failed responsibility toward the Palestinian refugees in the Sabra and Shatila camps: "Emmanuel Levinas, you are the philosopher of the 'other.' Isn't history, isn't politics the very site of the encounter with the 'other,' and for the Israeli isn't the 'other' above all Palestinian?"[46] Levinas's response takes the form of a philosophical lesson in phenomenology:

My definition of the other is completely different. The other is the neighbor [*prochain*], who is not necessarily my kin [*proche*] but who may be. But if your neighbor attacks another neighbor, or treats him unjustly, what can you do? Then alterity takes on another character, in alterity we can find an enemy, or at least we are faced with the problem of knowing who is right and who is wrong, who is just and who is unjust. There are people who are wrong.[47]

Levinas resists Malka's determination of the Palestinian as Israel's political other. His emphatic "no" to his interlocutor is not only compatible with this phenomenological ethics, but also is required by it. As he says damningly elsewhere: "The best way of encountering the Other is not even to notice the color of his eyes!"[48] In the interview, we quickly learn that difference or alterity is *not* relational. Race, racism, and racialization are strictly speaking ontic matters, better addressed in sociology than in ethics. Even the conflict of duties (which of my neighbors [fellow Jews or Palestinians] am I [more, first] responsible to?) is about justice, which falls under the jurisdiction of politics. And yet by insisting that ethics—not politics—is first philosophy, Levinas assigns the Palestinian question (Malka's own question, "is the Palestinian the other of the Israelis?" and the more general question, "how to address and redress the wrongs committed to the Palestinian people?") to at best a secondary consideration. Operating at a high level of abstraction ("there are people who are wrong"—who? why?), Levinas seems to default to a register where the Jews of Auschwitz are humanity's universal or timeless Victims, making the Palestinian, in turn, the Israeli's political victimizer. Difference here is ironically relational, an ontical designation; the enemy is historicized and culturalized (i.e., racialized).

Faced with the Palestinian question, Levinas's rhetoric of alterity falls flat. "What Levinas is basically saying," according to Žižek, "is that, as a principle, respect for alterity is unconditional (the highest sort of respect), but, when faced with a concrete other, one should nonetheless see if he is a friend or an enemy. In short, in practical politics, the respect for alterity strictly means nothing."[49] What is at stake in Žižek's critique of Levinas is the latter's *substantialization* of the other; the fascination with the Levinasian other blinds us to the structural suffering of concrete others: "The true ethical step is the one beyond the face of the other, the one of suspending the hold of the face, the one of choosing against the face, for the third."[50] True, emancipatory ethics, then, resists the lure of subjective violence, and steps back to attend to the objective violence; it transcends the dyadic moment of the face-to-face encounter (the ethical proper) to an incorporation of the other's others (the political proper).

Deciding "who is right and who is wrong, who is just and who is unjust" and recognizing that "there are people who are wrong" are not what disqualifies Levinas. Žižek does not have misgivings about determining enemies. As we saw in the previous chapter, Žižek repeatedly asserts the need for the Left to identify its true enemy: "What we need is *even more hatred*, but proper *political* hatred: hatred directed at the common political enemy."[51] What is problematic in Levinas's response is the ideological structure of priority. All things being equal (everyone is my neighbor, *tout autre est tout autre*), attachment to Israel tips the scale. Zionism provides the justification for the idea of Israel. As the Promised Land for the chosen people, Israel emerges for many Jews as immune from critique. Levinas to his credit is critical of this position and also rejects the argument (well-circulated after the Sabra and Shatila massacres) that if you are not living in Israel, you don't have the right to criticize its policies and actions. Levinas's Zionism appears more measured. Israel is more than a "political entity" (always susceptible to fetishization); it represents a "spiritual community."[52] Michael L. Morgan explains the thrust of Levinas's Zionism in terms of its priorities: "it is about helping Jews and not oppressing others."[53] Against the temptation to mystify Israel, Levinas still prioritized the relationship to the other over the relationship to the Promised Land: "a person is more holy than a land, even a holy land."[54]

Amanda Loumansky even suggests that Levinas admits, albeit obliquely, that Israel wronged the Palestinian people:

> [Levinas] reminds us that "a person is more holy than a land, even a holy land, since faced with an affront made to a person, this holy land appears in its nakedness but stone and wood." Levinas has no need to identify that person as a Palestinian because who else can the person be who has suffered the affront? But I think also Levinas intends (as he often does) for there to be a *double entendre*. Jews are also a people who are more holy than the land. The land to which Zionism lays claim is not the be all and end all for the Jewish people who will survive an expulsion from the land, a fate that Levinas recognizes might befall them if they prove themselves to be unworthy if it.[55]

Loumansky's reading of the *double entendre* is more than plausible. Levinas is not only prioritizing the relationship to the other over the relationship to the Promised Land, as his insistence that ethics is still first philosophy. But does this really save Levinas, redeem his position for a Left eager to recruit him for its cause? We must cut through its ideological appeal and reinterpret Levinas's statement even more critically, to read its vagueness not as a sign of the virtues of self-critique but as a fetishization of self-reflexivity (Levinas's "quandary of the self's conscience before the other") at the expense of a further silencing of the (unnamed) Palestinians. This is a repeated trope in philosophical and popular discourses about Israel where multifaceted complexity—an ability to question one's worthiness and recognize one's own depth and layered contradictions—is on the side of the Israelis, while a flattened two-dimensionality characterizes the side of the Palestinians.[56]

Loumansky contextualizes further Levinas's position by attending to Levinas's immediate audience, namely, his less tolerant Zionist interlocutors, whom he seeks to win over by his measured comments about Israel's culpability: "[Levinas] has in mind a (potentially critical) Zionist audience whom he wishes to reassure by confirming that he is keeping faith with the founding principles of the State of Israel and acknowledging that politics establishes that 'there is certainly a place for defence,' which is necessary in order to confront 'all those who attack us with such venom.'"[57] Again, this is a plausible reading, but it hardly paints Levinas as a courageous philosopher, a thinker willing to speak truth to power. Where is the labor of thought? Does ethics as first philosophy take a back seat to norms—or worse, to those in power? The supreme good turns out to be not the other as such but the Israeli status quo—synonymous with the ongoing repression and racialization of Palestinians—a defense of the nation-state, fueled and legitimized by Zionist claims of exceptionality. Even when Israel disappoints as in the events in Sabra and Shatila, Levinas sees it, self-servingly, as pointing to its better nature: "Israel has not become worse than the surrounding world, whatever the anti-Semites say, but it has ceased to be better. The worst thing is that this was precisely one of its ambitions."[58] From "the standpoint of its victims," to borrow Edward Said's formulation, Levinas's acknowledgment of Israel's misdoings, or Zionism's setback, provides little comfort.

The least that can be said is that Levinas fails to properly deconstruct Zionism and its racializing effects. Israel's messianic promise (the dream of a spiritual Zionism) was and is not only threatened by its Prime Ministers—from Menachem Begin to Benjamin Netanyahu—but was seriously tainted almost immediately by the dispossessions of Palestine's indigenous population. Levinas forgets, represses, or never really entertains the fact that the Zionist dream was from the start a Palestinian nightmare.[59] Levinas has on occasion even refused to recognize the existence of the Palestinians, preferring to assimilate them to the homogenizing category of Arabs, in an echo of the late nineteenth-century Zionist-colonial fantasy of *terra nullius*,[60] that is, of a Palestine free of Palestinians, a fantasy subtending Israel's ongoing necropolitics (its subjugation of Palestinian life to "the power of death"[61]), its brutal occupation[62] and routinized humiliation of Palestinian populations:

The origins of the conflict between Jews and Arabs go back to Zionism. This conflict has been acute since the creation of the State of Israel on a small piece of arid land which had belonged to the children of

Israel more than thirty centuries before and which . . . has never been abandoned by the Jewish communities . . . . But it also happens to be on a small piece of land which has been inhabited by people who are surrounded on all sides and by vast stretches of land containing the great Arab people of which they form a part. They call themselves Palestinians.[63]

In line with a long Zionist tradition that denies the existence of the Palestinian people,[64] Levinas raises doubts about the referential accuracy of the signifier "Palestinians," questioning their legitimacy as a people, those who merely "call themselves Palestinians." Juxtaposed with the Jews and their well-established lineage as the "children of Israel," the Palestinians are impostors who simply pale in comparison.

Levinas, like liberal Zionists, cannot see that the racialization of the Palestinians coexisted with the creation of the State of Israel. Israel's violence toward the Palestinians was and continues be constitutive of Israeli existence. Shahid Alam ingeniously inverts Israeli exceptionalism: "Critics of Zionism and Israel—including a few Israelis— have charted an inverse exceptionalism, which describes an Israel that is aberrant, violates international norms with near impunity, engages in systematic abuse of human rights, wages wars at will, and has expanded its territories through conquest."[65] To be sure, all nations engage in forms of what Walter Benjamin describes as state-founding violence (of which the racialization of the indigenous people is one prevalent model). But as Žižek critically observes, what makes Israel's case unique today is that this violence is ongoing and contested, and thus its memory is still very much alive. Israel "hasn't yet obliterated the 'founding violence' of its 'illegitimate' origins, repressed them into a timeless past. In this sense, what the state of Israel confronts us with is merely the obliterated past of every state power."[66]

An anti-racist critique of Israel must attend not only to the current abhorrent realities of life under occupation but also to Israel's "original sin"—the Nakba, the Arabic word for "catastrophe," denoting the forced mass expulsion of 800,000 Palestinians between 1948 and 1949.[67] The work of anti-racism must keep this link between "founding violence"— the arbitrary and groundless division of the social field between Jews and non-Jews (of which the Palestinians are the lowest manifestation)—and "objective violence"—the rules and practices that sustain the existence of the Zionist status quo[68]—visible. Take for example the July 2018 law passed by the Knesset, the Israeli Parliament, declaring Israel the "nation-state of the Jewish people." Predictably liberals were quick to condemn the law, stating that it jeopardizes Israel's identity as a Jewish *and* democratic state, and further endangers the prospects of a two-state solution, that cruel fantasy that only prolongs the unacceptable state of affairs.[69] What the liberal reaction ignores is Zionism's undemocratic legacy, fervent tribalism, and racial dehumanization of Palestinians.[70] The new law seeks to fully naturalize Israel's founding violence. For the critical eye, the law makes Zionism's unpalatable legacy explicit; its aggressive lobbying for Jewish settlements only accelerates Israel's "quasi-ontological segregation"[71]—or apartheid. As the law itself reads, "the state views the development of Jewish settlement as a national value and will act to encourage and promote its establishment and consolidation."[72]

# De-Racializing the Palestinians, or the Palestinians as Neighbors

If Levinas lacked the moral courage to tackle the problems of a messianic Zionism (never doubting its claims of exceptionalism), Žižek boldly calls for abandoning any mythic or transhistorical pretensions of origins and exclusionary claims of rooted-identity:

> The lesson is simply that every form of legitimization of a claim to land by some mythic past should be rejected. In order to resolve (or contain, at least), the Israeli-Palestinian conflict, we should not dwell in ancient past—we should, on the contrary, forget the past (which is in any case basically constantly reinvented to legitimize present claims).[73]

Seeing that "Zionism was a historical construction,"[74] as Gianni Vattimo and Michael Marder point out—and not the realization of Israel's Manifest Destiny—is a first step to deconstructing Zionism, to seeing it as an ideological concept. Zionists constantly argue that the connection between Jews and the land of Israel is both intrinsic and essential, that Jews dwelling in Israel is a necessity that had to happen. But the historical record of Zionism is more complicated: Palestine was by no means the only option for the Promised Land considered by early Zionists. Uganda, Azerbaijan, and Argentina were also some of the destinations seriously explored.[75] A second step to deconstructing Zionism is to address and redress the injustices committed against Zionism's victims, who are "not only the Palestinians . . ., but also . . . the anti-Zionist Jews, 'erased' from the officially consecrated account of Zionist history."[76]

Žižek turns to the figure of the *refuseniks*, Israeli soldiers who refuse to complete their compulsory military service in the Occupied Territories, for a *critique of Zionism from within*. The *refuseniks*, like any Israeli citizen, inherit a racist ideology that instructs them to treat Palestinians "not *as if* a racial group, not simply *in the manner* of a racial group, but *as* a despised and demonic racial group." Goldberg calls this "racial Palestinization."[77] What can only emerge from this racist ideology is the bestialization of the Palestinian, the genocidal view that *a good Palestinian is a dead Palestinian*.[78] Palestinians simply lack any ontological worth. In the Zionist fantasy of *terra nullius*, Palestinians, as Elias Sanbar argues, are encountered but not really there: "In order to succeed, the emptiness of the terrain must be based in an evacuation of the 'other' from the settlers' own heads."[79] But the *refuseniks* decline such interpellation into the Zionist social body. They decline the pathos of Zionism, its messianic pull: the ways it inculcates Jewish Israelis with a belief that their brutal treatment of Palestinians ultimately serves a redemptive end and that they answer only to a higher cosmic calling.[80] Refusing to serve as instruments of Israel's brutal necropower, the *refuseniks* reject blind allegiance to the nation-state, opting for a more just Israel. *Refusenik* Haggai Matar spoke in the early 2000s against Israel's disproportionate response[81] to the second Palestinian intifada or uprising in the following words:

> Today, militarization and racism among the Jewish population have reached a fascist level. The repression of critical thinking, the total acceptance of the occupation's crimes, the idolization of the army and the gradual acceptance of the principle of "ethnic cleansing"— all these constitute only part of our society's collapse. To this list one should add the systematic mistreatment of the Palestinian citizens of Israel, the hateful violence addressed at peace demonstrators, and the heartless attitude towards the abnormal and the weak.[82]

These conscientious objectors intervene in the politics and ethics of Jewishness. Declining to perpetuate Israel's state of exception—that is, its sovereign power to remove Palestinians from the protection of the law—the *refuseniks* seriously take up, if not fulfill, the injunction to "Love thy neighbor":

> What the *refuseniks* have achieved is the passage from *Homo sacer* to "neighbour": they treat Palestinians not as "equal full citizens," but as *neighbours* in the strict Judeo-Christian sense. And, in fact, that is the difficult ethical test for Israelis today: "Love thy neighbour!" means "Love the Palestinian!" (who is their neighbour *par excellence*), or it means nothing at all.[83]

After their act, Zionist life is out of joint, even if temporally. Palestinian lives are transfigured from *homines sacri* (individuals stripped of their rights, and deprived of the means of articulating their very exclusion or demanding redress) into neighbors (individuals who solicit an ethical response despite, or because of, their racialized otherness). The *refuseniks'* treatment of Palestinians calls for a reinvention of the Symbolic—infusing doubt into the racial separation of Jews and Arabs, which, in turn, unsettles the phantasm of a pure racial Zionist identity. It constitutes an anti-racist "ethical act," something of a "miraculous moment in which eternal justice momentarily appears in the temporal sphere of empirical reality."[84] As a virtually contagious miracle, though "downplayed"[85] by the mainstream media, the *refuseniks'* "No!" holds a genuinely emancipatory promise.

Domick LaCapra criticizes Žižek's jubilant reading of the *refuseniks* for its idealism and ahistoricity:

> Žižek can offer the totally speculative, implausible interpretation of the acts of refuseniks in Israel, refusing to fight in the occupied territories, not only as a move away from seeing Palestinians as Agamben's *homo sacer* toward a vision of them as Judaeo-Christian neighbors (what happens to Islam here?), but also as designating "the miraculous moment in which eternal justice momentarily appears in the temporal sphere of empirical reality"—in effect as acts of transcendent grace conflated with (or incarnated in) this-worldly miracles.[86]

LaCapra's disciplinary preference for situating causality and the possible within a particular historical framework forecloses the very possibility of an *act*, of that which makes the impossible possible. Žižek is not saying *refuseniks* are all revolutionary subjects calling for the destruction of the

Zionist order of things. It is very likely that most of the *refuseniks* fall under the category of liberal Zionists (they are only refusing to serve *in the Occupied Territories*), continuing to believe in Israel as a Jewish State living side by side with a free Palestine one. Still, in the act of refusal, Žižek perceives a disturbing excess that reveals the lack in the Symbolic, a gap whose revolutionary potential he seeks to exploit, challenging Israelis to live up to their own ideal,[87] to exert pressure on their Zionist communal life, and treat the Palestinians as neighbors.

To treat the Palestinians as neighbors is, of course, not simply to acknowledge their ontological opacity, to acknowledge, that is, the truth that "we are all opaque subjects"—*it is that and more*. It is to underscore and attend to their historical racialization, their state of precarity, or, in other words, the symbolic order's contingent distribution of vulnerability and unfamiliarity (an unfamiliarity increasingly taken as bestial and threatening, as a sign of Palestinian primitivism). The *refuseniks*, on Žižek's account, also decline the liberal or humanist remedy, which would mean conceiving of the neighbors through a limiting framework as "equal full citizens." The injunction to "Love the Palestinian" goes further in insisting on the challenges posed by the other. The Palestinian as a neighbor—the Palestinian stripped of his or her symbolic veneer via Israeli racialization—continues to arouse anxiety, compelling a different kind of affective relationality, a relationality that exposes the limits of relationality: when confronted with Palestinians, the *refuseniks* encounter "a blind wall, a lack of depth"[88] and act ethically toward them. Acting on the neighborly injunction de-racializes the Palestinians, decompletes Zionist reality and its apparatus of racial classification: *Zionist ideology is not all.* "Love the Palestinian" produces an affective excess, a visceral ethical feeling, that is, a noncoincidence between a compulsory hatred of Palestinians (what cultural norms tell soldiers they should feel for the enemy, for the racialized other) and how they actually respond to the (real) Palestinians: to de-racialize the Palestinians is to insist on treating them on equal footing.

To treat and relate to the Palestinian as a neighbor is, however, also to reject the faux universality of an "equal full citizen" model, a model that relies on a logic of sovereignty, a structure through which a sovereign power dictates who is included in Israel's modern state (applying the Law of Return), and who is excluded from it (denying the right of return). The enlightened sovereign self decides on the exception; he or she is driven to act by a masculine logic. That self would make the Palestinian other grievable (no longer designated as a *homo sacer*, not-quite-human or nonhuman[89]) on the basis of an implicit identification with the formerly excluded, now brought fully into the polity and the "privileges" of humanity, into the realm of intersubjectivity and sameness, controlled and contained under the umbrella of an inclusive humanism (a false universalism). By contrast, if there is identification, we might say that the *refuseniks* identify with Zionism's symptom: the Palestinians as symptoms, the excluded "part of no-part." Israel's racialized other here is never ontologized or divorced from the economic and political field of power. Quite the opposite, the example of the *refuseniks* repoliticizes the Symbolic, opening up new possibilities and modalities. It challenges Zionism as the unquestioned and ultimate horizon of Jewish political practice, delegitimizing the Zionist/colonizer settler narrative that racially frames or structures Israeli knowledge and experience of the Palestinian people, that decides "who matters and who does not, who is *disposable* and who is not."[90]

The *refuseniks'* important disidentification with the State of Israel inscribes them in a rich Jewish tradition, aligning them with the cosmopolitan Jew who, as Žižek observes, always kept a critical distance vis-à-vis his or her community:

> The privileged role of Jews in the establishment of the sphere of the "public use of reason" hinges on their subtraction from every state power. Theirs is this position of the "part of no-part" in every organic nation-state community, and it is this position, not the abstract-universal nature of their monotheism, that makes them the immediate embodiment of universality. No wonder, then, that, with the establishment of the Jewish nation-state, a new figure of the Jew emerged: a Jew resisting identification with the State of Israel, refusing to accept the State of Israel as his true home, a Jew who "subtracts" himself from this State, and who includes the State of Israel among the states towards which he insists on maintaining a distance, to live in their interstices.[91]

As the "part of no-part," the cosmopolitan Jew stands for "the empty principle of universality"[92] (in the next chapter we will look at the exilic Palestinian as similarly occupying the position of the "part of no-part," producing a critique of Zionism from without). Praise for this "uncanny Jew,"[93] of course, comes with a risk. Non-Jews who offer such praise risk the charge of anti-Semitism, while Jews risk the charge of pathological self-hatred (or in more patronizing terms, the charge of serving as a "useful idiot of anti-Semites"[94]). Contemporary Zionists treat Jews (like the *refuseniks*) who do not fully identify with Israel and accept its racial regime as a "foreign excess disturbing the community of the nation-state."[95] In declining organicist attachment, this universalist Jew experiences a new form of racism and racialization, which Žižek aptly dubs "Zionist anti-Semitism."[96]

Bruno Chaouat dismisses Žižek's claim of "Zionist anti-Semitism," seeing in the idea of an "uncanny Jew"—the Jew who does not (want to) belong to his or her given community—"a mirror of the antisemitic topos": "the common trope of antisemitism, the trope that traverses Western history, is that Jews . . . are never where they ought to be, they are always in an awkward, somewhat anachronistic position vis-à-vis the dominant ideology—cosmopolitan in a nationalistic Europe, capitalist in communist Russia, Bolsheviks in Nazi Germany, nationalist in post-national Europe, etc."[97] Žižek and other post-Heideggerian theorists are blamed for "Jew-splitting," for creating a mythic, dichotomous caricature: the good uncanny Jew versus the bad Zionist Jew. But there is an irony here to extent that Chaouat is guilty of creating his own split: the good Jew who appreciates Israel's historical necessity and the bad Jew like Judith Butler who fetishizes diasporic Judaism and falsifies the history of Zionism. In fact, Chaouat never really deals with Žižek's characterization of "Zionist anti-Semitism" that there is anti-Semitism at work when Jews who courageously disidentify with the State of Israel are vilified, described as traitors to their own race.[98] Chaouat draws instead a facile analogy between the old racist anti-Semites who malign Jews as outsiders and Žižek (the new anti-racist anti-Semite) who privileges the Jew as an outsider.[99]

If the creation of Israel was supposed to put an end to, or at least curtail, this anti-Semitic topos (since all Jews in principle can claim Israel as their home), Žižek's insistence on this "uncanny Jew" is read as a desire to keep open the wound of anti-Semitism. What Žižek is saying is quite the opposite. Žižek is not inventing or phantasmatically projecting anti-Zionist Jews. What he is pointing out is the ironic situation in which supporters of the State of Israel are themselves recycling anti-Semitic topoi—you don't belong in our community, you collaborate with our enemies, you are a threat to our way of life, etc. Žižek's sympathies clearly lie with Jews who object to Israeli policies toward the Palestinians, who question an aggressive Zionism that silences opposition at home and abroad. This does not stem however from a desire to perpetuate anti-Semitism—the hatred of Jews in the guise of a noble defense of the marginalized, excluded, and dispossessed other—but from what Judith Butler has called "a passion for justice," a genuine desire to see, and fight for, universal equality and freedom (*égaliberté*) for Jews and Arabs alike.[100]

# Žižek with Derrida

In light of the example of the *refuseniks*, we can return to the refugee crisis with which we opened the chapter and now ask, paraphrasing Žižek: isn't the difficult ethical test for Europeans today precisely to see the refugees as neighbors? "Love thy neighbor!" means "Love the refugee!," or it means nothing at all. As a corollary question: what kind of hospitality does justice to the biblical injunction? Here, thinking Žižek with Derrida might prove resourceful.

While Žižek is often critical of deconstruction, seeing it as failing to confront today's true antagonisms, he does perceive a convergence between Derrida's early notion of *différance* and his own account of "minimal difference":

> Since I have written many pages in which I struggle with the work of Jacques Derrida, now—when the Derridean fashion is fading away—is perhaps the moment to honor his memory by pointing out the proximity of this "minimal difference" to what he called *différance*, this neologism whose very notoriety obfuscates its unprecedented materialist potential.[101]

What both ideas have in common is the insistence on an internal division in the thing itself, "the constitutive noncoincidence of a thing with itself."[102] Žižek couples his praise for the materialist potential of *différance* with a dismissal of the late Derrida's rhetoric of the messianic. When "radical" liberals advocate open borders in order to let in all the refugees, an idea Žižek rejects, we can hear in their call an echo of Derrida's discussion of openness to the other:

> Let us say yes *to who or what turns up*, before any determination, before any anticipation, before any *identification*, whether or not

it has to do with a foreigner, an immigrant, an invited guest, or an unexpected visitor, whether or not the new arrival is the citizen of another country, a human, animal, or divine creature, a living or dead thing, male or female.[103]

Derrida may have increased the range of the "face"—it is no longer restricted to living humans and also includes racial others (the other as immigrant or foreigner)—but what we have here from a Žižekian vantage point is more of the same, more Levinasianism, more fascination with difference—the endless awaiting of the other. The messianic other looks a lot like the Levinasian other, plagued with similar political problems. Deconstruction is, at best, a remedy for subjective violence; at worst, it ignores objective violence, consigning the other's others to oblivion.

But this is to ignore Derrida's critical distance from Levinas and his rejection of Levinas's "*dream* of a purely *heterological* thought."[104] Against what we might call the Levinasian blackmail, Derrida insists that the question is not one of choosing between "the opening and the totality,"[105] that is, between infinity and sameness. Derrida keeps returning to the *relationality* of the other/the face. Though there is always something surprising about the other, something "wholly other [*tout autre*],"[106] a pure or unmediated encounter with the other remains something of a *phantasm*. And to be sure, we find Derrida, at times, all-too-captivated by this *phantasm* of a "pure ethics":

> Pure ethics, if there is any, begins with the respectable dignity of the other as absolute *unlike*, recognized as nonrecognizable, indeed as unrecognizable, beyond all knowledge, all cognition and all recognition: far from being the beginning of pure ethics, the neighbor as like or as resembling, as looking like, spells the end or the ruin of such an ethics, if there is any.[107]

Yet we must attend carefully to Derrida's self-puncturing moments of doubt here, to moments such as the one above, where Derrida entertains thoughts of a pure ethics while qualifying such observations with the repetition of the words, "if there is any"—thematizing, as it were, the phantasmatic character of such a notion.

We can reread Derrida's account of the other in terms of the Lacanian Borromean knot, which unites the three orders of the Real, the Imaginary, and the Symbolic. When Derrida evokes "the neighbor as like or as resembling, as looking like," he is referring to the imaginary-symbolic neighbor. His account of the other aligns with the real neighbor, the neighbor as a "monstrous Thing"—unaltered or domesticated by the symbolic order. Again, the injunction "Love thy neighbor" is about loving the real neighbor, not the decaffeinated other of liberal multiculturalism: "the idealized Other who dances fascinating dances and has an ecologically sound holistic approach to reality."[108] This neighbor disturbs me at my core. The challenge is how to politically and ethically engage the non-European other.

Of course, not all monsters are created equal. Evoking the "monster" for Derrida is about resisting the reduction of the other to the already known (the other is without abyss, phantasmatically transparent); it is to maintain a relationless relation with the other. Each other is radically monstrous, and yet each other shares the identity of monstrosity. Conceptualizing the relation to the other as a "relation without relation" renders problematic the choice between pure otherness or pure sameness, and serves to block or forestall the (illusory) hermeneutic security that the "is" (the other is . . .) might provide.

And there is the monstrosity of the refugees. This monstrosity is doubled: it is constituted by racist fantasies of intruding foreigners (of course, referring to them as "monsters" can easily play into the hands of racist right-wing populists) and by the neighbor's anxiety-producing unknowability and unpredictability: Who are the refugees? What do they want from me? To consider refugees as real neighbors is not to dehistoricize or ontologize their condition, nor is it to minimize their racially dehumanized condition. On the contrary, "Love thy neighbor" takes up the difficult—even traumatizing—task of identifying with society's/globalism's desubjectivized others, those others whose faces fail to disclose their humanity. It is also to avow and come to terms with the fact that "refugees are the price humanity is paying for the global economy."[109] Today's large migrations in Europe are the direct result of Western interventions and neocolonial expansions. Most refugees originate from "failed states," severely lacking "public authority."[110] If some in the West conveniently promote timeless explanations of the unrest in Syria, Iraq, Libya and elsewhere ("ethnic warfare fuelled by old passions"), Žižek locates the source for the failed states in the global economy, as "the result of international economics and politics."[111]

The refugees desperately need their own *refuseniks*, Europeans citizens and politicians who will refuse to serve the interests of global capitalism.

Žižek praises German chancellor Angela Merkel's 2015 "invitation to accept the refugees—more refugees than any other European state," considering it "a genuine ethical miracle, one that cannot be reduced to the capitalist strategy of importing cheap labor force."[112] Merkel knew that she would take a political hit for her decision—and increase the popularity of anti-immigrant right-wingers—but still did it because it was the right thing to do. At the same time, Žižek knows that it is going to require the election of more than liberal politicians to change the current path of the global economy. More "radical" liberal politicians only fuel the fantasy of a capitalism with a human face, that is, a postracial capitalism capable of accommodating the occasional influx of refugees and still function as "efficiently" as before. In his exchange with John Caputo, Žižek throws into starker relief the fault lines separating a Marxist critique from its liberal deconstructive counterpart. Caputo first responds to Žižek and Badiou's alarming concern about the spread of global capitalism with the following patronizing reassurance:

I would be perfectly happy if the far left politicians in the United States were able to reform the system by providing universal health care, effectively redistributing wealth more equitably with a revised IRS code, effectively restricting campaign financing, enfranchising all voters, treating migrant workers humanely, and effecting a multilateral foreign policy that would integrate American power within the international community, etc., i.e., intervene upon capitalism by means of serious and far-reaching reforms . . . . If after doing all that Badiou and Žižek complained that some Monster called Capital still stalks us, I would be inclined to greet that Monster with a yawn.[113]

Žižek counters that this "Monster" is precisely untamable within the existing economic structures. Cosmetic reforms that pretend to stabilize capitalism can only prolong the disastrous reign of the postpolitical:

The problem here is not Caputo's conclusion that if one can achieve all that within capitalism, why not remain within the system? The problem lies with the "utopian" premise that it is possible to achieve all that within the coordinates of global capitalism. What if the particular malfunctionings of capitalism enumerated by Caputo are not merely accidental disturbances but are rather structurally necessary? What if

Caputo's dream is a dream of universality (of the universal capitalist order) without its symptoms, without any critical points in which its "repressed truth" articulates itself?"[114]

Caputo's universality is a universality without refugee crises, a universality that exists alongside the fantasy of a "frictionless"[115] capitalism.

Žižek sees the mainstream Left as critically impoverished— abandoning its call for "the ruthless critique of all that exists,"[116] tacitly acquiescing to the permanent reality of today's global economy. He ironically labels them "leftist Fukuyamaists."[117] Žižek urges the Left to shift focus back to the material realities that brought us this refugee crisis. Humanitarian aid is a *pharmakon*; it is "both cure and poison."[118] It does address the suffering of the refugees. But, as with a Žižekian critique of privilege theory, the point here is to redress their suffering. This will not happen merely by increasing humanitarian intervention, which prolongs the exposure and suffering of the refugees by obfuscating the global causes of the crisis. Nor do lofty proclamations suffice, as when leftist liberals, or "Beautiful Souls," assert that "Europe should show solidarity, should open its doors widely."[119] Such claims smack of fake radicalism. The call for open borders is an empty act.[120]

What prevents a confrontation with the problem at hand is a series of distortions about what the problem is. We (Europeans and the rest of the Western world) are asked to choose between terrorism or anti-terrorism, a humanist identification with refugees or a racist rejection of refugees, the defense of Western values or the rejection of Western values, Islam or a critique of Islam, and so on. This binary logic confuses the refugee problem. What is needed is more lucidity over the Left's short-term and long-term goals:

> The political consequence of this paradox [when it is the religious fundamentalists or right-wing populist factions, and not Western, or Western-backed, liberal forces, who are dealing with class matters] is the properly dialectical tension between long-term strategy and short-term tactical alliances: although, in the long-term, the very success of the radical-emancipatory struggle depends on mobilizing the lower classes that are today often in thrall to fundamentalist populism, one should have no problems with concluding short-term alliances with egalitarian liberals as part of anti-sexist and anti-racist struggles.[121]

The anger of anti-immigrant populism toward global capitalism gets "displaced and mystified,"[122] redirected against refugees and other scapegoats. But populism is not an exclusive problem of the Right. The Left has its own versions, such as the one expressed in the recent Yellow Vests movement. Like right populism, left populism—though far less racist and xenophobic than its counterpart[123]—foregrounds economic pain by demanding lower taxes, higher pensions, increased salaries, and even "Frexit" (the exit of France from the European Union). But for Žižek the Yellow Vests ultimately have not offered "a feasible alternative to the system."[124] Their demands can only receive a "conditional yes."[125] Žižek fully endorses only leftist projects that include a recognition that "the whole paradigm will have to change."[126] In this respect, the Yellow Vests are really no better at dealing with the refugee problem and racism than the anti-immigrant populists. They are vulnerable to the same type of ideological manipulation:

> How to deal with the flow of refugees? The solution is not to just open the borders to all who want to come in, and to ground this openness in our generalised guilt . . . . If we remain at this level, we serve perfectly the interests of those in power who foment the conflict between immigrants and the local working class (which feels threatened by them) and retain their superior moral stance . . . Again, the "contradiction" between advocates of open borders and populist anti-immigrants is a false "secondary contradiction" whose ultimate function is to obfuscate the need to change the system itself: the entire international economic system which, in its present form, gives rise to refugees.[127]

Long-term humanitarian help—though less of a priority for left populism (if it becomes a priority, then there would really be no difference between it and right populism)—is for this reason detrimental for both the refugees and the Europeans: "The more we treat refugees as objects of humanitarian help, and allow the situation which compelled them to leave their countries to prevail, the more they come to Europe, until tensions reach boiling point, not only in the refugees' countries of origin but here as well."[128]

For Žižek, the long-term solution for Europe is to fundamentally rethink hospitality as solidarity:

Don't just respect others: offer them a common struggle, since our problems today are common; propose and fight for a positive universal project shared by all participants. . . .

So let's bring class struggle back—and the only way to do it is to insist on the global solidarity of the exploited and oppressed . . . . Maybe such global solidarity is a utopia. But if we don't engage in it, then we are really lost. And we will deserve to be lost.[129]

At a time when both the Left and the Right are (re)turning to the nation-state (as a means of resisting global capitalism by minimally subtracting yourself from it), global solidarity would make the impossible possible. Only such solidarity can effectively deal with populist hostility. Only such solidarity can counter Europe's hitherto "'autoimmune' responses."[130] But here we might want to give the term "autoimmune" a Derridean twist.[131] As with *différance*, the notion of autoimmunity embodies for Derrida a certain "minimal difference" as Žižek understands the term. Autoimmunity entails a process through which, as Derrida puts it, "a living being, in a quasi-*suicidal* fashion, 'itself' works to destroy its own protection, to immunise itself *against* its 'own' immunity."[132] Yet while autoimmunization refers to the attempt to gain pure immunity, the attempt to wall off the self—an individual, a community, a nation—from external forces and influences, autoimmunity also names the condition of the self, that introduces a noncoincidence between the self and itself, that makes such attempts at self-enclosure impossible.

In describing the self as autoimmune, Derrida redefines the term, understanding it not as an illness or disability to lament or overcome, but rather as a condition of malleability and openness—a condition that involves vulnerability to harm but that also makes intersubjective contact and relation possible. Derrida cautions against the dangerous fantasy of a pure community, insisting that for a community to stay "alive," it must remain "open to something other and more than itself."[133] European communities are living in a state of paranoia, which compulsorily fuels the immunitary attitude. "Everywhere we look, new walls, new blockades, and new dividing lines are erected against something that threatens, or at least seems to, our biological, social, and environmental identity," writes Roberto Esposito.[134] The refugee crisis has triggered and is triggering such immune disorders in one European nation after another.

What is Europe? And what is happening to it? The liberal Left, ashamed of its colonial past, adopts a generous humanitarian perspective vis-à-vis the refugees, willing to assimilate them in an ever-expanding capitalist Europe. The anti-immigrant populist Right wants to shrink Europe, to deglobalize it; the extreme Right fully endorses the virtues of the immunology paradigm. European lives ought to be immunized, purified, and protected, whereas refugee lives ought to be left disposable, exposed, and precarious. The Right's message is clear: *Europe for Europeans—or even better, France for the French, Germany for the Germans, Italy for the Italians, and so on.*

Both the Left's and the Right's responses are to be rejected. We must go beyond humanitarian concerns or security concerns. Ilan Kapoor justly decries "the overwhelming tendency . . . to tackle the symptoms rather than the causes, the quick and efficient managerial fixes rather than more complex political struggles, the media-friendly 'personal stories' rather than the wider and recurring patterns of inequality and dispossession."[135] Against this depolitization of violence, where one talks about refugee suffering without needing to address the world's economic and political landscape, the Left must reorient its critical focus on the *causes* of global injustice and inequalities. The refugee crisis provides Europe "a unique chance to redefine itself."[136] This crisis has exposed to the world Europe's "pervertability"[137]—its universal image as the defender of human rights and its practices (treatment of the refugees) hardly coincided. But Europe's "strange illogical logic"[138] of autoimmunity, its self-destructive propensity, is also what enables Europe to improve, to endlessly perfect itself.

Žižek's bold advice for Europeans is to take "Love thy neighbor" to heart. To love the refugees is to decline an embrace of the other based on charity, sentimentalist humanism, or empathy. There is no "friendly neighbor"[139] behind the mask of cultural difference. "Love thy neighbor" means acknowledging the radical alterity of the neighbor, the refugee's singular form of *jouissance*, accepting that "most of the refugees are *not* 'people like us.'"[140] There is no "harmoniously indifferent coexistence."[141] But as if to block the impulse to reify this difference (Us versus Them), Žižek is quick to add, "not because they are foreign, but because *we* ourselves are not 'people like us.'"[142] This point is crucial. The "we" is always already irreducibly inconsistent. The same holds for *jouissance*: "It is not only that different modes of *jouissance* are incongruous with each other without a common measure; the other's *jouissance* is insupportable for us because (and insofar as) we cannot find a proper way to relate to our own *jouissance*."[143] The fundamental division is not between Europeans and refugees (popularized in the racist "clash of civilizations"[144] narrative)—rather, the division exists within each one of us. We share with the neighbor an inhuman core, an "abyss of impenetrability."[145]

Žižek also rejects the patronizing respect or soft racism of the liberal Left who suspend any critical judgment of the refugees and other marginalized groups, refusing to treat them on equal footing, keeping them at a comfortable distance.[146] Žižek obviously does not want to add to their suffering by joining the chorus of the anti-immigrant populist right. But, at the same time, he does not want to speak for the other; he does not want a toothless, depoliticized respect of the other that only fetishizes the racialized refugees and their way of life. This homogenized other, reduced to the status of a "passive bystander,"[147] makes liberal Europeans feel good about their anti-racism—which is nothing but the flipside of the extreme right's enjoyment of hating the refugees. If the Left wants to bring about genuine change in Europe, in the lives of the refugees, and the rest of the world, it must seek out "the global solidarity of the exploited and oppressed."[148] What prevents this "global solidarity" from becoming yet another leftist empty gesture is internal critique. The Left must reaffirm and reclaim its commitment to anti-capitalism—and carefully tie its struggle against racism and other forms of oppression to that commitment—which it has inadvisably all but surrendered to the extreme right populist movements. Pure hospitality or pure hostility is ultimately a false choice in the refugee crisis. Of course, what is happening to the refugees is catastrophic. They need immediate protection from xenophobic groups, and they need to be afforded hospitality, but this cannot become an end itself; this is not a problem solvable by humanitarian aid alone. The Left must also engage critically and honestly with the refugees and other oppressed groups. As Edward Said used to say, "never solidarity before criticism."[149] The Left must insist (and strive to convince others) that some European values and ideas— egalitarianism, human rights, the welfare state, and so on—are worth saving and (collectively) fighting for.

# 3 POSTCOLONIALISM: FROM THE CULTURALIZATION OF POLITICS TO THE POLITICIZATION OF CULTURE

*Postcolonial theory emerged as the dominant paradigm for understanding collective "struggle" over the same years that witnessed the massive and sustained asset-stripping of the third world. The properly political value of this theory needs to be assessed in terms of the way it responds to this situation.*

**PETER HALLWARD**[1]

*The structure of the universe of commodities and capital in Marx's Capital is not just that of a limited empirical sphere, but a kind of socio-transcendental a priori, the matrix which generates the totality of social and political relations.*

**SLAVOJ ŽIŽEK**[2]

One symptom of neoliberal capitalism's triumphant reign is the alleged "return to ethics" that made its way into Western universities, particularly in the humanities. On Žižek's account, with the return to ethics, the Left's project of radical democracy fell victim to a pervasive type of intellectual blackmail:

The moment one shows a minimal sign of engaging in political projects that aim to seriously challenge the existing order, the answer is immediately: "Benevolent as it is, this will necessarily end in a new Gulag!" The "return to ethics" in today's political philosophy shamefully exploits the horrors of the Gulag or Holocaust as the ultimate bogey for blackmailing us into renouncing all serious radical engagement.[3]

For the liberal multiculturalist and deconstructionist, steady reform—rather than the violent burst of revolution—is the reasonable and moral way of proceeding, a position to which Žižek, as we have seen, is entirely opposed, insisting that "the point of emphasizing morality is to prevent the critique of capitalism."[4] This "return to ethics"—fueled by a fetishization of cultural hybridity, a gentrified figure of otherness which is, as Jameson sardonically puts it, "merely added mechanically onto some individual psychology," "evaporat[ing] into Levinassian sentimentalism"[5]—is symptomatic of a more general "culturalization of politics,"[6] which displaces the economic focus on class struggle, a struggle easily dismissed as a form of economic essentialism or what cultural studies theorist Stuart Hall dubs "economism."[7]

The position of postcolonialism within this debate is conflicted. On the one hand, political struggle is in the DNA of postcolonial theory, which is committed to "the creative cultural engagement with imperialism in all its forms,"[8] to critiquing the exercise of neocolonial power and its ongoing impacts. We could say that postcolonialism takes politics as first philosophy—to paraphrase and pervert Levinas. But what kind of politics postcolonial theorists espouse—is Homi Bhabha's "deep collaboration between aesthetics, ethics and activism" adequate to the task of critique? how efficacious is it?—remains a contested question both within the field and without, as Peter Hallward's remarks above attest.[9] There is indeed something unnerving about witnessing the rise and dominance of postcolonialism (a discourse about defending the voices of the Third World) during a period when global capitalism (an economic system geared toward the systematic appropriation of Third World goods) proceeded unchecked. For Žižek, despite its avowed commitments, postcolonialism, like multiculturalism and deconstruction, is guilty of depoliticizing social reality, of turning "Marxism into cultural analysis,"[10] and of unduly psychologizing the politico-economic struggle:

The problem of postcolonialism is undoubtedly crucial; however, "postcolonial studies" tends to translate it into the multiculturalist problematic of the colonized minorities' "right to narrate" their experience of victimization, of the power mechanisms that repress "otherness," so that, at the end of the day, we learn that the root of postcolonial exploitation is our intolerance toward the Other and, furthermore, that this intolerance itself is rooted in our intolerance toward the "Stranger in Ourselves," in our inability to confront what we repressed in and of ourselves. The politico-economic struggle is thus imperceptibly transformed into a pseudo-psychoanalytic drama of the subject unable to confront its inner traumas.[11]

The "stranger in ourselves" might seem analogous to the monster in the Western self that an encounter with the real neighbor (the refugee, the Palestinian) discloses. Where the postcolonial reading stops short, for Žižek, is in not linking this monstrous division that exists within each one of us—that fantasy invariably but impossibly tries to resolve—back to society's class antagonism. Its lesson remains one-sided so long as class struggle remains unaddressed.

In *Violence*, Žižek also faults the postcolonial critique of liberal ideology for stopping at demystifying the abstract universality of European modernity. And more recently in *Trouble in Paradise*, Žižek objects to decoloniality's even more categorical denunciation of Eurocentrism (which he views as an offshoot or intensification of postcolonial theory, rather than a departure from it). Seeing themselves as correcting postcolonial theory's Eurocentric biases—lamenting the latter's all-too-narrow archive, its overt reliance on European modernism and poststructuralism—decolonial theorists like Walter D. Mignolo hunger for the local, a reality uncontaminated by European thought and its capitalist regime.[12] Against Europe's "geopolitics of knowledge," they emphasize "epistemic disobedience" and reject wholesale modernity's universality.[13] This modernity committed what José Medina dubs "epistemtic death," silencing non-Europeans, expunging their agency, and excluding them from any hermeneutic involvement in official knowledge production.[14]

Žižek readily concedes that postcolonial and decolonial critics are fully justified in denouncing the false ideological universality that masks, naturalizes, and legitimizes a racist and neocolonial condition and agenda, but he also insists on the need to go further, seeing these competing progressive movements as limiting themselves to resisting only false universality and abstractions such as "Man" as the bearer of human rights. At best, their intervention constitutes only half of the Marxist critique (its moment of demystification); at worst, it succumbs to "a non-reflective anti-Eurocentrism"[15] manifested as a depoliticized call to respect difference, an indulgence in a cult of victimhood, a retreat behind communitarian boundaries, or a nostalgic desire for a return to authentic precolonial or indigenous realities.[16]

In this, Žižek doubles down on a Marxist approach that has come under fire in postcolonial circles and perhaps most prominently in the debates over Jameson's now infamous article "Third-World Literature in the Era of Multinational Capitalism." Jameson's piece now typically serves as a warning lesson, a cautionary tale for Marxists who would export their critical hermeneutics to the Third World, who would fail, that is, to suspend the impulse to homogenize and translate colonial wounds and nationalist struggles into well-known symptoms of capitalism. Critically reacting to Jameson's argument that Third World texts "are necessarily . . . allegorical, and in a very specific way," that "they are to be read as what I will call national allegories,"[17] R. Radhakrishnan underscores the former's simultaneous will to mastery and inattentiveness to his historical differences:

> During the course of this essay, Jameson talks all too glibly about "the return of nationalism" in the Third World as though nationalism were enjoying a re-run in the Third World. The confident use of the term "return" suggests that within the universal synchronicity of Western time, nationalism is repeating itself in the Third World, whereas, historically, "nationalism" is new to the Third World. Throughout this essay (in spite of an initial gesture of unease), Jameson has little difficulty in maintaining his official conviction that the Third World histories are a predictable repetition of the histories of the "advanced world"; hence, the masterly confidence with which he "allegorizes" the Third World on its own behalf.[18]

Does Žižek learn from Jameson's "error"?[19] "No" is the short answer. Žižek displays even less interest in investigating the specificities of the postcolonial, or decolonial, condition. Žižek repeats instead Jameson's insistence on the economic, on viewing Third World national cultures as "locked in a life-and-death struggle with first-world cultural imperialism—a cultural struggle that is itself a reflexion of the economic situation of such areas in their penetration by various stages of capital, or as it is sometimes euphemistically termed, of modernization."[20]

Critics invested in a cultural politics emphasizing difference and local specificity may find this repetition frustrating or puzzling to say the least, yet if one patiently moves through the layers of Žižek's argument (without, e.g., getting shaken by his uncharitable and frequent conflation of postcolonial theory with multiculturalism and political correctness), one can observe valid objections to postcolonial and decolonial theories, motivated by a desire to enrich the debate on the Left, as well as a commitment to engage specificity otherwise.[21]

As we will see in this chapter, an effective critique of late capitalism cannot proceed without a commitment to the language and practice of universality. To this, however, Žižek adds the important qualifier: it is a universalism that has learned from and is marked by its violent colonial history. A genuinely anti-colonial, anti-racist critique requires a dialectical next step. Žižek finds the path of universality more rewarding and productive than any rigorous defense of difference (cultural or otherwise), insisting that the Left must move beyond the postcolonial exposure of the processes of othering in Western discourses. If Angela Davis is right in arguing that "any critical engagement with racism requires us to understand the tyranny of the universal,"[22] this engagement cannot end with a divestment from universality and a (re)investment in particularity. The Left must appropriate and harness the gap between formal democracy and the economic reality of exploitation and domination. This appearance—the experience of the gap—must be rearticulated to mean more than an illusion, more than an ideological lie. Žižek posits the pursuit of Hegelian "concrete universality"[23]—rather than a reactionary defense of racial or ethnic/religious difference, which can only lead to an ineffective political correctness or a defunct "identity politics"—as the real alternative to abstract, ideological universality.

## A Universalism That Is "Non-All"

In opposing the camp of cultural/ethnic difference and championing that of Marxist universality, Žižek arguably returns us to the now classic exchange between Jean-Paul Sartre and Frantz Fanon over the status and long-term viability of the *Négritude* movement. "Black Orpheus," Sartre's preface to Léopold Sédar Senghor's 1948 anthology of *Négritude* poetry, and Fanon's critical gloss of it in his 1952 *Black Skin, White Masks*, stage an encounter between existential-Marxism and anti-colonial theory. Sartre clearly praises Senghor's anthology, seeing it as a productive form of engaged literature. But Sartre also highlights what he perceives as its shortcomings, namely its philosophical insufficiency, how "Negritude appears as the weak state of a dialectical progression."[24] *Négritude* suffers from a "particularistic logic."[25] On the road to emancipation, *Négritude* is only the point of departure, not the final destination. For Sartre, a truly emancipatory critique does not preserve but dissolves all differences; accordingly, anti-colonialism must "lead to the abolition of racial differences."[26] Fanon objects to Sartre's paternalistic reading, rejecting Sartre's "helleniz[ing]" of *Négritude*, his "Orpheusizing" of the black colonial body.[27] Against Sartre's interpretive machinery, Fanon affirms the sufficiency of his singular otherness:

> The dialectic that introduces necessity as a support for my freedom expels me from myself. It shatters my impulsive position. Still regarding consciousness, black consciousness is immanent in itself. I am not a potentiality of something; I am fully what I am. I do not have to look for the universal.[28]

Fanon's objection to Sartre's dialectical reading is twofold. First, Fanon denounces Sartre for the latter's unmarked and unqualified universal perspective, which, he argues, blinds Sartre to a careful consideration of the specificity of the black lived experience, of "the fact of blackness." He decries the fact that "Sartre forgets that the black man suffers in his body quite differently from the white man."[29] Sartre's intervention, predicated on a narrow European *telos* of history, ends up "destroy[ing] black impulsiveness."[30] Second, Fanon points to a deficiency in the application of the dialectical method. Sartre's cognitive explanatory framework—which dutifully discerns the epiphenomenal from the real determinants, the symptoms from the causes—fails to account for the effects of *Négritude*, for the movement's impact on the psyche: "When I tried to claim my negritude intellectually as a concept, they snatched it away from me. They proved to me that my reasoning was nothing but a phase in the dialectic."[31] That is to say, subjecting *Négritude* to a cold dialectical reading neglected to record the movement's affective appeal, the utter joy "in the intellectualization of black *existence*."[32]

Mignolo might have been thinking of such an exchange in his response to Žižek's provocatively titled 1998 article, "A Leftist Plea for 'Eurocentrism.'" In his dismissal of Žižek's relevance (for decolonial subjects), Mignolo singles out the opening sentence of the essay: "When one says *Eurocentrism*, every self-respecting postmodern leftist intellectual has as violent a reaction as Joseph Goebbels had to culture—to reach for a gun, hurling accusations of protofascist Eurocentrist cultural imperialism."[33] To which, Mignolo counters:

> A self-respecting decolonial intellectual will reach instead to Frantz Fanon: "Now, comrades, now is the time to decide to change sides. We must shake off the great mantle of night, which has enveloped us, and reach, for the light. The new day, which is dawning, must find us determined, enlightened and resolute. So, my brothers, how could we fail to understand that we have better things to do than follow that Europe's footstep."[34]

In Mignolo's version, Fanon's message for fellow anti-colonialists is loud and clear: Europe is a relic of the past, even a detriment to our intellectual growth. Decolonizing the mind necessitates a rupture with Europe and its hegemonic universalism. Whereas Sartre, according to Mignolo, recognized this shift in Fanon, today's Sartre (Žižek) fails to acknowledge the anti-colonial's need for a different path of resistance, one that does not follow the script of Modernity.[35] Casting Žižek exclusively as the would-be Sartre of "Black Orpheus," however, only gives us part of the picture, and Mignolo's attempt to recruit Fanon to the cause of decoloniality is, at best, forced or one-sided, and, at worst, self-defeating. Protecting Fanon from Western contamination is a fool's errand. In his rebuttal of Mignolo's reading, Žižek points out that, far from authorizing a decolonial retreat from universality into non-Western particularity, Fanon frequently engaged with European thinkers and was quite hospitable to Western thought: "Fanon himself . . . dealt extensively and intensively with Hegel, psychoanalysis, Sartre, and even Lacan."[36] Indeed, making Fanon available only for decolonial identification is arguably un-Fanonian to the extent that it ignores or flattens the author's complex intellectual heritage and, more importantly, passes over his investment in a global solidarity that did not exclude Europeans.

Hamid Dabashi defends Mignolo's line of argumentation by saying that there is plenty of Fanon to go around, that Žižek can keep his

Europeanized Fanon: "Žižek can have his Fanon all to himself. There is plenty of Fanon left for others."[37] Yet this is an odd line of defense, for Dabashi does not then elaborate on what such a decolonial Fanon, a Fanon for the rest of us, really looks like. Is this an essentialist Fanon, whose decoloniality can be neatly decoupled from the European thought he engages? Is this a Fanon who repeats Western discourses before moving away from this error, expunging its trace from his thinking, or is it a Fanon who repeats with a difference, who means something wholly different by the Western concepts he deploys? Though Dabashi's central argument is certainly true—that "the point . . . is not to have any exclusive claim on Fanon, or to fetishize him (or any other non-European thinker for that matter) as a frozen talisman for Europeans to cite to prove they are not philosophically racist. The point is not to dismiss but to overcome the myth of 'the West' as the measure of truth"[38]—this does not advance our understanding of Fanon's contribution to this overcoming. Rather, Dabashi's suggestion that a "Western" Fanon can be neatly cordoned off from a "decolonial" one again produces something like a decolonial blackmail: either we (the non-Europeans affected by the legacies of colonialism and imperialism) criticize Western modernity and try to escape its hegemonic orbit by reorienting our gaze to non-European thinkers, or else we are celebrating its virtues, and thus betraying and turning our back on our specific history and locality. A Žižekian answer to Mignolo's implicit question, decolonial particularity or abstract universalism?, is a resolute, *No, Thanks!*

Rather than advocating identity politics or "identity *in* politics"[39]—Mignolo's wrong answer to a wrong question—Žižek formulates a model of universality that confronts the exclusionary logic of Eurocentrism, a logic that produces subjects who count and others who do not, subjects who benefit from the "Rights of Man" and those who fall outside the liberal umbrella, deemed less relevant, less grievable and so forth. In opposition to an ideological universalism, Žižek turns to Saint Paul's famous statement from Galatians 3:28: "There is no longer Jew nor Greek, there is no longer slave nor free, there is no longer male and female; for all of you are one in Christ Jesus."[40] To be clear, what Žižek privileges in Paul is not his religious message, that is, his displacement of Judaism with Christianity, but his formulation as an endless source and locus of negativity. It is Paul's principle of *adiaphora* (an ethical indifference toward ethnic and cultural particularities) that Žižek harnesses in his politics of subtraction.

Fanon practices this kind of *adiaphora* when he sustains a critical distance from *Négritude* and other similar movements, resisting the impulse for rootedness, the phantasmatic impulse to ontologize or homogenize black experience:

No, I have not the right to be black. It is not my duty to be this or that. . . . I acknowledge one right for myself: the right to demand human behavior from the other. . . . The black man is not. No more than the white man.[41]

The shift from difference as experiential rootedness (the stuff of tribalism and identity politics) to difference as experiential relatedness helps to revive a universalist humanist framework where what ultimately matters is to be treated humanely. It also might be tempting to read Fanon as offering his own version of Pauline cosmopolitanism: *there is neither white nor black*. But here we must not forget about the material conditions of colonial life. There is no transcendence of race without the dismantlement of the colonial system, and there is no dismantlement of the colonial system without an affective and cognitive transvaluation of the *difference* of the colonized. Coloniality is not destiny, but it is lived as if it were. A politics of subtraction weakens coloniality's hold on the psyche. This is the Eurocentrism—synonymous with a universalism at odds with (the ideological complacency of) identitarian thinking—that Žižek unabashedly defends.

# Solidarity with the Palestinian: A Decolonial Answer

The question of who counts, and how to relate to their universal singularity, animates Fanon's work. Fanon's solidarity is always supplemented by a universalist orientation; even when accounting for one's own trauma or the trauma of *a* people, Fanon fights hard against the myopic impulse to fetishize that suffering, to reify the singular into the particular, preferring to orient his discussion toward a universalist framework that takes up the plight of the dispossessed, of those who *do not count*, the "part of no-part."[42] Decolonial critics have adopted a narrower perspective on solidarity, however. Mignolo's intervention on the Palestinian question will serve as a case study for thinking anti-racist solidarity today (building on our discussion in Chapter 2), a case study for imagining solidarity or decolonial relationality beyond universalism and Eurocentrism. In Gianni Vattimo and Michael Marder's edited volume *Deconstructing Zionism*, which also includes an essay by Žižek, Mignolo attends to the dispossession of the Palestinians, laying out a convincing case against Zionism's logic of coloniality, linking the source of the conflict to Zionism's alignment with European thinking, with its unwavering attachment to the idea of the nation-state: "To solve the conflict of Palestine/Israel would require more than peace agreements— it would require decolonizing the form of the modern European nation-state."[43] Zionism is the ideological commitment to the slogan "one state, one nation" that forecloses any possibility of coexistence between Palestinians and Israelis. What is needed, for Mignolo, is a decolonization of the State of Israel, which "means first and foremost unveiling the logic of coloniality implicit in the state form, along with its rhetoric of salvation and democracy."[44] With the creation of the State of Israel, the formerly dispossessed did not become the purveyors of democracy but rather the dispossessors of the Palestinians, reaping the benefits of "the modern/colonial racial matrix."[45] Racialized as Europe's barbaric other, the Palestinian (and the rest of the Arab population) stood on the other side of modernity, dutifully kept in check by Israel—itself racially upgraded and now fully enjoying the privileges of whiteness, enjoying the virtues of moral superiority—as an outpost of European civilization/coloniality, "a villa in the jungle," as many Israelis are fond of saying.[46]

Phantasmatically shielded by a belligerent messianism—that is, by the myth of a sacred origin and Manifest Destiny, the return to the Promised Land—Israel, far from being immune to the contradictions of the nation-state, displays (in an amplified form) all the ills and shortcomings of European modernity. It has been beset from the start by the intractable problem of every modern nation-state: "to look after the well-being of its citizens and to deem everyone else as suspicious or as a lesser human and dispensable in relation to a given nation-state."[47] Israel's self-definition as a Jewish State only compounds the problem, or more precisely, reveals and reinforces the ideological lie of European democracy, which is at heart built on exclusionary self-other binaries. There is no solution to the conflict unless Israel frees itself from "the prison-house of religion, the nation, and the state,"[48] unless it jettisons the rhetoric of "one state, one nation."[49] This requires "the politicization of civil society."[50] But this is where the limitations of decoloniality come into view. Mignolo's envisioned politicization can only be conceived as a clear break with European thinking and its logic of the nation-state. Palestinians and critics of Zionism must look elsewhere for alternative models of nationalism and coexistence (e.g., Ecuador's or Bolivia's pluri-national states). Mignolo omits from analysis European counter-discourse to the legacy of nationalism. He talks of the nation-state as if it is withering on its own ("what is known as the form nation-state is nearing its exhaustion"[51]), unaffected, as it were, by any critique *from within*. This is of course not to say that a critique from within is sufficient on its own, only that foreclosing it a priori is unhelpful and unwarranted. In this (European) counter-tradition, for example, the diasporic Jew (Žižek's "uncanny Jew")—anathema to Zionism's identitarian logic—has been a foil to the organicity of the nation. And perhaps more surprisingly, Mignolo fails to take up the idea of binationalism (likely due to its European origins), the radical alternative to the "two-state solution" (though in 2007 he signed his name in support of the one-state solution[52]).

An alternative model of solidarity and resistance interweaves a critique from within and a critique from without, drawing precisely on a diasporic or exilic mode of critique to conceive of solidarity as a form of radical relationality. In one of his last interviews, Edward Said boldly affirmed such a model of the self in solidarity. Responding to his Israeli interlocutor's observation that "[he] sound[ed] very Jewish," Said concurred: "Of course. I'm the last Jewish intellectual. You don't know anyone else. All your other Jewish intellectuals are now suburban squires. From Amos Oz to all these people here in America. So I'm the last one. The only true follower of Adorno. Let me put it this way: I'm a Jewish-Palestinian."[53] By adopting and adapting the figure of the diasporic Jew, Said embraces a postcolonial exilic modality of being, in contradistinction to an "ideology of difference,"[54] harnessing the force of a Jewishness other than Zionist, of a Jewishness defined by its negativity, by its power of subtraction. As noted in Chapter 2, this is what Žižek champions in the Jewish tradition:

> The privileged role of Jews in the establishment of the sphere of the "public use of reason" hinges on their subtraction from every state power. Theirs is this position of the "part of no-part" in every organic nation-state community, and it is this position, not the abstract-universal nature of their monotheism, that makes them the immediate embodiment of universality. No wonder, then, that, with

the establishment of the Jewish nation-state, a new figure of the Jew emerged: a Jew resisting identification with the State of Israel, refusing to accept the State of Israel as his true home, a Jew who "subtracts" himself from this State, and who includes the State of Israel among the states towards which he insists on maintaining a distance, to live in their interstices.[55]

The "part of no-part" stands for "true universality"—a "struggling universality," as he puts it elsewhere[56]—representing "the whole of society": "we—the 'nothing,' not counted in the order—are the people, we are all, against others who stand only for their particular privileged interest."[57] They challenge the existing order of things. They recognize that the authority of the symbolic order is not absolute—"there is no Other of the Other, no ultimate guarantee of the field of meaning"[58]—unsettling political sovereignty à la Carl Schmitt, defined by its capacity to decide the exception, to determine the friend/enemy dyad.

Against the attempt to counter Israeli (European) identity with Palestinian (Indigenous) identity, Žižek sees a greater chance for emancipatory politics if Palestinians (like Said) align themselves with those Jews who reject the phantasmatic lure of their insular communities, who consider the idea of Israel as a racist or anti-Semitic project encouraged by Western powers for the purpose of emptying Europe of its Jewish population.[59] Palestinians are "today's 'universal individual.'"[60] They are the globally excluded, Israel's historical other, occupying the position of the "part of no-part." As Jamil Khader rightly observes: "Precisely because Palestinians have been reduced to this undead position in the global capitalist system, Palestinians can be said to represent the truth of the system, its constitutive injustice and inequality. In their inherent exclusion and abjection, therefore, Palestinians can be considered, in Žižek's words, the 'very site of political universality.'"[61] Palestinians are ethically invisible for many Israelis, and for some they are only visible in their destruction, experienced as an utterly obscene source of enjoyment.[62] Palestinian existence thus registers and embodies the void in Israel's social body, functioning simultaneously as a threat and obstacle to Israel's Zionist dream of fullness—of a Greater Israel—and as an index (to rest of the West) of Israel's restless domination and *un*democratic regime. But the solution to Israel's democratic woes is not a two-state solution, which would only legitimize and fortify Israel's regime of "Jewish supremacy,"[63] as well as perpetuate its fantasy of wholeness, of a social life without Palestinians (even now the Palestinians legally living in Israel are transfigured as Arab Israelis), keeping Zionist privilege invisible while encouraging Palestinian nativism—a depoliticized retreat into identity politics, patriotic fervor or a reactionary defense of difference. The other solution is binationalism.

# Binationalism as a Universalist Project

Binationalism originates in the writings of early European Zionist intellectuals (including Martin Buber, Judah Magnes, and Arthur Ruppin), and its relevance as a political position—its answer to the then Jewish question—has been "occluded by the changing history of the meaning of Zionism."[64] The sad irony is that now binationalism is an index of anti-Zionism, or even anti-Semitism.[65] Though binationalism was first introduced in the lexicon by Jewish intellectuals prior to the creation of Israel in 1948, Said reappropriated the concept—which in its original formulation did not fully break with settler colonialism— deploying it for emancipatory ends in a significantly different context: its status as a potential answer to what is now the Palestinian question. Said's binationalism solicits the labor of decoloniality, calling for a decolonized view of European nationalism and the abandonment of any mythic or transhistorical pretensions of origins and exclusionary claims of rooted identity. You can still live your life as a Zionist (be emotionally attached to the land) but you must not preclude others from sharing and caring for the same land. You must decline the rhetoric of Israeli exceptionalism, disaffiliate from the state's racist practices, give up your colonial/Zionist privilege, and transform the system that sustains it. Your claim is not metaphysical (the appeal to Scriptures) but *historical*, just like mine. "They can be Zionists," Said writes, "and they can assert their Jewish identity and their connection to the land, so long as it doesn't keep the others out so manifestly."[66]

Similarly, Žižek cautions against phantasmatic appeals to the past. What the past needs is not fetishization but (re)interpretation:

> According to the standard view, the past is fixed, what happened happened, it cannot be undone, and the future is open, it depends on unpredictable contingencies. What we should propose here is a reversal

of this standard view: the past is open to retroactive reinterpretations, while the future is closed, since we live in a determinist universe . . . . This does not mean that we cannot change the future; it just means that, in order to change our future, we should first (not "understand" but) change our past, reinterpret it in a way that opens up toward a different future from the one implied by the predominant vision of the past.[67]

Against the hermeneutics of "Manifest Destiny," which interprets historical contingencies teleologically as necessities—and thus solidifies Israel's past while seamlessly foreclosing Palestinian futurity—Žižek turns to the past in order to dereify it, so as to unsettle the present horizon of possibilities. To open the "determinist universe" of the Palestine/Israel conflict, to combat the "cruel optimism" of the two-state solution—and the "slow death"[68] that it entails for the Palestinians—Žižek returns to the "lost cause" of binationalism. Against the grain (the common objection that it is not practical, it cannot be done, and so on), Žižek points to the current reality that a one-state model is already in place: "What both sides exclude as an impossible dream is the simplest and most obvious solution—a bi-national secular state comprising of all of Israel plus the occupied territories and Gaza. To those who dismiss the bi-national state as a utopian dream disqualified by the long, Manichean history of hatred and violence, one should reply that, far from being utopian, the bi-national state already is a fact."[69] Israel and the Occupied Territories constitute a single state, but one that habitually abjects, racializes, and pathologizes Palestinians. Palestinians' perceived lust for violence and disregard for their own (collateral damage is always blamed on the Palestinian resistance, on their willingness to let their own die) is deemed incompatible with Israel's European way of life), and thus only Israelis count as fully human, and fully citizens. Jewish Israeli lives are in this framework the only liveable and grievable lives.

As we saw in Chapter 2, right-wing Zionists and their supporters often circulate the stereotype that the Left is anti-Semitic—the face of the new racism—and that it wants to destroy the State of Israel and its Jewish way of life. The enlightened liberal Zionists earnestly correct this "appearance" of hostility to the Jewish state by pleading: "no, no, that's not the case. The Left only wants a reduction of Palestinian suffering, less unnecessary violence, no more Gaza wars," and so on. The universalist-Left project of binationalism compels a dialectical return to the reality of the appearance: right-wing Zionists were correct after all, for a true leftist vision does involve radically restructuring the very identity of the nation, outside the logic of the nation-state. Israel as a Jewish state and Israel as a democratic state cannot coexist. Non-exclusive Jewish attachment to the land can stay, but Jewish supremacy (and its apparatus of objective violence) as a way of life cannot.

So, again, we must resist false oppositions. The question is no longer, if it has ever been, a one-state versus a two-state solution, a European versus a non-European solution (for the decolonial critic), but instead what kind of one-state should prevail. As it stands, Israel aggressively discriminates in access to land, resources, and housing, and is wholly incompatible with the universality of democracy, captured by the civil rights slogan, "one person, one vote"—whence the need "to abolish the apartheid and transform it into a secular democratic state."[70] In politicizing *égaliberté*, Palestinians for binationalism make clear that they are not satisfied by merely demystifying Israel as a democratic state, by denouncing its rhetoric of equality as a falsehood or an illusion. Rather, they delegitimize Israel as a racist state by performing concrete universality, by transcending local identities (religious, national), and by abandoning the multiculturalist playbook of resistance.

As an intervention into the hegemonic reality of the occupation, Žižek proposes something of a thought experiment: What if Jerusalem became a site for such coexistence? What if Israelis and Palestinians severed their phantasmatic attachment to Jerusalem and renounced their exclusive claim to the land? What if Jerusalem became "an extra-state place of religious worship controlled (temporarily) by some neutral international force"?[71] This would constitute "a true political act," an act that "renders the unthinkable thinkable,"[72] the impossible possible. Whereas Donald Trump's decision to recognize Jerusalem as the capital of Israel only reinforced the predominant vision of the past (despite the cries of Western liberals in the United States and abroad who mistakenly claim that this unilateral action was a game-changer, jeopardizing the protocols of negotiation, the status quo, the pacifying pragmatism of the two-state solution), Žižek's proposal would derail the logic of sacrifice and compromise, asking the two parties instead to understand their contribution (their release of political control and religious claim over holy lands) as a mutual gain.[73] For both Israelis and Palestinians, this political act would entail traversing their fundamental fantasy of an "ethnically 'pure' nation-state" (the dream—or rather nightmare—of living without others) and would thus be tantamount to undoing their ego—a "strik[ing] back at themselves"[74]—to short-circuiting their affective investment in exclusionary nationalism.[75]

If the *refuseniks*, from a position of power, offer one response to this intractable conflict, countering Zionist nationalism with neighborly or agapic love, and frustrating a nationalist sovereignty obsessed with its securitization by dismantling the friend/enemy dyad (a critique of Zionism from within), Palestinian writer and poet Mahmoud Darwish proposes another, one that shifts registers from agape to eros, where the question of power is more dynamic and less asymmetrical (a critique of Zionism from without). In *Memory for Forgetfulness*, a collection of poems dealing with Israel's siege of Beirut in 1982, Darwish's narrator recounts a scene with his Jewish lover, which brings to the forefront the dilemmas involved in relating to your enemy at the erotic register, that is, when that enemy is also your enigmatic lover.

Anxiety permeates the poem: after making love to his Jewish lover, the narrator becomes preoccupied with having to check in with the Haifa police in order to avoid being jailed or permanently banned. This impeding reality along with the more generalized existential knowledge that "*each would kill the other outside the window*" weighs heavily on the narrator. A shared self-sabotaging compulsion to return to vexed topics (Do you hate Jews? Do you love Arabs?) only exerts further pressure on the imaginary barrier separating them from the social conflict outside, a barrier immunizing their love from intractable difference. Suspicion and resentment accompany desire and tenderness. When they try to engage in small talk for example (he asks her what she usually dreams about), her answer sparks a digression to biblical times:

> – I usually don't dream. And you? What do you dream about?
> – That I stop loving you.
> – Do you love me?
> – No. I don't love you. Did you know that your mother, Sarah, drove my mother, Hagar, into the desert?
> – Am I to blame then? Is it for that you don't love me?
> – No. You're not to blame; and because of that I don't love you. Or, I love you.[76]

Bulter comments on "this final conjunctive disjunction,"[77] on the paradoxical formulation of loving and not loving the other: how the narrator's relation to his Jewish lover entails "both proximity and aversion; it is unsettled; it is not of one mind. It might be said to be the affect, the emotional tenor of an impossible and necessary union, the strange logic by which one wishes to go and insists upon staying."[78] Butler at once negates and offers a connection between this version of love and binationalism: "Surely binationalism is not love, but there is, we might say, a necessary and impossible attachment that makes a mockery of identity, an ambivalence that emerges from the decentering of the nationalist ethos and that forms the basis of a permanent ethical demand."[79]

I appreciate Butler's hesitation, her reluctance to easily identify love with binationalism. Postcolonial critics might also credit Butler for not repeating Jameson's problematic Third World hermeneutics, which would read Palestinian literature as national allegory. And yet Butler arguably closes the door too quickly on national allegory and the connection between binationalism and love. If binationalism is not strictly speaking identical to love, it might be said to be at once the embodiment and the need for a particular kind of love, one that is akin to neighborly love, that is, to a love that interpellates and hysterizes the proximate other. So, we might ask again: What kind of love is binationalism? What kind of love does it solicit from the Palestinians and the Israelis? In this light, reading Darwish's poem as a national allegory *about* binationalism attests to the poem's political saliency and overtones without simultaneously denying its inventiveness and singularity. The poem's staging of the "national situation"[80] is precisely *not* a repetition of a tired and predictable European narrative. Quite the contrary, Darwish's poem does not merely use sexual relationality to talk about national/racial identity. Rather, the two are deeply interwoven in the poem, each affecting and supplementing the meaning of the other.

As Žižek reminds us, "since sexuality is the domain in which we get closest to the intimacy of another human being, totally exposing ourselves to him or her, sexual enjoyment is real for Lacan: something traumatic in its breathtaking intensity, yet impossible in the sense that we cannot ever make sense of it. This is why a sexual relation, in order to function, has to be screened through some fantasy."[81] But fantasies are not foolproof; they do falter, making dissatisfaction constitutive of sexuality as such. Moreover, Žižek argues each subject is from the start "barred," incomplete: " 'Man' and 'woman' together do not form a Whole, since *each of them is already in itself a failed Whole*."[82] Likewise, the enemy—as the "timeless" source of antagonism—is always already within me:

To grasp the notion of antagonism, in its most radical dimension, we should *invert* the relationship between the two terms: it is not the external enemy who is preventing me from achieving identity with myself, but every identity is already in itself blocked, marked by an impossibility, and the external enemy is simply the small piece, the rest of reality upon which we "project" or "externalize" this intrinsic, immanent impossibility.[83]

Failure here is, then, not the result of an incompatibility between two identities or races: *Israelis are from Mars, Palestinians are from Venus*. Rather, the problem is real and structural, both in myself and compounded by my relationality: "there is no automatic, unmediated, or untroubled connection between sexual partners . . . Because each subject connects with others only through fantasy, no natural coupling of man and woman can take place."[84] As a deadlock in the Real, sexual difference is an interpretive impasse that necessitates its own paradoxical hermeneutics/ethics of the Real.

What follows from the impossibility of sexual relationality is not only the lack of a harmonious resolution to amorous relations but the possibility of excess, of love as a supplement: "What makes up for the sexual relationship is, quite precisely, love."[85] Here love as supplement can be read in two ways, mapping onto two ways of understanding binationalism. The first interpretation of love remains purely at the level of the Imaginary. Love phantasmatically covers over the disjunction between sexual partners; love purports to heal, removing the "barredness" of sexual relationality. Love reassures and promises the fusion and union of the lovers. Its correlative version of binationalism reads as follows: it entails a commitment to an ideal, postracial Oneness, a removal of all antagonisms, a healing and resolution of prior wrongs and traumas. This is the version of binationalism that political realists love to dismiss as unreasonable and utopian, a deception or dangerous lure for liberals,[86] arguing instead for a pragmatic separation over an idealistic union of the two communities.

The second interpretation of love does not iron out the disjunction. It insists on the Real, on the fact that there is no sexual relationality. Love requires "an acceptance of this truth";[87] the subject must be "willing to live with the antagonism."[88] Consequently, for a correlative version of binationalism this lack of relationality does not prompt a reductively pessimistic assessment of human relations (a narcissistic wound—the trauma of realizing that you are not my specular image, that your fantasies are not mine), but enacts the condition for binationalism as such. Binationalism supplements the lack of a harmonious existence between the Palestinians and the Israelis. It is an ethico-political response to the existential fact that "fantasies cannot coexist peacefully."[89] Binationalism fosters a relationality that is "non-all," *otherwise than nationalistic*: it is a relationality that, as Said might put it, does not exhaust itself through filiation (relation which "belongs to the realms of nature and 'life'") but also insists on affiliation (relation which "belongs exclusively to culture and society").[90] It is a form of relationality at odds with a nationalism myopically defined, a nationalism aligned exclusively with a particularist identity (one nation, one people).

In Darwish's poem, the union of the lovers is socially prohibited (*each would kill the other outside the window*); the Imaginary opens itself as a temptation—their forbidden love functions as a fetish. The world outside can be in ruins as long as they are together. But when the fantasy of immunity falters—he has to return home and he resents her people for putting him in that situation; she wants to understand his frustration but is also narcissistically driven by her own insecurities, and so on—the "barredness" of their relationship takes on a more "real" or permanent dimension. The poem ends with the Jewish lover asking again for the recognition of his love:

– And you don't love me?
– I don't know.
And each is killing the other by the window.[91]

On one decolonial reading, the narrator's doubt could be construed as evidence of his "colonial difference," producing a kind of subaltern knowledge: knowledge of life under Israeli hegemony, a life that voices its irreducible objections to the coloniality of power, to the colonial order of things (of which his Jewish lover is an agent). What we have here, Mignolo might say, is a shift from Descartes's "I think therefore I am" to the decolonial thesis, "I am where I think." Whereas Descartes's saying produces a unity in thinking and being, and helps to foster and promote an economy of sameness (we all have the same *cogito*), Mignolo's formulation brings to the forefront Darwish's "border thinking" ("the moments in which the imaginary of the modern world system cracks"[92]), and foregrounds geography in any questions of knowledge and biography. The word "where" pluralizes (= democratizes) meaning, legitimizes subaltern experience, and thus declines "the universality to which everyone has to submit,"[93] reorienting us to history and locality, to the narrator's positionality in relation to "the epistemic and ontological racism of imperial knowledge."[94]

But if "where" is meant to counter modernity's fantasy of a universal "I," Darwish's poem complicates the decolonial elevation of "where" by figuring place as entangled with the Real. The last line positions the reader in the room, marking a move from the virtual to the actual: each sexual partner now is in the process of killing the other *by* the symbolic window. The threat is no longer coming from the outside but from within, a grasp that the deadlock of sexual difference is *in* the Real. What form of binationalism will supplement the lack of complementarity between Palestinians and Israelis is, I believe, the poem's allegorical question.

The couple's failure is of course not yet a fact. They *are killing* each other—they haven't *killed* each other. The narrator's doubt, which rewrites his earlier *I don't love you/I love you*, continues to offer no certainties or guarantees. "I don't know" indexes the logic of desire, since for Lacan, "so long as I desire, I know nothing of what I desire."[95] Binationalism supplements this situation (Palestinians and Israelis are killing each other) not by offering the certainties and guarantees that are lacking, but by soliciting both communities to will/desire the impossible. Analogous to Žižek's thought experiment on internationalizing Jerusalem, willing binationalism can be said to constitute an act. It suspends "the reign of the pleasure-reality principle"[96] and performs a kind of madness, the madness of the decision: "'the moment of decision is the moment of madness' precisely in so far as there is no big Other to provide the ultimate guarantee, the ontological cover for the subject's decision."[97] For the Palestinians, opening themselves to the unknown, giving up what they *cannot not want*[98] (international recognition of their identity), is what one deciding on binationalism wills. The subject of binationalism is willing to desire something that goes against the interest of their would-be-nationalist ego, against the committed belief that an independent state will put an end to their daily miseries. This subject is willing to traverse the fantasy of the two-state solution: the transparent background for many Palestinians that structures the way they relate to the occupation and their attitude toward futurity. This belief that things will get better—the debilitating pragmatism[99] of the two-state solution that grips the Palestinians—must be countered by what Žižek calls the "courage of hopelessness" (a formulation that he borrows from Agamben[100]). Traversing the fantasy of the two-state solution does not mean to see through it and "perceive the reality obfuscated by it," but rather "to directly confront the fantasy as such . . . [F]antasy remains operative only insofar as it functions as the transparent background of our experience—fantasy is like a dirty intimate secret which cannot survive public exposure."[101] Palestinians overcome the fantasy the moment they have the courage to realize that the light at the end of the tunnel is not statehood but more dispossession, killing, and maiming—that is, the moment their attitude toward their current environment and future is effectively denaturalized, taken not as a given (of course, we want a Nation) but as a problem (what does coexistence with my neighbor look like?).[102]

## Base–Superstructure Redux

But isn't binationalism for all of its radical demands just the last culturalization of politics? To be sure, it might be preferable to the current hegemony of "Levinassian sentimentalism" (to evoke again Jameson's, along with Žižek's, disdain for the subordination of politics by ethics), but isn't it still a superstructural concern that, not unlike the ones emanating from decoloniality, does little to confront society's economic antagonisms? Or to state the question more bluntly: What is the relationship of binationalism to class struggle? We might respond to this question in a couple of ways. First, binationalism can be described as "class struggle at the level of ideas,"[103] to borrow from Terry Eagleton. Binationalism is an *idea*—a lost cause—that possesses the force of a political act, capable of re-structuring the very symbolic coordinates of one's situation. At the very least, a superstructural concern can still impact the economic base. Žižek himself revisits Marx's much-discussed base–superstructure metaphor, and gives it a Lacanian twist, turning again to Lacan's claim that there is no sexual relationality: "If . . . there is no sexual relationship, then, for Marxism proper, there is *no relationship between economy and politics*, no 'meta-language' enabling us to grasp the two levels from the same neutral standpoint."[104] Indeed, this is what Žižek calls the "parallax view," a "constantly shifting perspective between two points between which no synthesis or mediation is possible."[105] If parallax is commonly understood as "the apparent displacement of an object (the shift of its position against a background), caused by a change in observational position," for Žižek, the parallax gap signifies far more, enabling him to reconceptualize the interpretive scene itself. As he puts it:

> The philosophical twist to be added [to the standard definition of parallax] . . . is that the observed difference is not simply "subjective," due to the fact that the same object which exists "out there" is seen from two different stances, or points of view. It is rather that . . . subject and object are inherently "mediated," so that an "epistemological" shift in the subject's point of view always reflects an "ontological" shift in the object itself.[106]

In parallax thinking, the classic base–superstructure couple takes on a new meaning:

> We should take into account the irreducible duality of, on the one hand, the "objective" material socioeconomic processes taking place in reality as well as, on the other, the politico-ideological process proper. What if the domain of politics is inherently "sterile," a theatre of shadows, but nonetheless crucial in transforming reality? So, although economy is the real site and politics is a theatre of shadows, the main fight is to be fought in politics and ideology[107]

Though the economy remains "a kind of socio-transcendental a priori,"[108] the "ultimately determining instance" (repeating Althusser-Jameson[109]), Žižek is not returning to "the nineteenth-century myth of a self-enclosed economic space," as Ernesto Laclau charges.[110] Quite the contrary, Žižek's "economism" is non-totalizable, subject to the Lacanian logic of the "non-all," allowing, in turn, for the (re)politicization of culture, for the superstructure to be a space for critical inventiveness—an engine for genuine transformation.

If the idea of binationalism is to mobilize change, to challenge Israel's apartheid regime, and infuse life into today's "theater of shadows," Palestinians must remain attentive to the "antagonism *inherent*" in their social structure, and not lose track of their true enemy. Žižek's cautionary tale is the rise of Nazism and the failure of the German people to identify their true antagonism and enemy: as a result, "class struggle is displaced onto the struggle against the Jews, so that the popular rage at being exploited is redirected from capitalist relations as such to the 'Jewish plot.'"[111] The real antagonism is externalized as a struggle between Aryans and Jews, as "a struggle for *domination* between *us* and *them*, those who cause antagonistic imbalance."[112] The Nazis phantasmatically identified the Jews as the fundamental cause of the German people's predicament; the Jews functioned as the Nazi's *object petit a* (the object-cause of [Nazi] desire). The Jews were not an object of Nazi desire but the ultimate obstacle that strictly speaking sustained Nazi desire/identity.[113] "What is a Nazi without a Jew?," astutely asks Žižek.[114]

Can we speak of a similarly displaced but irreducible social antagonism in Palestine? How are Palestinians to understand the violence directed toward them? What is the fundamental antagonism spurring the Israeli drive for domination? Are the Palestinians the *objet petit a* of the Israelis? On the one hand, it is impossible to ignore the reality of Israeli brutalization, and thus the enemy has *not* been misperceived: it is the Israeli government and its unrelenting state violence, described by Žižek as Israel's "Kafkaesque network of legal regulations" where "the condemnation of 'illegal' settlements [Israel's performance of justice as fairness to the Western world] obfuscates the illegality of the 'legal' ones."[115] Here binationalism becomes the culmination of a fight that seeks to end Palestinian racialization, to abolish Israeli apartheid and to put pressure on the world to see Israel as a neocolonial regime, as an undemocratic and unjust state. On this account the only enemy is the racist Zionist, the Israeli colonial settlers, fighting for their exclusive right to the land and its resources, which the binationlists want to share peacefully. The problem with this account is not with its content, but its *insufficiency*. Naming Israeli governments and colonial settler politics the enemy is at once necessary and incomplete. In this it is reminiscent of the decolonial critique of Israel.

Exposing and criticizing Zionism as an ideology that seeks to *dominate* the Palestinians only gives a partial explanation for the continuing brutality of the Israeli government. Žižek follows Jameson in stressing that the struggle against domination is, as Jameson put it, "an essentially moral or ethical one which leads to punctual revolts and acts of resistance rather than to the transformation of the mode of production as such."[116] There is also an important *economic* disincentive to halting Israel's necropolitics—its regulation of Palestinian death and maiming.[117] If, according to Israel's imaginary narrative, Israel would be happy living side by side with its peaceful Arabs, without fantastic Muslims, without irritant Palestinians (a stain on its moral profile), Israel's highly successful and influential military–industrial complex turns the irritant Palestinian/

the Islamic peril into a necessity, a justification for the existence and perpetuation of its muscular identity. For to sustain itself, the military–industrial complex needs the racialized Palestinian "threat," fueling, in turn, a need for security, a permanent war model, a permanent state of exception. Hamas (an organizational embodiment of the most irritant Palestinian) guarantees Israel's permanently militarized identity. The over decade-long blockade of Gaza "put[s] the Palestinians on a diet," freezing them in a state of bare life (humanitarian aid, which gives Israel cover from full Western outrage, is intrinsic to this management of bare life[118]), producing, in turn, a large number of unemployed, disposable, and unassimilable bodies, a racialized surplus population, to test and showcase its latest awesome weapons to a global audience.

Yotam Feldman's 2013 documentary film, *The Lab*, makes a compelling case for economic profit driving hawkish Israeli policies. "Israel's weapons industry has tripled its profits to more than [US] \$7 billion a year over the past decade, making a country about the size of New Jersey into the fourth largest weapons exporter in the world," writes Max Blumenthal.[119] Israel's profitable necropolitics thus complements quite smoothly the Zionist-colonial fantasy of *terra nullius*, as long as it remains purely an ideological fantasy: *it wants a Palestine free of Palestinians—but not quite.* Palestinians are the object-cause of Zionist desire, the *objet petit a*, the obstacle that arguably sustains Israeli desire/identity.[120] What is a fervent Zionist without an abject Palestinian?

At this juncture, keeping with the economic focus requires a further step, a parallactic shift on the enemy, in order to better apprehend the scene of Palestinian struggle. What sustains the misery of the Palestinians is not only the Israeli government and its draconian policies, but also the economic structures that currently regulate Palestinian life in the Occupied Territories. In *The Battle for Justice in Palestine*, Ali Abunimah warns of the neoliberalization of Palestine, of the ideological traps of political domesticity:

> In tandem, with the assistance of the United States and Israel, the Palestinian Authority in Ramallah built a repressive police-state apparatus that sought to suppress and disarm any resistance to Israeli occupation and to crush internal Palestinian dissent and criticism with increasing ferocity. [. . .] But behind a smokescreen of "state-building" rhetoric and flag-waving, a small Palestinian elite has continued to enrich itself by deepening its political, economic, and military

ties with Israel and the United States, often explicitly undermining efforts by Palestinian civil society to resist. This catastrophic assault on Palestinians has been masked with the language of "technocratic" government and marketed as nothing less than the fulfillment of the Palestinian "national" project. . . . If these are indeed the foundations of a future Palestinian state, then a people who have struggled for so long for liberation from Zionism's colonial assault can only look forward to new, more insidious forms of economic and political bondage.[121]

The consequences of Palestinian neoliberalization are significant.[122] First, by making the status quo economically lucrative for *some*—those in power, those especially in charge of security cooperation with the Israeli government—neoliberalization forecloses, or at least minimizes, possibilities for imagining social reality and coexistence with the Israelis outside the framework of a two-state solution. Second, by opening the Occupied Territories to global capitalism (under the terms set by the Oslo Accords), "economic 'development,'" as Abunimah alarmingly observes, "has been channeled away from indigenous Palestinian business and into industrial zones where foreign and Israeli exporters can exploit unskilled Palestinian workers cheaply and without any accountability, a model enthusiastically financed and promoted by the United States, the European Union, Turkey and Japan."[123]

Taking "capitalism itself as the ultimate horizon of the political situation"[124] enables us to reframe binationalism and the Palestinian question. It helps to underscore binationalism as a universalist project, engaged in a fight against both domination and exploitation (postapartheid South Africa arguably addressed racial domination but has not sufficiently attended to economic exploitation, since South Africa, as David Harvey points out, "after years of fierce struggle against apartheid, is no better off now than it ever was in achieving basic freedoms from want and need"[125]). Seeking economic justice at home invariably links the Palestinian plight to other labor movements in Israel and elsewhere in the region.[126] The solidarity of workers can effectively challenge the interests of the few, *de*naturalize their exploitation (i.e., contest the ways exploitation is effortlessly built into the functioning of the economy), and foreground binationalism as a socio-economic project, not limited to its own particularist interests, but "grounded in the 'part of no-part,' the singular universality exemplified in those who lack a determined place in the social totality, who are 'out of place' in it."[127] If decoloniality and others fetishize the enemy ("the elevation of Zionism into the neo-imperialist racism par excellence"[128]), overemphasizing his or her exceptionality (Israel as the embodiment of modernity/coloniality and its racist ideology), and thus always risk reifying the antagonism, binationalism, if it is to be transformative, must embrace its role as a supplement to the Palestinian/Israeli antagonism, taking the task of coexistence, of living together with each other's (real) neighbor, as an urgent ethico-political challenge, fully cognizant that there is no guarantee of success. *And each is killing the other by the window.*

# 4 CRITICAL RACE THEORY: THE SUBJECT SUPPOSED TO LOOT, RAPE, AND TERRORIZE

*Your friend is speaking to your neighbor when you arrive. The four police cars are gone. Your neighbor has apologized to your friend and is now apologizing to you. Feeling somewhat responsible for the actions of your neighbor, you clumsily tell your friend that the next time he wants to talk on the phone he should just go in the backyard. He looks at you a long minute before saying he can speak on the phone wherever he wants. Yes, of course, you say. Yes, of course.*

**CLAUDIA RANKINE**[1]

*Palestinian resistance is cited as proof that we are dealing with terrorists. This paradox is inscribed into the very notion of a "war on terror"—a strange war in which the enemy is criminalised if he defends himself and returns fire with fire.*

**SLAVOJ ŽIŽEK**[2]

Originating in US legal thought, Critical Race Theory (CRT) makes race a cornerstone of analysis. For CRT, racism is intrinsic to American culture and its laws. Racism is not an aberration or an anomaly but an integral part of the "normal" state of affairs.[3] And while CRT acknowledges that racial progress does happen—with the civil rights movement functioning for liberals as the paradigm for understanding such racial change—it remains alert to racism's long-lasting effects, foregrounding the continuing reality of racial dominance and structural racism, a view of reality Derrick Bell dubs "racial realism," or "this mind-set or philosophy [that] requires us to acknowledge the permanence of our subordinate status."[4] CRT thus paints racial progress, at best, as fragile, and, as worst, as delusional. The belief in slow and incremental racial progress serves the interest of the powerful, not its victims: "We must first recognize and acknowledge (at least to ourselves) that our actions are not likely to lead to transcendent change and may indeed, despite our best efforts, be of more help to the system we despise than to the victims of that system whom we are trying to help."[5] Racial progress does not proceed in a linear fashion nor does it herald postraciality. Far from it, "a commitment to racial equality merely perpetuates our disempowerment."[6] An anti-racist future is not on the horizon of American culture. All that can be achieved is a lessening of black disappointment, a curbing of emancipatory aspiration, and the fleeting enjoyment of "harass[ing] white folks."[7]

CRT adopts a hermeneutics of suspicion when it comes to the interpretation of racial gains. Its "interest-convergence thesis," championed by Bell, argues that for the interests of domestic minorities to be heard and acted upon they must first align with the greater interest of the dominant racial group. Consequently, we must resist the "feeling good" moments of racial progress; they are not signs of white altruism or epiphanic breakthroughs, but always qualified, always driven by the interests of the white elite. As such, racial gains are precarious, unavoidably susceptible to backlash and reversal. Indeed, no racial gains are irreversible: in 2013 the Supreme Court struck down key provisions of the landmark 1965 Voting Rights Act, severely weakening its enforcement powers.[8] And after eight years of Barack Obama, America—with the Tea Party and the Trump presidency preparing a "correction" of racial progress—has gotten a culture backlash, or a "whitelash," as Van Jones famously put it,[9] while racist economic structures remain for the most part in place. Racial capitalism persists—a capitalism with a white face.

CRT's sobering, skeptical view of racial realism resonates with Žižek's insistence on objective violence. Both Žižek and CRT counter the narrative of racial progress (as a decline in subjective violence) with accounts of persistent structural racism and racial antagonism. The intractable fantasy of black criminality structures the American imaginary, touching the minds of whites and blacks alike. As Claudia Rankine pointed out well before the recent media attention to the phenomenon of whites alerting the police to black people going about everyday activities, to be black is to be an object of suspicion, to be perceived as thuggish merely for occupying public space. Blacks internalize the cultural script: *Thou shall not make white people uncomfortable.* Rankine thematizes the impulse to blame the victim: "you clumsily tell your friend that the next time he wants to talk on the phone he should just go in the backyard." The desire to fit in—to fit into a world governed by white supremacy—compels you to compromise your values, prompting a pointed and devastating reminder: "He looks at you a long minute before saying he can speak on the phone wherever he wants. Yes, of course, you say. Yes, of course."

One obvious remedy to the fear of the racialized other is to point out that the facts do not support your fear. Although evidence-based counterarguments have a role to play in combatting racism, demystification misses something crucial about the pathology of racism. As Žižek observes, "a suspicious gaze always finds what it is looking for."[10] Žižek turns to Lacan's musings on the jealous husband to demonstrate the need to keep the pathology of suspicion separate from the fact of suspicion. The racist suspicious attitude remains pathological regardless of whether the suspicion is confirmed or not:

> Jacques Lacan wrote that, even if what a jealous husband claims about his wife (that she sleeps around with other men) is all true, his jealousy is still pathological. Why is this? The more pertinent question is not "Is his jealousy well-grounded?" but "Why does he need jealousy to maintain his self-identity?". Along the same lines, one could say that, even if most of the Nazi claims about the Jews were true (they exploit Germans, they seduce German girls . . .)—which they are not, of course—their anti-Semitism would still be (and was) pathological since it represses the true reason why the Nazis *needed* anti-Semitism in order to sustain their ideological position.[11]

Confronting anti-Semites with evidence of the "commonness" of Jews—showing they are like ordinary Germans—does not dispel the racists' prejudices but works paradoxically as further confirmation of their validity: "You see how dangerous they really are? It is difficult to recognize their true nature. They hide it behind the mask of everyday appearance—and it is exactly this hiding of one's real nature, this duplicity, that is a basic feature of the Jewish nature."[12]

Likewise, asking the question "Are blacks really a threat to white America?" holds little promise for challenging white racist fantasies about blackness. The evidence that it yields, if not dead on arrival, is all too often merely rationalized away. Unsettling antiblack racism requires us to reframe the question, that is, to politicize the question of fear. The true question is "What does this obsessive fear of blacks tell us about the hegemony of whiteness?" Why do whites, like the neighbor in Rankine's anecdote, need this obsessive fear of blacks to retain their identity? Why doesn't the evidence of living peacefully next to a black woman compel the neighbor to identify and combat her prejudices? Whites' paranoid fear—more often expressed privately or obliquely, rather than in the kinds of mass public demonstrations seen in Germany in the late 1930s or in Europe today concerning the refugees—tells us more about white America than it tells us about blacks and other marginalized groups. The hegemony of whiteness is arguably faltering but the cause of the problems is again distorted and displaced, projected onto an internal intruder (blacks, non-white Americans). Racist whites misperceive the weakening of their powers as a consequence of liberal empowerment of blacks, through special privileges given to blacks and other minorities at the expense of whites. Blacks in power are seen as an aberration of how things ought to be (recall the Tea Party's slogan "I want my country back" shortly after Obama's election).

This chapter takes up the role of racist fantasies, looking at the ways they distract us from confronting the cause of the problems "immanent to today's global capitalism" by projecting these problems, time and time again, onto internal–external intruders. Žižek draws on Lacan's formulation, "the subject supposed to know," adapting it to expose the unconscious mechanisms at work in the racialization of others through their identification with criminality or barbarity. His paradigmatic example comes from the stories about black criminality that circulated in the aftermath of Hurricane Katrina. If the "subject supposed to know" denotes the function of the analyst rather than the analyst as such, the "subject supposed to loot and rape" refers not to black subjects themselves and what they have actually done or not (evidence-based suspicion) but denotes instead the phantasmatically projected black body. The "subject supposed to loot and rape" embodies the workings of ideology, and the enjoyment racists get from finding their speculation and suspicion "confirmed."

Abroad, this projected unruly subject of terror remerges in the 2005 French Riots and in the post-9/11 global environment—in the figures of blacks and *beurs* (slang for Arabs/French youths of North African descent) and the Palestinian, respectively. Žižek makes the structural similarities between American blacks and Palestinians explicit: "In US slums and ghettos, police effectively functions more and more as a force of occupation, something akin to Israeli patrols entering the Palestinian territories on the West Bank."[13] Both are in a constant state of surveillance. But while a veneer of equality exists in the United States, bolstered by post-Jim Crow statutory changes, the Palestinians dwell in a racial apartheid, in a settler-colonial setting where racial dehumanization and subjugation are part of the very fabric of Israel's Zionist reality.[14] Palestinians are cynically criminalized by their very desire to survive, by their will not to consent to Israeli occupation: the audacity "to return fire with fire" (resisting subjective violence), to foolishly refuse their allocated position in the Zionist order of things (resisting objective violence). Similarly, in France's *banlieues* (or urban periphery) an increased population of disenfranchised French youth are the object of suspicion and control, perceived—by France's racists—as a stain on the French republic, the result of the failure to properly instill in them the virtues of its past, which for some even include colonialism. "We no longer teach that the colonial project also sought to educate, to bring civilization to savages," laments Alain Finkielkraut.[15]

Žižek's intervention follows a different path from Finkielkraut's ideological Eurocentrism. The latter's solution can only further cement France's racial realism. Žižek's critique is twofold: first, to short-circuit the ideological machinery that produces the other as a racialized menace, a "stranger danger," a "subject supposed to loot, rape, and terrorize," and, second, to globalize the struggle against racism. While surely appreciative of CRT's dismissal of the ideological narrative of racial progress, and its challenge to the stifling optimism of white liberals (be patient, things will get better; enthusiastically citing Martin Luther King Jr.'s hopeful saying: "the arc of the moral universe is long, but it bends toward justice"), Žižek does not rule out the possibility for "transcendent change." What is taking place in the United States, Occupied Palestine, and France speaks to the same need: to develop a radical emancipatory politics, that is, a critique of our socioeconomic existence that moves beyond toothless resistance or resistance as an impotent act of frustration that attends to society's endemic racism and racial wrongs by touching the Real of its antagonism.

## Under Suspicion

For blacks in America, living under suspicion means living racial realism. CRT sees this reality as a permanent feature of American cultural life. If the Civil Rights movement appealed to the sensibility of whites to reform its racist social order, CRT argues that soliciting white empathy for black pain turned out to be a losing strategy. As Tommy Curry observes, "it is no longer acceptable to philosophically converse and politically pontificate legal strategies that are built on the possibility of whites abandoning white privilege, when it is the passivity and acceptance of Black deaths that give these conversations with whites moral suasion. In other words, the suffering of Black people can no longer be the moral impetus behind attempts to persuade whites to act right."[16] Any anti-racist liberal project can only repeat the humanitarian logic governing the West's relation to the Third World. The immediate aftermath of Hurricane Katrina is a case in point. Blacks in New Orleans emerge as the included excluded of global capitalism; they are America's homegrown "third-worldish" subjects. White America's witnessing of the abjection of blacks was "unsettling":

> The images coming out of New Orleans showed "victims" who were desperately poor and predominantly black. Turn on any television, open any newspaper: the exhausted, desperate, sad, and sometimes angry faces looking back at us were poor and black. Those images made many of us uneasy about our system and ourselves.[17]

As if to manage this uneasiness—to resolve the "injustice dissonance" resulting from the juxtaposition of the suffering of poor black Americans with the image of America as a "just" society—white America resurrected racial caricatures of earlier years to "make sense" of what they were seeing on television. Jon Hanson and Kathleen Hanson document the recycling of racist stereotypes from slavery and Jim Crow deployed to assuage the "troubled psyches" of whites: "many in the media and the public seemed almost eager for evidence of our old friend, the untamed black brute— the 'savage, animalistic, destructive, and criminal' beast, who is incapable of self-governance, and ready to rape and plunder the moment the lights go off."[18]

The chaos was effectively naturalized;[19] the catastrophe confirmed white America's suspicion of black people, its deep fantasies about black criminality (there is a gang-banger in every black man), putting on display its repressed feelings about the continuous menace of blackness—despite, or because of, the putative progress of racial relations after the Civil Rights movement. Like critical race theorists, Žižek is attentive to the unconscious mechanism by which blacks are never fully assimilated to the American mainstream, always, as it were, an inch away from slipping (back) into barbarism:

> New Orleans is one of those cities within the United States most heavily marked by the internal wall that separates the affluent from ghettoized blacks. And it is about those on the other side of the wall that we fantasize: More and more, they live in another world, in a blank zone that offers itself as a screen for the projection of our fears, anxieties and secret desires.[20]

The "subject supposed to loot and rape" here refers not to black subjects themselves and what they have actually done or not (most of the reports and rumors about the lawlessness and excesses of violence, gangs, and rapes in the Superdome were actually false) but instead about the perception of black bodies: "'You see, Blacks really are like that, violent barbarians under the thin layer of civilization!' "[21] The evidence of some violence works as *ideology*; racist whites are "*lying in the guise of truth*."[22]

With its "subject supposed to loot and rape," white America could have its cake and eat it too. It could affirm the fairness of neoliberal capitalism and blame blacks for their misery. Hostile to the welfare state, neoliberals proselytize private voluntarism and personal responsibility. Neoliberal ideology "normatively constructs and interpellates individuals as entrepreneurial actors in every sphere of life."[23] By this logic the system did not fail the black citizens of New Orleans. What failed them were social welfare policies that only fueled their bloated sense of entitlement, their addiction to handouts, keeping them, in turn, in a perpetual state of immaturity. Consequently, the argument goes, the failure of responsibility lies squarely on the side of New Orleans' black population: they are society's parasites and criminals. Blacks are ultimately responsible for their laziness and bad judgment, for not heeding the advance warnings.

And it is their "natural" propensity for violence and criminality, coupled with their (historically produced state of) immaturity, that made not only the rescue efforts so difficult and painful to watch, but that was also retroactively posited as the cause for their poverty and abject condition in the first place.

The abjection of blacks after Katrina became, then, an occasion to revive and circulate familiar racists tropes (blacks are lazy and violent, uncivilized and uncivilizable) and an economic cautionary tale of sorts addressed to *all* Americans (don't rely on the government for help; be independent, decline the entitlement mentality, and affirm your entrepreneurial subjectivity). If the first use of the victims is blatantly racist, the second "purport[s] to harbor no racial hostility."[24] The fact that it is blacks who are turned into anti-examples, examples not to emulate but to flee, is deemed accidental to the argument. Those who reject this line of argumentation are often met with the false charge of race-baiting or playing the race-card. What CRT does is to carefully point out how race infiltrates all aspects of our economic system and social reality. Charles Mills and others talk of "racial capitalism" and "white-supremacist capitalism."[25] Neoliberals depoliticize the system when they reduce the highs and lows of capitalism to the failure and valor of each of its individual economic subjects. Blacks are perceived on the whole as bad economic subjects (consider Ronald Reagan's trope of the welfare queen who drains the system of its economic possibilities), whereas whites adopt the appropriate work ethic and are compensated for it. Again, for neoliberals and white supremacists, white privilege is something *earned*, either by personal hard work or genetic superiority. To counter the fetishization of whiteness, Mills treats it not as a "color at all, but a set of power relations."[26] Mills effectively de-ontologizes whiteness. What matters is not what whiteness *is* but what it *does*: how whiteness (synonymous here with white supremacy or racism) helps whites "secure material advantages."[27] Whiteness is a promise of white economic prosperity: even if I (a white blue-color worker) am now struggling, my whiteness will advantageously open doors and foreclose options for (non-white) others. The "subject supposed to loot and rape" gives me "moral" cover; it helps me rationalize my (racist) outlook and sense of deservedness. Such futurity secures and reproduces the status quo, or, as with the Tea Party and Trumpism, seeks to revitalize a supposedly beleaguered status quo, weakened by laws and regulations (crystalized in affirmative action) that favor unappreciative minorities.

It buttresses America's racial order and distorts more viable modes of resistance to economic exploitation. Like Žižek, Bell laments the missed rapprochement between the economically disadvantaged whites and their black counterparts:

> Almost always the injustices that dramatically diminish the rights of blacks are linked to the serious economic disadvantage suffered by many whites who lack money and power. Whites, rather than acknowledge the similarity of their disadvantage, particularly when compared with that of better-off whites, are easily detoured into protecting their sense of entitlement vis-à-vis blacks for all things of value. Evidently, this racial preference expectation is hypnotic.[28]

If the economically belabored whites continue to cling to their white privilege, to the lingering benefits that they still enjoy from capitalism, black vulnerability is compounded. Under racial capitalism, blacks are not only economically exploited, they are also culturally dominated, experiencing, as it were, the full wrath of objective violence.

## Resisting Violence/Violent Resistance

The 2014 unrest in Ferguson, ignited by the fatal shooting of an unarmed eighteen-year-old black youth, Michael Brown, on August 9, brings to light the challenges in resisting state violence. The police (mis) treatment of blacks harkens back to a pre-Civil Rights era, validating CRT's warning about the fragility of America's racial gains.[29] For Žižek, it is also reflective of the changing face of capitalism. Global capitalism's ideological investment in democracy and equality (the capitalism that emerged during the European Enlightenment) is waning; it can no longer entice you with formal equality, which, of course, was and is always and necessarily at odds with its material expression:

> For Marx, capitalist exploitation has to take place in conditions of legal freedom and equality. That is to say, we all have the same rights formally and legally and we are free, but then, in effect, if you don't have money, you have to sell yourself and you are *exploited*. But now, I claim that worldwide capitalism can no longer sustain or tolerate this *global equality*. It's just too much.[30]

With neoliberal capitalism the erosion of formal equality is taking place all across the world. Who is deemed disposable—a *homo sacer*, an individual life "reduced to bare existence outside the polis"[31]—is multiplying at an alarming rate. In the United States, it is blacks and other vulnerable minorities who bear the full force of neoliberalism's devastating effects. As Henry Giroux points out, "The spectacle of neoliberal misery is too great to deny anymore and the only mode of control left by corporate-controlled societies is violence, but a violence that is waged against the most disposable such as immigrant children, protesting youth, the unemployed, the new precariat and black youth."[32] If CRTs' interest-convergence thesis helps to explain America's changing attitude toward blacks as a result of its desire to increase its soft power during the Cold War, Žižek's reflections on global capitalism help to explain how the erosion of equality, when not confronted directly (what are the true causes of society's democratic ills? what are we doing to counter neoliberalism's brutal logic? are we seriously exploring alternative politics? are you sure you have correctly identified your enemy in blacks or the immigrants?), is disproportionally felt by society's most vulnerable bodies. Racism and racialization function here, again and again, as scapegoating mechanisms; they intensify people's otherness, deprive them of their substance, and facilitate their exclusion from society's protection, turning large bodies of the population into quasi-*homines sacri*. In this respect, Michael Brown's heinous killing is "symptomatic of the neoliberal, racist, punishing state emerging all over the world, with its encroaching machinery of social death."[33]

The Ferguson demonstrations and riots defy America's necropower, its indiscriminate maiming and destruction of black lives. Michael Brown's killing disclosed the police not as "the agent of law, of the legal order, but as just another violent social agent."[34] It shattered the social order's veneer of justice. As Žižek observes, "the poor black majority of the town took the killing as yet more proof of systemic police violence against them."[35] Justice for blacks broke down.[36] An emancipatory belief that things cannot stay the way they are quickly set in. The objective violence of the status quo—masquerading as postraciality—became newly and crushingly visible (to those, i.e., unaffected by it on a daily basis) and illegitimate (to the many watching the events unfold—from the shooting to the acquittal of the white police officer Darren Wilson). With the situation becoming unbearable, the protesters took to the streets, destroying private property, damaging businesses, disobeying curfews, and so on. Reuters reported that there were more than 400 arrested after Wilson's acquittal as Ferguson protests spread to other US cities (including Boston, New York, Los Angeles, Dallas, and Atlanta).[37] The killing of Michael Brown was, of course, not an isolated mediatic event. Two notable national events had recently preceded it: on July 13, 2013 George Zimmerman was acquitted for the shooting death of an unarmed black teenager, Trayvon Martin, sparking the transformative "Black Lives Matter" movement, and, about a month prior to the killing of Brown, Eric Garner was choked to death by NYPD officer Daniel Pantaleo on Staten Island on July 17, 2014 (a grand jury failed to indict the officer). Each event produced violent demonstrations.

Žižek cautions that we should not read the violent demonstrations in Ferguson as mere instances of subjective violence (thus adopting the perspective of the police whose business is to preserve and protect the legal order). The unrest is better understood as an explosion of "'abstract negativity'—in short, raw, aimless violence."[38] It is violence that results from the "'negativity' of untying social ties."[39] The crowds that spontaneously formed acted "'irrationally,'" in the sense that they displayed outbursts of destructive energy with no programmatic end and concrete set of demands, registering only a "vague call for justice."[40]

Žižek juxtaposes the Left's use of the energy unbound by this "untying"—the raw energy unleashed in crowds—with that of the New Right. Since the rise of the Tea Party in the United States, the Right has masterfully exploited this "'untying' energy": channeling it for the purposes of reestablishing law and order (crystalized in Trump's "Make America Great Again"), and rallying the people by projecting a nostalgic past, a phantasmatic lost age where whiteness reigned supreme, and promising protection from internal threats (the perceived excesses of the Civil Rights movement, which is only tolerated so long as it doesn't infringe on white privilege) and external ones (the perpetual threat of immigrants or undocumented aliens "stealing" American jobs).[41] The liberal Left remains on the fence, struggling with the violence laden in any "untying energy" (a violence with the troubling potential to "hurt the innocent," concerned leftists worry). Žižek's message for the Left is quite clear: you must counter this "Rightist untying" with an untying of your own. As the "pre-political condition of politics," this untying "opens up the space for political intervention."[42]

The Ferguson protests and riots are a case in point. Žižek characterizes the violent demonstrations that erupted from this leftist untying as an example of what Walter Benjamin calls "divine violence." Unlike "mythic violence," which is "law-founding" state violence, "divine violence" is "law-destroying." The term "divine violence" is admittedly misleading. To be clear, it "has nothing to do with the terrorist violence executed by today's religious fundamentalists who pretend they are acting on behalf of God and as instruments of Divine-Will."[43] If "divine violence" unavoidably evokes God, it is rather "*a sign of God's (the big Other's) own impotence*."[44] Against "decaffeinated"[45] readings of Benjamin by liberal leftists, Žižek underscores the *violence* in "divine violence":

> "Well and good, gentlemen critical theorists, do you want to know what this divine violence looks like? Look at the revolutionary Terror of 1792–94. That was the Divine Violence." (And the series goes on: the Red Terror of 1919 . . .) That is to say, one should fearlessly identify divine violence with positively existing historical phenomena, thus avoiding all obscurantist mystification. When those outside the structured social field strike "blindly," demanding *and* enacting immediate justice/vengeance, this is "divine violence"—recall, a decade or so ago, the panic in Rio de Janeiro when crowds descended from *favelas* into the rich part of the city and started looting and burning supermarkets—*this* was "divine violence" . . . . Like the biblical locusts, the divine punishment for men's sinful ways, it strikes out of nowhere, a means without end.[46]

Divine violence does not give its perpetrator the higher moral ground. "Divine violence is *brutally* unjust: it is often something terrifying, not a sublime intervention of divine goodness and justice."[47] Divine violence "serves no means"[48] and has no preconceived idea, thus preventing it from sliding into mythic violence—violence in the service of law and social order. There were obviously protesters in Ferguson who were making specific requests to the police and elected representatives (end the unjustified use of lethal force, end the practice of racial profiling, implement the use of police officer body-worn cameras, etc.). Žižek is not denying this but only stressing that these nonviolent, reformist gestures still operate within the existing legal order. Divine violence rejects the available modes of action; to paraphrase Kant, the maxim "*protest* as much as you want *but obey!*"[49] is no longer an option.

What makes divine violence *divine* is its "destructive" rather than its founding character.[50] It happens "with no cover of the big Other,"[51] without any guarantees or transcendental authorization. It involves exposure, risk, and decision: it is "the heroic assumption of the solitude of the sovereign decision."[52] How can the Left critically and creatively tap into this destructive energy? Though there is nothing *intrinsically* emancipatory about it, the unrest in Ferguson attests to a heroic enactment of divine violence; it suspended, if momentarily, the hold of power, *opening* a space for anti-racist politics—a politics that would undermine society's law-preserving violence and racial realism. Žižek cautions that raw violence can also take the form of "impotent rage and despair masked as a display of force," as in the case of the 2005 French riots, which, he says, embody "a spirit of revolt without revolution."[53] Revolt is a form of reform, which "means changes *within* the existing order. . . . On the contrary, revolution is where the basic rules of society change."[54] "The real revolution," Žižek argues, "is when you change the balance itself: *the measure of balance*."[55]

Thinking Ferguson with the Paris *banlieues*, and vice versa, brings to light the challenges in transforming anti-racist rage into political intervention, raw violence into a "positive programme of sociopolitical change."[56] Put slightly differently, what is to be done to convert the untying energy of anti-racist crowds into a political act (as opposed to a *passage à l'acte*, the impotent expression of violence and loss of control)? What is to be done to covert it into an act that radically reconfigures the contours of the socio-symbolic system?

On October 27, 2005, Ziad Benna and Bouna Traoré were electrocuted as they fled the police in the Parisian suburb of Clichy-sous-Bois. The deaths of these two *beurs* ignited almost three weeks of rioting in the *banlieues* of Paris, causing damage exceeding 200 million euros in torched cars and buildings. In turn, the riots generated a series of interpretations from liberals and conservatives alike, interpretations that revolved around the problem of how to properly diagnose and rectify the situation. Liberals argued for the need for better integration of young immigrants into French culture, for an improvement of their social and economic prospects, whereas conservatives underscored the necessity of upholding law and order—of protecting the dignity of France's Republican universalism against what was perceived as an "ethnic-religious revolt," in the words of Alain Finkielkraut.[57] For Finkielkraut and others, France's migrant youths—always already suspect—are simply angry and ungrateful Muslims.

But according to Žižek, each of the dominant readings fundamentally erred in its presuppositions, misconstruing the problem, confusing symptoms for causes, and ultimately failing to attend to the real antagonism of French society. The media rhetoric of violence—how we talk about violence—framed the ideological situation and reception of the rioters, and it is to this that Žižek directs his intervention. Skeptical through and through, this intervention declines the media's framing of the riots as yet another case of subjective violence (with all its ethico-political trappings). Žižek opposes the humanists' and liberals' call to cultivate empathetic imaginings as the remedy to this subjective violence, enjoining his readers to resist the ideological pull of subjective violence itself: "My underlying premise is that there is something inherently mystifying in a direct confrontation with [violence]: the overpowering horror of violent acts and empathy with the victims inexorably function as a lure which prevents us from thinking."[58] To think critically about the 2005 French riots is to think about their violence *obliquely*, to look at it awry, that is, to look at violence from a multiplicity of incommensurable perspectives. In contrast, media outlets treated the riots as a spectacle, interpreting them exclusively as an instance of subjective violence. As Paul A. Taylor insightfully observes: "The media is symbolically most violent when it presents itself as a neutral conduit for reporting actual physical violence like the *banlieues* riots. That explicit *subjective* violence is presented with a misleading sense of urgency. Misleading because the very urgency with which you the viewer/listener are asked to respond is the very thing that will prevent you from recognizing the causes (*objective* violence) of the scenario you are witnessing."[59]

If the reception of the riots was problematic, the proposed solutions to the situation were no less so. Žižek cautions against the symptomatic approach and its temptation of depth, the temptation to see in the actions of the rioters a hidden, *latent* political message, awaiting deciphering from the anti-racist liberal-minded cultural critic:

What needs to be resisted when faced with shocking reports and images of the burning Paris suburbs is what I call the hermeneutic temptation: the search for some deeper meaning or message hidden in these outbursts. What is most difficult to accept is precisely the riots' meaninglessness: more than a form of protest, they are what Lacan called a *passage a l'acte*—an impulsive movement into action which can't be translated into speech or thought and carries with it an intolerable weight of frustration.[60]

Drawing explicitly on Lacan, Žižek insists that a *passage à l'acte* is not a strategic deliberation, but a blind outburst. Yet Žižek also insists, paradoxically, on the need to interpret this ambiguous *action*: "The fact that there was no programme behind the burning Paris suburbs is thus itself a fact to be interpreted."[61] On the one hand, Žižek maintains that the rioters' action lies outside the interpretive framework of the symbolic order. On the other hand, Žižek politicizes the non-meaning of the rioters' *passage à l'acte*, interpreting the riots as a case of phatic communication: *Hey Paris, you have a problem!*

The rioters' violence concerns Žižek, but not because it conflicts with a humanist sensibility. The riots exposed France's racial realism, its callous indifference to minorities. The liberal Left's proposed racial remedies are insufficient (how do we correct failed integrationists policies?), covering over the impasse (the antagonism within French culture), offering superficial alterations to France's racial order, "merely different versions of the same thing."[62] In their genuine desire to empathize with society's racially excluded—

> Can we even imagine what it means to be a young man in a poor, racially mixed area, *a priori* suspected and harassed by the police, not only unemployed but often unemployable, with no hope of a future?[63]

—liberals overstress the *objective* conditions determining their existential life, neglecting, in turn, to attend to the rioters' agency and subjectivity: "To riot is to make a subjective statement, implicitly to declare how one relates to one's objective conditions, how one subjectivize them."[64] The rioters are reified and pathologized as damaged goods, broken by the French system that was supposed to care for them.

Lamenting the rioters' impasse, their lack of options, Žižek writes:

> The sad fact that opposition to the system cannot articulate itself in the guise of a realistic alternative, or at least a meaningful utopian project, but only take the shape of a meaningless outburst, is a grave illustration of our predicament. What does our celebrated freedom of choice serve, when the only choice is between playing by the rules and (self-)destructive violence?[65]

What Žižek finds even more tragic in the rioters' actions is their (lack of) effectiveness: a *passage à l'acte* is precisely not a genuine act. They were not motivated by a political vision—a vision of racial and economic justice that is sought without the guarantee of success. They were not willing, in other words, to look into the terrifying "abyss of the act."[66] Their "authentic rage"[67] manifested itself as a sign of impotence, a failure to change the coordinates of their social being. Their actions were not active but reactive: "an authentic political gesture is *active*, it imposes, enforces a vision, while outbursts of impotent violence are fundamentally *reactive*, a reaction to some disturbing intruder."[68]

The situation of the rioters is hermeneutically slippery. What we need is more questions (a skeptical desire to rethink the situation) and fewer answers (a "refusal to offer placebos,"[69] which seem to be compounding the problem). Yet, far from dismissing or ignoring the rioters' plight, Žižek does seek to understand and then to formulate a solution, albeit an oblique one, to their predicament. Or rather, to be more precise, what Žižek offers us is interpretive patience rather than easy and quick solutions. Understanding the rioters' actions as a "blind acting out," "carr[ying] with it an intolerable weight of frustration,"[70] recalls Beauvoir's important qualifier to the Sartrean moral category of "bad faith." As Beauvoir puts it, "Every time transcendence lapses into immanence, there is degradation of existence into 'in-itself,' of freedom into facticity; this fall is a moral fault if the subject consents to it; *if this fall is inflicted on the subject, it takes the form of frustration and oppression.*"[71] Facticity and immanence have been inflicted upon the rioters. Žižek intimates that social, political, and economic circumstances are the real causes of their shortcomings. But he does not treat the blacks and *beurs* as mere victims of the racist social order. Neither passive victims nor autonomous rational beings, the rioters occupy an ambivalent, compromised position.

The rioters' compromised situation reflects to some degree the complexity of their *ressentiment*, their attitude toward France's Republican ideals. Their *ressentiment* may not be purely slavish—(self-)destructive violence is presumably preferable to a servile state of absolute docility—but, at the same time, Žižek argues that it falls short of being transformative, a true act. A solution, Žižek maintains, must begin with an acknowledgment that the rioters' refusal was not radical enough.[72] Their violence possessed elements of divine violence but remained stuck at the level of revolt.[73] It was a necessary violence but not a sufficient one—not the revolutionary violence needed—for effecting genuine change in the symbolic order: "Their aim was to create a problem, to signal that they were a problem that could no longer be ignored. This is why violence was necessary. Had they organised a non-violent march, all they would have got was a small note on the bottom of the page."[74] The efficaciousness of violence is a double-edged sword, since violence is what registers in today's media-obsessed society and it is also what is most co-optable as a form of subjective violence by mainstream media, which covers not the socioeconomic conditions (the systemic violence) that gave rise to the problems at hand, but the scenes of destruction and transgression, such as car burnings and looting.

Looking awry at the riots enables Žižek to offer his own "belated" interpretation of the rioters' aims, which were, he argues, to seek greater ideological integration. The rioters did not fully divest themselves from the existing symbolic structure. They were not short-circuiting the Republican ideals of *Égalité*, *Liberté*, *Fraternité*, demanding the inclusion of *Diversité*, for instance. Cultural pluralism is not the antidote to French racism. Quite the contrary; the blacks and the *beurs* wanted to be fully recognized as *citizens* of France:

> Within the space of French state ideology, the term "citizen" is opposed to "indigene," [which] suggests a primitive part of the population not yet mature enough to deserve full citizenship. This is why the protesters' demand to be recognised also implies a rejection of the very framework through which recognition takes place. It calls for the construction of a new universal framework.[75]

The desire to be recognized—to count, so that their lives may be regarded as liveable and grievable—by a current system that has systematically excluded them necessitates an alternative framework. Žižek insists that this framework must remain a universal one.

As we in saw in Chapter 3, the answer is not a framework grounded in a particular non-European way of life. The desire to resurrect an obliterated pre-colonial identity (an identity prior to contact with Europe) is a fraught enterprise. Žižek's message recalls that of Fanon, who questioned, in *The Wretched of the Earth*, the colonized who, "hotheaded and with anger in their hearts," "relentlessly" yearn to "renew contact once more with the oldest and most pre-colonial springs of life of their people."[76] Roots—the return to "Mother Africa," for instance—serve as a fantasy that promises to put an end to the colonized's suffering and humiliation.[77]

In America, this temptation for roots is visible in Black Panther leader Stokely Carmichael's embrace of African heritage, changing his name to Kwame Ture and encouraging black folk to similarly liberate themselves from white culture: "We have to fight for the right to invent the terms which will allow us to define ourselves and to define our relations to society, and we have to fight that these terms will be accepted. This is the first need of a free people, and this is also the first right refused by every oppressor."[78] Meditating on the workings of language clearly resonates with Žižek, who insists on the deceptive and ideological character of language: "Words are never 'only words.' They matter because they define the outlines of what we can do."[79] Language manipulates us by making us believe that we are free, unqualified agents of our world: "We 'feel free' because we lack the very language to articulate our unfreedom."[80] The work of anti-racist critique lies in patiently making us aware of such "unfreedom." Žižek upholds and expands on Carmichael's position. Something inventive does need to take place to unsettle the current social order and its "institutional racism"[81] but that critical inventiveness lies not beyond the European legacy but *through* it. A more effective blow to white supremacy is to "deprive the whites of the monopoly on defining their own tradition."[82] As in his critical engagement with postcolonialism and decoloniality, Žižek urges a next dialectical step:

> What the oppressors really fear is not some totally mythical self-definition with no links to white culture, but a self-definition which, by way of appropriating key elements of the "white" egalitarian-emancipatory tradition, redefines that very tradition, transforming it not so much in terms of what it says as in what it does not say—that is, obliterating the implicit qualifications which have *de facto* excluded Blacks from the egalitarian space.[83]

While Carmichael turns to Africa for a mythic non-white cultural and linguistic identity, Žižek sees in Malcolm X's renaming a more revolutionary gesture. Adopting X in place of the patronymic Little represents a universalizing move that does not limit black radicalism to a reified vision of the past as the basis for an anti-racist critique. This is the Malcolm X alluded to in Aimé Césaire's *A Tempest*.

Césaire is, of course, one of the fathers of the *Négritude* movement, which enacted a nostalgic and redemptive return to Africa. *Négritude*, in its infatuation with Africa, relies on a logic of exemplarity that prevents blacks outside of Africa from engaging in the necessary work of critical self-fashioning, doing no less damage to the colonized than their prior infatuation with Europe: "Fifteen years before, they [the West Indians] said to the Europeans, 'Don't pay attention to my black skin, it's the sun that has burned me, my soul is as white as yours.' After 1945 they changed their tune. They said to the Africans, 'Don't pay attention to my white skin, my soul is as black as yours, and that is what matters.' "[84] If *Négritude* was a necessary "black mirage"[85] to block French cultural assimilation, its emancipatory value has run its course. And yet Césaire's *A Tempest* also suggests "a universal, non-identitarian Négritude."[86] The drama is a critical and creative adaptation of William Shakespeare's early modern play, *The Tempest*. *A Tempest* follows a now familiar anti-colonial path, rehearsing the racial antagonism between the colonizer (Prospero) and the colonized (Caliban and Ariel). Against Ariel's ideological universalism, Caliban insists on the enemy ("You don't understand anything about Prospero. He's not the collaborative type. He's a guy who only feels something when he's wiped someone out. A crusher, a pulveriser, that's what he is! And you talk about brotherhood!"[87]), on the incommensurable gap, the antagonism between Caliban (and Ariel) and Prospero, between the Third World and Europe. Again, attentiveness to this antagonism does not necessarily translate into a form of identity politics, or one identity (*Négritude*) fighting against another other (white supremacy). In a key moment in the play, however, Caliban tells Prospero of his desire to be renamed "X"—with clear allusion to Malcolm X and the Black Panthers. What Malcolm X accomplished with his own renaming is not a move on behalf of sectarianism. Quite the contrary, as Žižek notes, "when he adopted X as his family name: he was not fighting on behalf of the return to some primordial African roots, but precisely on behalf of an X, an unknown new identity opened up by the very process of slavery which made the African roots forever lost."[88] Declining the phantasmatic lure of local traditions, to which global capitalism is all-too-accommodating, Malcolm X opts for a revolutionary universality.[89] The move from Prospero's Caliban to Caliban's X is a move toward a universal Caliban. To answer the Paris rioters' demand for recognition is precisely to follow the path of a universal Caliban, to adopt and adapt a new universal framework emerging from a "de-whitened," decolonized egalitarian-emancipatory tradition.

# The Fetish of Liberal Nonviolence

Is this appropriation of the egalitarian-emancipatory tradition any less violent than the riots on the streets of Paris and Ferguson? Žižek is here forcibly clear: *no, it is even more violent!* One of Žižek's most frequently misunderstood quotes is "Gandhi was more violent than Hitler."[90] How can one of the most exemplary historical figures of nonviolence exceed in violence the evil incarnated by Hitler? The highly fetishized idea of nonviolence needs hermeneutical scrutiny. The choice is never simply between violence (burning cars, damaging businesses) and nonviolence (peacefully protesting your grievances within the contours of the law). What matters is not the *realpolitik* of violence and the moral purity of nonviolence, but whether these practices actually bring about changes in the coordinates of the social field. This is Žižek's main point. A true change to the social order is by definition violent. Hitler scapegoated the Jews as the cause of Germans' economic ills rather than confronting Germany's capitalist economic structure, whereas Gandhi led a movement that "effectively endeavored to interrupt the basic functioning of the British colonial state."[91] Gandhi's "non-violence" transformed the coordinates of the entire field. It is not sufficient to kill or banish the tyrant (or in this case the British colonizer): "It is not enough simply to get rid of the tyrant; the society which gave birth to the tyrant [or the society that has internalized the ideology of the colonizer] has to be thoroughly transformed."[92] Likewise, against Martin Luther King Jr.'s fetishized appropriation by liberals, Žižek reminds us of the violence of King's nonviolence since it took on America's capitalism and militarism:

> As Harvard Sitkoff put it, "[King] took on issues of poverty and militarism because he considered them vital 'to make equality something real and not just racial brotherhood but equality in fact.'" To put it in Badiou's terms, King followed the "axiom of equality" well beyond the topic of racial segregation: he was working on antipoverty and antiwar issues at the time of his death. He had spoken out against the Vietnam War and was in Memphis when he was killed in April 1968 in support of striking sanitation workers. As Melissa Harris-Lacewell has put it, "Following King meant following the unpopular road, not the popular one."[93]

A true anti-racism must decidedly follow the unpopular road to the uneasiness of white liberals.

In any case, demanding nonviolence from an oppressed group is both obscene and ineffectual. It is, at a minimum, a failure to acknowledge the differential allocation of vulnerability and the possible modes of resistance that are available, and foreclosed, by such a positionality.[94] Take for example, Žižek's description of the typical liberal Zionist attitude toward Palestinian violence.

> Many peace-loving Israelis confess to their perplexity: they just want peace and a shared life with Palestinians; they are ready to make concessions, but why do Palestinians hate them so much, why the brutal suicide bombings that kill innocent wives and children? The thing to do here is of course to supplement this story with its counter-story, the story of what it means to be a Palestinian in the occupied territories, subjected to hundreds of regulations in the bureaucratic microphysics of power.[95]

The demand for nonviolence (the elimination of subjective violence perpetuated by Palestinians) blinds liberal Zionists to the objective violence constitutive of Palestinian social existence. This violence happens not in the spectacular, large-scale showdowns between the Israeli military and Palestinians fighters, but in the quotidian existence of its indigenous population. It takes place in the military's "hyperregulation of everyday life"[96] through its checkpoints, road blockades, permits and passes, and so on. This, as Saree Makdisi argues, is "occupation by bureaucracy"; it is also *racialization by bureaucracy*. At almost every moment of daily life, Palestinians are repeatedly racialized as subhumans, subjected to endless arbitrary control and unnecessary scrutiny. Serving as the "background music of the occupation,"[97] Israeli bureaucracy sustains an ideological space for liberal Zionists to distinguish themselves from their more fervent counterparts without, however, interrupting the de-Palestinification of the land in any significant way.

Liberal Zionists are also likely to be amenable to a two-state solution and may be more comfortable with approaching the issues of race and racism as personal problems than structural ones. They personally do not consider the Palestinians a priori ruthless. They envisage living with them peacefully—as long as the arrangement coincides with their interests: no Palestinian refugee right of return (Israel must remain a Jewish state), no acknowledgment of any historical wrongs (continued denial of the Nakba), a demilitarized Palestinian statehood, no relinquishment of Jewish supremacy in Israel proper, and so on. The two-state solution illustrates nicely Bell's Interest-Convergence-Thesis. Israel's global image has weakened over the last decade. The world's indictment over its Gaza Wars (with the notable exception of the United States) and the success of the Boycott, Divestment and Sanctions (BDS) movement make Israel ripe for a "compromise" (although the fervent right-wing political factions in Israel hold out for a Greater Israel, still dreaming of its version of a one-state solution, an Israel with no Palestinians). What liberal Zionists fear is precisely the violence of binationalism and its universal framework. For binationalism to be discussed (not only by academics but by people in Palestinian and Israeli neighborhoods) as a real possibility is to actively ignore those in power who uphold the status quo, those who say that binationalism is impossible, that it is a leftist, utopian, anti-Semitic idea. It is to change the rules of negotiation: it is to do "*symbolic* violence"[98] to the so-called peace process—and inevitably to the identity of the self, Palestinian and Israeli, that this process sustains. If Palestinians do not give way to their desire,[99] if equality is made axiomatic, as binationalism would make it, Jewish supremacy—which currently fosters and sustains Israel's basic social infrastructure—would lose its appeal: Jews, committed to *universal* justice, would find the idea of an exclusively *Jewish* state unjust and disrespectful. Ironically, liberal Zionists, and like-minded supporters of Israel, constantly ask for a "Palestinian Gandhi"[100]—not realizing that this figure would surely be endorsing the unpopular road of binationalism.

The problem as liberal Zionists sees it lies with the Palestinians themselves. If political Zionists prefer to Nazify Palestinians, to ontologize Palestinian evil—Netanyahu circulated the spurious story that it was a Palestinian who gave Hitler the idea of exterminating the Jews, making Palestinians, in effect, worse than Hitler![101]—liberal Zionists only suggest it by their puzzlement about the killing of the innocent. What is missing in their analysis of the situation, as Žižek points out, is that "violence is *already* here."[102] The violence that Palestinians endure is irreducible to Israeli airstrikes on Hamas posts in the Gaza Strip (or in its prolonged form, the Gaza Wars). There is always a base level of violence happening when nothing new is happening: occupation violence, violence in "normal times."[103] To account for this violence requires a critical confrontation with the legacy of Zionism. Zionist principles underpin current power relations and the state as an institution itself. Failing to address this further contributes to the invisibility of Zionist privilege and obfuscates the fact that the racial problem lies at the very root of Israel's foundation and the institutionalization of its discriminatory practices. Liberals, too, enjoy and benefit from Zionist privilege and the social power that it affords (regardless of one's individual attitude toward its privilege or Palestinians).

Israel's racial realism has everything to do with the racial politics of Zionism. As a regime of power, Zionism produces a particular kind of arrangement of the "partition of the sensible" (to use Rancière's language[104]), a form of intelligibility that values Jewish lives (especially those of Ashkenazi or European Jews) and devalues non-Jewish lives (especially Palestinian ones). More importantly still, Zionist discourse tries to fix or reify Palestinian difference: "Inside Israel, the 'difference' that counts is that between Jew and non-Jew. So far as land in Israel is concerned, for instance, much of it (nearly 90 percent) is held in trust for the Jewish people, whereas non-Jews cannot juridically derive equal benefits from it simply because they are not Jews," writes Edward Said.[105] Simply put, Palestinians will never gain full equality in Israel.

After 9/11 Israel capitalized on the opportunity to depict Palestinians as irrational and dangerous—as *subjects supposed to terrorize*. The global "War on Terror" necessarily flattens historical and political differences in the attribution of terrorism to many disparate acts of violence. The "War on Terror," with its clear and distinct logic of good and evil, facilitated a closer identification of the West with Israel, and swept Palestinians into the broad category of international terrorists. While the Israelis were depicted as a mirror image of the Americans, unjustly shocked and traumatized by the violence of the Islamic other, Palestinians—like the "Islamo-fascists" who attacked America on 9/11—were racialized as profoundly evil, hating the freedom of Israelis and their democratic way of life. As Keith Feldman insightfully observes, "Islamo-fascism . . . emerged as a new articulated expression of race war, one whose genealogy was shaped by durable symbolic and material links between Israel, Palestine, and US imperial culture. Islam, according to this logic, is figured as pathology and distilled into an overdetermined figure essentially incompatible with the exemplary life of liberal democracy expressed in the United States and Israel."[106] As subjects supposed to terrorize, Palestinians stand behind the gates of civilization; their predictable violence is "a product of cultural pathology," framed as a disorder or disease to be eradicated.[107]

Again, for Žižek, the counter to Israeli racist fantasies is not a retreat into religious particularism. He refuses to align Hamas and Hezbollah with the global Left. The answer to Israeli domination is not a retrenched or regressive form of identitarianism, but a secular mode of critique—a binationalist vision—that foregrounds justice and equality for all, that makes the land available to Muslims, Jews, Christians, atheists, and others alike:

> The big question for me—and here I am an unashamed Eurocentrist— is the political solution in Palestine, namely the necessity of a single, secular state. Is the goal of Hezbollah or Hamas a single, secular state, or not? I totally support the Palestinian cause, and even Palestinian "terror," provided it is publicly oriented toward a single, secular state. The option proposed by Hamas and Hezbollah is not a single secular state; but the destruction of Israel, driving the Jews "into the sea." I don't buy the anti-imperialist solidarity with these forces.[108]

Žižek briefly comments on the recent phenomena of Palestinians stabbing Israelis with knifes as possible instances of divine violence.[109] Such actions do terrorize Israelis, disrupting their comfort, giving them a taste of daily Palestinian trauma, but, at the same time, Netanyahu and others have successfully co-opted this type of Palestinian terror, using it to fortify their "symbolic authority"[110] (only the Likud party, and its right-wing coalition allies, can protect Israeli Jews), folding it into their propaganda machine ("see, they can't be trusted as peace partners!"), solidifying and exporting the Palestinian image as "a subject supposed to terrorize"—placing, in turn, the cultural pathology squarely on the side of the Palestinians and BDS activists.

# Racialized Subjects of the World Unite

How, then, does an anti-racist critique combat the proliferation of "subjects supposed to loot, rape, and terrorize"? How do you stop the seemingly effortless production of *homines sacri* at home and abroad? What are racialized subjects to do? Žižek paints a rather pessimistic view of the world in its current trajectory: "I see explosions everywhere."[111]

This is the necessary outcome of dwelling in a "global apartheid society,"[112] in which participation in public life is increasingly becoming a luxury, restricted to the few and powerful. Such conditions can only breed anger and resentment—whence the proliferation of (often impotent) violent rage. This raw violence, viewed from the perspective of those in power, people who enjoy the privileges afforded to them by the status quo, cements society's racial realism. The projection of the subject supposed to loot, rape, and terrorize is validated again and again.[113] Breaking from this vicious circle necessitates a better understanding of the global situation.

If the extreme Right has doubled down on fear mongering, the liberal Left is sadly ineffective in their eagerness to help, to implement better integrationist policies to alleviate the pangs of racial realism. These pervasive moments of crisis are also moments of revolutionary potentialities. To block the Right's exploitation of such moments, Žižek urges us to "think more radically to arrive at the real root of the problems."[114] It will not come as a surprise that for Žižek the main cause is capitalism. But we must resist the crude conclusion that *capitalism causes racial realism*. Rather, to paraphrase Benjamin: "Every rise of racial realism bears witness to failed revolution." The fact of racial realism—that blacks in the United States, blacks and *beurs* in France, and Palestinians in Occupied Palestine and Israel will always have a subordinate status—points to the global Left's failure to secure *égaliberté* for all. The racial realist perspective's strength—it demystifies liberal accounts of racial progress—is also its weakness: it always risks congealing and perpetuating racial inequalities (the symbolic order *is* racist), reifying, in turn, the political landscape. Paul Gilroy makes a slightly different point about breaking with the "pious ritual in which we always agree that 'race' is invented but are then required to defer to its embeddedness in the world and to accept that the demand for justice nevertheless requires us to enter the political arenas that it helps mark out."[115] The idea of racial realism—or any attachment to the dubious category of race—always risks reproducing the presuppositions of the racist system that is being critiqued and generating in us "resignation to the world as it appears."[116]

CRT powerfully exposes white and Western racial fantasies of criminality: the subject supposed to loot, rape, and terrorize. But the next move is to traverse such fantasies and impact the political terrain itself. Racial realism is not destiny; it is "non-all." An anti-racist critique cannot remain at the level of the Imaginary (unmasking the images that fuel a politics of fear) and the Symbolic (uncovering the way civil rights laws serve white interests); it must also touch the Real of antagonism. This can only be done, for Žižek, by politicizing and mobilizing the excluded, the racialized subjects of global capitalism. These subjects can come to occupy what Žižek calls the "proletarian position."[117] What blacks, *beurs*, and Palestinians have in common is that they are the "part of no-part," the "'supernumary' elements"[118] of their respective society: "those who belong to a situation without having a specific 'place' in it; they are included but have no part to play in the social edifice."[119] Žižek breaks here with the classic Marxist identification of the proletariat with the working class. There is no longer only one agent of revolution, "a 'predestined' revolutionary subject,"[120] as in the days of Marx; now, we have "*different proletarian positions.*"[121] Yet for blacks, *beurs*, and Palestinians to fully assume the proletarian position they need not only to breach the racial script—to jettison the liberal playbook of pragmatic reform—but also to impose and enforce that emancipatory wager, the revolutionary leap into the "abyss of the act."

# 5 AFRO-PESSIMISM: TRAVERSING THE FANTASY OF THE HUMAN, OR REWRITING THE GRAMMAR OF SUFFERING

*Political ontology, as imagined through Humanism, can only
produce discourse that has as its foundation alienation and
exploitation as a grammar of suffering, when what is needed
(for the Black, who is always already a Slave) is an ensemble of
ontological questions that has as its foundation accumulation and
fungibility as a grammar of suffering.*

**FRANK B. WILDERSON III[1]**

*In spite of our differences, we can identify the basic antagonism
or antagonistic struggle in which we are both caught; so let us
share our intolerance, and join forces in the same struggle. In
other words, in the emancipatory struggle, it is not the cultures in
their identity which join hands, it is the repressed, the exploited
and suffering, the "parts of no-part" of every culture which come
together in a shared struggle.*

**SLAVOJ ŽIŽEK[2]**

Afro-Pessimism shares Critical Race Theory (CRT)'s unflinching
skepticism regarding racial progress. The formal emancipation of blacks

did not translate into equality and full membership in civil society. While CRT's hermeneutic orientation calls for destabilizing the hegemony of whiteness, and the legal order that buttresses it, so as to make room for marginalized voices, Afro-Pessimism concerns itself with the uniqueness of the constitutive exclusion of blackness. As Saidiya Hartman avers:

> Legal liberalism, as well as critical race theory, has examined issues of race, racism, and equality by focusing on the exclusion and marginalization of those subjects and bodies marked as different and/ or inferior. The disadvantage of this approach is that the proposed remedies and correctives to the problem—inclusion, protection, and greater access to opportunity—do not ultimately challenge the economy of racial production or its truth claims or interrogate the exclusion constitutive of the norm but instead seek to gain equality, liberation, and redress within its confines.[3]

Afro-Pessimism sustains its focus on the crushing reality of antiblackness and the metaphysical suffering of blacks. In the words of Frank Wilderson, one of the movement's major contributors, "the Afro-pessimists are theorists of Black positionality who share Fanon's insistence, that, though Blacks are sentient, the structure of the entire world's semantic field . . . is sutured by anti-black solidarity."[4] Afro-Pessimism explains the ongoing racial fantasies of black criminality and parasitism discussed in the previous chapter through a critical analysis of modernity and its construction of blackness as nonhuman. Today's racism is not an unfortunate residue of prior days that only occasionally manifests itself in hate crimes and excessive police brutality (all instances of subjective violence). For Afro-Pessimists, anti-racist scholars have systematically misconstrued the enemy as white supremacy. An anti-racist critique must go deeper and engage the legacy of modernity itself: how modernity defined human subjectivity through its constitutive exclusion of blacks— understood and ontologized as slaves. Though slavery existed at several historical periods and in different geographical sites, the paradigmatic slave for Europeans came to be identified exclusively with black flesh. As Wilderson powerfully puts it, the Middle Passage ontologically changed African lives in a way that even exceeded the existential imprints left by the Shoah: "Jews went into Auschwitz and came out as Jews, Africans went into the ships and came out as Blacks. The former is a Human holocaust; the latter is a Human *and* a metaphysical holocaust."[5] Wilderson adds,

"That is why it makes little sense to attempt analogy: the Jews have the Dead (the *Muselmann*) among them; the Dead have the Blacks among them."[6]

By juxtaposing the Middle Passage with the Shoah, Wilderson tacitly provincializes the analysis of Auschwitz as the site for understanding exceptional violence. If the Shoah attests to modernity's trauma, to the psychic blow to its (white) humanist self-image, racial slavery provides an alternative analytical model that speaks more directly to the concerns and existential lives of blacks. It is not to enough to say that biopolitics under National Socialism takes a turn for the worse "when the state of exception starts to become the rule."[7] What is the relevance of biopolitics when blacks were unqualifiedly relegated to what Fanon called the "zone of nonbeing"?[8] Biopolitical investment in lives is wholly foreign to racial slavery, which does not manage death for the sake of life. Rather, the abjection of racial difference is the operative logic of transatlantic slavery, making it constitutively necropolitical. Orlando Patterson foregrounds the destructive impact of slavery:

> Slavery . . . is a highly symbolized domain of human experience. While all aspects of the relationship are symbolized, there is an overwhelming concentration of the profound natal alienation of the slave. The reason for this is not hard to discern: it was the slave's isolation, his strangeness that made him most valuable to the master, but it was his very strangeness that most threatened the community . . . On the cognitive and mythic level, one dominant theme emerges, which lends an unusually loaded meaning to the act of natal alienation: this is the social death of the slave.[9]

And "a living death is as much a death as it is a living," writes Jared Sexton.[10] Unlike other forms of slavery which were temporary (the result of military defeat, for instance), the chattel slavery of Africans did not take the form of a contingent event that could, in time, be redressed or overcome: "Chattel slavery, as a condition of ontology and not just as an event of experience, stuck to the African like Velcro."[11] Racial slavery transmuted "the African body into Black flesh."[12] Divorcing Africans from culture and history, modernity invents the ontology of blackness (the human-cum-object).[13] Achille Mbembe concurs: "The Black Man, despised and profoundly dishonored, is the only human in modernity whose flesh has been transformed into the form and spirit of merchandise—the living crypt of capital."[14] By racializing the fleshly condition of blacks, Europeans condemned black lives to a permanent, and seemingly irreversible, state of inferiority, enslavement, and meaninglessness.

Blacks not only served as "the burning fossil that fueled capitalism during its primitive era"[15] but also played an instrumental role in defining the contours of bourgeois labor, bringing to light the ontological difference between the Human and the slave.[16] The former could sell his or her labor-power as a commodity (and, in turn, taste the pleasures of agency from his or her paid labor and ability to buy things), whereas the latter's being-object—accumulable and fungible—was used and exchanged as a commodity.[17] To be human, then, is to be able to enter into a relation of labor and not be subject to enslavement or what Marx called "primitive accumulation."[18] It is to be recognized as nonblack, not as a slave with whom only a relation to property is available: "work is not an organic principle for the slave."[19]

Antiblackness takes on its meaning in relation to the "Human," which operates as a "master signifier" or "quilting point" anchoring it; though in itself meaningless, the master signifier "Human" quilts the field of meaning, around which other signifiers (freedom, recognition, democracy, subjecthood, whiteness, blackness, and, so on) can crystallize or stabilize. For Wilderson and other Afro-Pessimists, the foundational meaning of antiblackness never went away; slavery was never simply replaced by freedom. Though the form of enslavement has obviously mutated—blacks no longer dwell in the plantation; they are afforded civil rights and *formal* equality before the law[20]—slavery's ontological mark persists, lingering as an intractable feature of black (non)being: the racialized black body is today's slave, a person with a certain sociopolitical status, whose existence and practices are never his or her own but "the expression of the master's prerogative."[21] Slavery conditions the horizon of all black folks.

There was no rebirth of the self after the end of slavery; slavery liquidated the *being* of black folks, irremediably altering them, condemning blacks to social death. Hartman writes in her memoir:

> Slavery annulled lives, transforming men and women into dead matter, and then resuscitated them for servitude. Toiling away in the aftermath of death could only be a curse, not a miracle.
>
> I, too, live in the time of slavery, by which I mean I am living in the future created by it.[22]

Accordingly, the violence experienced by blacks is altogether of a different order, reflecting both the singularity of their past trauma and their subjection to civil society's libidinal economy, which the editors of *Afro-Pessimism: An Introduction*, define as

> the economy, or distribution and arrangement, of desire and identification, of energies, concerns, points of attention, anxieties, pleasures, appetites, revulsions, and phobias—the whole structure of psychic and emotional life—that are unconscious and invisible but that have a visible effect on the world, including the money economy.[23]

For this reason, an anti-racist stance that abstracts too much, seeing all minorities as victimized by the same out-of-control white supremacy, will obfuscate the nature of black subjection and the workings of civil society's libidinal economy. Liberals as much as white supremacists partake of this libidinal economy. The latter perversely enjoy gratuitous violence and black suffering; the former empathize with black suffering while simultaneously enjoying their own anti-racism—indulging in a brand of anti-racism that can only imagine racism as instances of subjective violence (the actions of rotten apples, rogue agents), never really questioning the foundational antiblackness of society nor the anti-blackness that informs Western nations' global outlook.[24]

Afro-Pessimism makes one thing clear: the operative antagonism of civil society is not between whiteness and its racialized others (with the various remedies involving the checking of white privilege, the deconstruction of white sovereignty, the demystification of white universality, the exposure of white interest, and so on), but between black and nonblack. The value of whiteness is predicated on black abjection; whiteness gains its desirability not as a result of its positivity but through its parasitic relation to blackness. Or as Jared Sexton formulates it, "it is racial blackness as a necessary condition for enslavement that matters most, rather than whiteness as a sufficient condition for freedom."[25] Without the subordination of blackness, white civil society would lack its current coherence.[26]

Afro-Pessimism displays here what Žižek describes as "the courage of hopelessness." Seeking an alternative to the status quo *within* the coordinates of the existing system is not evidence of critical inventiveness but "a sign of theoretical cowardice."[27] Again, "the true courage," as Žižek argues, "is to admit that the light at the end of the tunnel is probably the headlight of another train approaching."[28] Pessimism enables as it disables and disabuses: "I'm a pessimist in the sense that we are approaching dangerous times. But I'm an optimist for exactly the same reason. Pessimism means things are getting messy. Optimism means these are precisely the times when change is possible."[29] Only after you realize that the existing civil society forecloses any attempt at genuine critique, and that all that the current post-political order offers are alternatives that ultimately only repeat the status quo, can genuine change take place. Afro-Pessimism's negativity is thus not a form of nihilism, or, worse, a reactionary form of *ressentiment*. Rather, we might characterize it as a life-affirming *ressentiment* that fuels the revolutionary desire for rupture, that compels you not "to play nice," that compels you to abandon the belief in postraciality, to reject the cruel pragmatism of reform (embraced by multiculturalism and qualified by deconstruction, postcolonial theory, and CRT in their own distinct ways), and to see the sociopolitical given as fundamentally antagonistic, irremediably unworkable.[30] There is no room for blacks to articulate their grievances within white civil society; their hunger for recognition will forever be unsatisfied: "Whereas Humans exist on some plane of being and thus can become existentially present through some struggle for, of, or through recognition, Blacks cannot reach this plane."[31]

Yet affirming the structural reality of antiblackness/social death,[32] the exceptionalism of antiblack violence—that it cannot be analogized—always risks ontologizing and dehistoricizing race, becoming, in turn, an end in itself, a "separatist ideology"[33] that can only yield an ineffective politics. A global anti-racist struggle cannot do away with solidarity; it cannot glibly dismiss coalition-building endeavors as "an anti-Black configuration, social formation," as Wilderson does.[34] If Afro-Pessimism is fully justified in resisting all-too-convenient cross-racial coalitions, it must *also* open a space for different forms of solidarity beyond the politics of recognition and identitarian coalitional movements. One of the questions that Žižek's analysis orients us to is *who is the neighbor?*[35] Afro-Pessimists like Wilderson and Sexton make a compelling case for understanding blacks as modernity's faceless others, its "real" neighbors—whose *grammar*[36] of suffering is utterly foreign to whites and their nonblack "junior partners of civil society"[37] (e.g., immigrants of color, white women, and workers). Liberal white America's promotion of diversity fails to account for black difference for the singularity of their suffering. Still, does this mean that, for Afro-Pessimists, blacks are beyond solidarity with nonblacks, let alone whites? This chapter pursues this question, asking whether we need to shift the very foundations on which we conceive and build solidarity and anti-racist politics.

## Life After Slavery: *plus ça change . . .*

With their humanity always already under suspicion, "social death" is the only symbolic destiny for blacks. Blackness has meant, and continues to mean, living in a state of "absolute dereliction."[38] There is in fact no *black* humanity. Humanity is on the side of the nonblack, of antiblackness. Blackness is an endless source of allergy for white America: "The Black is a phobic object because he or she presents me with a problem that is beyond language, that leaves me with no way to redress what this person represents. This person is the antithesis of Humanity."[39] It is not the *doing* of blacks that arouses anxieties but their very *being*. For Afro-Pessimists and many others, the Trayvon Martin case brought to light civil society's antiblackness—the structural conditions that enabled and justified (at least in the eyes of his jury) George Zimmerman's fatal shooting of a seventeen-year-old unarmed black teenager in Sanford, Florida—and the failure of humanist discourse to read and remedy the situation—its proposed redress for black suffering is more of the same: condemn the contingent expression of antiblack violence as an aberration and call for better assimilation of black youth in civil society. On this view, there is nothing wrong with white liberal America. To take up such a stance is to disavow the contention that "White people are not simply 'protected' by the police, they *are* the police,"[40] and to hold instead that "the arc of the moral universe is long, but it bends toward justice."

Consistent with an antiblack social script, Zimmerman, the neighborhood watch captain of his gated community, perceived Martin as a racialized black body, out of place, not belonging—we might say as a "subject supposed to trespass and rob"—and thus as a threat to his life. Zimmerman's social phantasmatic fear of blackness found structural support and ideological justification in Florida's "Stand Your Ground" law, which states that a citizen (a Human, Afro-Pessimists would point out) may use deadly force if he or she feels threatened. With Zimmerman, it was not only his life but his property, or "more symbolically, white American neighborhoods or 'good neighborhoods' that needed protection from 'these thugs who always get away.' "[41] To be sure, the initial incident and the subsequent acquittal were met with social outrage and denounced as racial injustice. Liberals asked themselves, *how could this still happen today?* For Afro-Pessimists and others, the answer is, *very easily!* Martin's death "confirmed suspicions"[42]; he was a "prison-slave-in-waiting."[43] America's postraciality was a fantasy out of joint with the daily experiences of black folks. The Trayvon Martin case may have been a shock to white liberals, but antiblackness is nothing new. In her powerful *The New Jim Crow*, Michelle Alexander carefully documents the manifestation of antiblackness in the crushing reality of mass black incarceration in the United States: "The fact that more than half of the young black men in any large American city are currently under the control of the criminal justice system (or saddled with criminal records) is not—as many argue—just a symptom of poverty or poor choices, but rather evidence of a new racial caste system at work."[44] The move from the plantation to the prison did not reflect a narrative of black emancipation. "Black time," as Calvin Warren states, "is the black hole of time that resists linear narrativity."[45] What we have, then, isn't postraciality or postblackness but "a single *carceral continuum*"[46]: antiblackness 2.0. This new antiblackness is the (objective or institutional) antiblack violence that is happening when nothing new is happening.

The extrajudicial killing of Martin did become something "new"—it was *made* new by its sustained coverage on social media—yet little effort was made to relate the Martin shooting back to society's antiblack libidinal economy, to the criminal justice system and its state-sanctioned violence against black bodies. Mainstream media did discuss racial profiling, stop and frisk, gun control, and the legalistic peculiarities of Florida's "Stand Your Ground" law, but it clearly felt more at ease in discussing the shooting as an instance of racist subjective violence.[47] So while it was significant that Martin's fatal shooting received coverage—that it was not just another statistic blissfully ignored by liberal America—the coverage did not completely disabuse its liberal audience of its postracial idealism but rather tended to convert the gratuitous antiblack violence into a kind of spectacle, an excessive and exceptional (contingent) criminal act. It is as though antiblack violence could only be apprehended through the depoliticized lens and captivating (and more profitable[48]) image of the victim–victimizer dyad, which ironically lures us away from society's "structures of subjugation"[49] and the "banality" of antiblack violence.

Media obsessions centered around the character of Martin, especially when news circulated about text-messages and pictures of drugs and guns found on Martin's cell phone. Circuit Judge Debra Nelson ruled against the defense lawyers' request to introduce such evidence during opening statements in Zimmerman's trial for second-degree murder, but she did allow the defense to bring up the marijuana found in Martin's system the night of the shooting. Just about everybody indulged in speculation about the (non)significance of these texts and images. As Bryan J. McCann points out, "audiences were asked to choose between Martin the angelic child victim and Martin the violent 'thug.'"[50] Wasn't Martin a would-be criminal, looking for trouble? asked right-wing outlets. Wasn't Martin just playing and deep down just an innocent—nonviolent—kid, armed only with iced tea and Skittles? asked the liberal Left media.[51] Conservative pundits followed the predictable path of blaming the victim, of putting Martin on trial: as a "subject supposed to trespass and rob," Martin was always already guilty of a crime.[52] A number of online articles with titles like *The New American*'s "Trayvon Martin Was No Innocent" proliferated during and after the trial. Right-wing news site *The Daily Caller* obtained Martin's Twitter feed and published selected tweets that made him appear thuggish.[53] Fox News contributor Geraldo Rivera commented, "You dress like a thug, people are going to treat you like a thug."[54] Liberal journalists and activists rightly objected to relevance of these details of Martin's life. For example, Ben Adler, writer from *The Nation*, exposes the Right's dubious and deceitful attacks on Martin's character:

> The DC [*The Daily Caller*] doesn't explain why Martin's tweets are even remotely relevant, because they are not. But the implication, just like reports that Martin was suspended from school for possessing an empty bag with traces of marijuana, is that by being a normal teenager he was a bad person who deserved what happened to him.[55]

And yet this line of argumentation has its limits; it is not without its ideological pitfalls. Hartman questions the impulse among white liberals to want to identify with the victim of racial violence ("Only if I can see myself in that position can I understand the crisis of that position") before actually objecting to that violence: "that is the logic of the moral and political discourses we see everyday—the need for the innocent black subject to be victimized by a racist state in order to see the racism of the racist state."[56] The representation of Martin—making him appear as their imaginary neighbor—becomes crucial to winning liberal sympathies. He has to be "exemplary in [his] goodness" and not an intimidating thug.[57] There is no place for appreciating and defending Martin's right to "'undeserved' happiness."[58] The liberal desire for identification with black goodness is the obverse side of the right-wing phantasmatic rejection of black badness—of perceiving blacks as "subjects supposed to trespass and rob."[59]

A liberal counter to the fear that Martin allegedly aroused in Zimmerman is to point out that the facts do not support his fear. Here again, Žižek would insist that liberal demystification does not get at the pathology of racism: "a suspicious gaze always finds what it is looking for."[60] In critically assessing the Trayvon Martin case we must keep Zimmerman's pathology of suspicion separate from the fact of suspicion. Zimmerman's racist suspicious attitude remains pathological regardless of whether the suspicion is confirmed or not. The same follows for Zimmerman's staunch, white right-wing defenders. Even if most of their claims about Martin had been true—even if he had been dangerous and intoxicated, a "thug wannabe"[61] looking for a violent confrontation—their antiblackness would remain pathological, helping to sustain an ideological position (compensating for the weakness of whiteness), and thus telling us more about white America than about blacks.

# Destroying the World, or the Courage of Negativity

If the pathology of antiblackness is ingrained in white America's libidinal economy, its collective unconscious, what does Afro-Pessimism offer as a corrective remedy to black social death? Afro-Pessimists typically proceed negatively by outlining what does *not* constitute a viable model of resistance to, and emancipation from, antiblackness. Wilderson and other Afro-Pessimists are critical, in particular, of Marxism and postcolonial theory for their failure to attend to the singularity of (anti)blackness and their complicity in the antiblack solidarity which gives coherence to the existing structure of domination: "Marxist and postcolonial armed struggle, though radically destabilizing of the status quo, are also endeavors which, through their narrative capacity to assimilate 'universal' frameworks of liberation and redress, unwittingly work to reconstitute the paradigms they seek to destroy."[62] Both paradigms are committed to a vision of the subject to come, currently shackled by the oppressive structures of capitalism or neocolonialism. Marxists can posit a *homo faber* unactualized in the current socioeconomic realities, and postcolonial theorists can recall a modality of being and plenitude before the tragic European encounter.

Neither vision of the subject, however, correlates with the situation of blacks, with their desire to destroy the world. The slave is not, and can never become, a *homo faber*—a type of being who creates and realizes himself or herself in labor. Alienation is experienced when workers are not given the opportunity to be human to enjoy their labor. This is the humanist Marxist objection to capitalism. The slave is not a tool-user, he or she is a "sentient being,"[63] a speaking tool, disciplined by "a scopic regime,"[64] reduced to an "image ontology,"[65] where the racialized black other is denied any depth, interiority, and source for creativity. Unlike the anti-colonial *Négritude* movement, which sought to resurrect a black *Dasein*—Léopold Sédar Senghor, for example, translates Martin Heidegger's "*Da-sein*" (literally, "being-there") into "*Neger-sein*"[66]— Afro-Pessimists assert that "black existence is marked as an ontological *absence*."[67] Blackness is "being-*not*-there"; to be black is to possess a non-*Dasein* nature.[68] The slave/black is not a subject—he or she is an object, narrated at will by white civil society.

If there is no shared understanding of the subject, of the world and its grammar, if the subject of Marxism and postcolonial theory brackets blackness from its constitution, then their proposed revolutionary projects must be approached with caution and suspicion. Who is their enemy? What are they proposing as the end goal of emancipation? And what and who have they ignored along the way? Wilderson identifies a tripartite structure in the emancipatory projects of Marxism and postcolonial theory:

> The arc of an emancipatory progression which ends in either equality, liberation, or redress, in other words, a narrative of liberation, is marked by the three generic moments that one finds in any narrative: a progression from equilibrium (the spatial-temporal point prior to oppression), disequilibrium (capitalist political economy or the arrival and residence taking of the settler), and equilibrium restored/ reorganized/ or reimagined (the dictatorship of the proletariat or the settler's removal from one's land).[69]

For Marxism and postcolonialism, the world is salvageable and reconcilable; its equilibrium can be restored. The emancipated world that they envision is a world that they already fundamentally know, a world still plagued by antiblackness: "Through their indisputably robust interventions, the world they seek to clarify and deconstruct is the world they ultimately mystify and renew."[70] But for Afro-Pessimism, the world is decisively beyond redemption. Wilderson enthusiastically quotes Fanon quoting Césaire's revolutionary call to start with "the end of the world," which is the "only thing . . . worth the effort of starting."[71] The "arc of an emancipatory progression" is an ideological lie. There is no looking backward, to a nostalgic and redemptive return to Africa. "Blackness cannot be disimbricated from slavery."[72] Accordingly, there was never an equilibrium, since blackness as such came ontologically into existence as a by-product of the Middle Passage. If the dominant paradigms on the Left acknowledge and denounce black oppression, they nevertheless relativize it. As they see it, there is a clear division between blacks as slaves and blacks post-slavery. Black oppression today belongs to a more generalized necropolitics, where some lives count and some don't.[73]

Many Afro-Pessimists are emphatic in their rejection of this line of argumentation. For them, the call for a solidarity of the oppressed (that refuses to acknowledge the uniqueness of antiblackness) attests to a misunderstanding of antiblackness. The call is both fake and mystifying. It is guilty of perpetuating an investment in the "*Human* subject" at the expense of the "Slave."[74] Rallying behind solidarity fails to appreciate the impossibility of what Afro-Pessimists are demanding: "We cannot enter into a structure of recognition as a being, an incorporation into a community of beings, without recognition and incorporation being completely destroyed. We know that we are the antithesis of recognition and incorporation."[75]

Moreover, Wilderson insists on the aporetic situation of black intellectuals in their struggle for liberation—"to say we *must* be free of air, while admitting to knowing no other source of breath, is what I have tried to do here"[76]—and on the analytic distinction between the "question of pure analysis" and the question Lenin poses, "What is to be done?" While the latter moves into the realm of actions and answers, the former dwells in negativity, in its unflinching questioning of what is, which can allow black people to "learn more about the totality and the totalizing nature of Black oppression."[77] Calls for solidarity, for cross-racial tactics aimed at reforming the racial order of things, distract blacks, unduly altering and corrupting their "space of pure analysis."[78] In this light, Wilderson offers a rather cynical interpretation of the organic solidarity that developed around the Ferguson protests, when Palestinians shared on social media tactics for dealing with police tear gas (since both Palestinians in the Occupied Territories and the Ferguson protestors were being hit with the same American-made tear-gas canisters). Wilderson accuses Palestinians of instrumentalizing black rage and negativity in order "to catalyze and energize their struggle."[79] His message to young fellow black activists is clear: don't be fooled by the Palestinian display of care. Black-Palestinian solidarity is, at best, fragile—at worst, a ruse. Palestinians are (only) using the black cause to further their own.[80] They want to destroy their Zionist-dominated world but not the world that blacks suffer, not the civil society structured by the Human and the antiblackness inherent to it. Against the ruse of analogy, Wilderson stresses the importance of preserving the difference between blacks and Palestinians not only because it is inaccurate to collapse the two (different histories, different enemies) but also because it blinds blacks to the conscious or unconscious anti-blackness of Palestinians:

> One of the things we need to deal with is the ways in which right reactionary white civil society and so-called progressive colored civil society really work to sever the Black generation's understanding of what happened in the past. So right now, pro-Palestinian people are saying, "Ferguson is an example of what is happening in Palestine, and y'all are getting what we're getting." That's just bullshit. First, there's no time period in which Black police and slave domination have ever ended. Second, the Arabs and the Jews are as much a part of the Black slave trade—the creation of Blackness as social death—as anyone else. As I told a friend of mine, "yeah we're going to help you get rid of Israel, but the moment that you set up your shit we're going to be right there to jack you up, because anti-Blackness is as important and necessary to the formation of Arab psychic life as it is to the formation of Jewish psychic life."[81]

For Wilderson, Žižek's comparison of the American police with the IDF to highlight the ways the former "functions more and more as a force of occupation"[82] vis-à-vis the black population can only add to the confusion of analogy (despite a history of counterterrorism collaboration between the IDF and the American police[83]). Žižek and others, bent on aligning the two struggles, are doing a disservice to blacks by occluding their unbearable situation.[84] For Palestinians, there is a way out (a Palestinian state); for American blacks, only social death awaits them. For Wilderson, there is a background here that cannot be taken for granted. Palestinians had a "spatial place that was lost"; there was a "prior plenitude," where they had "spatial integrity."[85] They now demand their sovereignty: "Free Palestine." The United Nations, for example, registers and recognizes "the spatial coordinates of that demand" (though the institution itself doesn't necessarily put any real pressure on Israel to comply with that demand). But for blacks no "auditor" exists, "because the collective unconscious is not ready to accept that Black people had something that could have been appropriated, which is to say that the collective unconscious is not ready to accept that Blacks are Human."[86]

Needless to say, Wilderson simplifies a great deal here. On one hand, there is an imputation of Palestinian motives that veers on Orientalism[87] (Palestinians are figured as the embodiment of "Arab psychic life") and pure speculation (he assumes an impending Palestinian betrayal,[88] whereas the long history of black-Palestinian solidarity[89] belies that belief), and, on the other, there is the unwarranted assumption that what Palestinians want is a return to the same by way of the ideological path of the nation-state. As we saw in Chapter 3, the idea of binationalism, far from a decolonial retreat into plenitude and particularism, not only poses a problem for Israel and its neoliberal allies but calls into question the libidinal economy of national sovereignty that intractably depends on racialization and domination for its operation.

# Traversing the Human via the Universal

It is in this context that Étienne Balibar once referred to the universality of the Palestinian question, arguing that this universality lies in its thematization of the stakes of global democracy itself: "[The Palestinian cause] is a *test* for the recognition of right, and the implementation of international law."[90] To insist on the universal dimension of a Palestinian grammar of suffering is to resist the containment of the Palestinian question to a regional dispute between Israel and its antagonistic Arab neighbors. The Palestinian question touches all of us, he argues, to the extent that we are all compelled to imagine and invent the conditions for justice and equality in our contemporary global world. This is precisely why Žižek considers Palestinians one of the embodiments of the "singular universal," the "part of no-part"—"those who lack a determined place in the social totality, who are 'out of place' in it and as such directly stand for the universal dimension."[91] They are effectively racialized by Israel's civil society, unprotected by its *human*ist umbrella. As "singular universal," the interests of Palestinians are not predetermined by their subject positions; when they struggle to redress their wrongs, they speak to universal concerns (including the wrongs experienced by blacks).

The Palestinians as "singular universal" clearly clashes with Wilderson's dismissive reading but finds some resonance with Sexton's theorization of the slave as occupying a "universal particular" (a concept that he extrapolates from his reading of Žižek). Sexton himself does not propose the analogy between blacks and Palestinians. Quite the contrary. Like Wilderson, Sexton expresses a strong desire to sustain the ontological difference of antiblackness and not dilute its political force by folding the plight of blacks under the umbrella of people of color. Sexton even faults Mbembe for diverting his hermeneutic focus from racial slavery and its aftermath in "African-derived populations" to a "'third worldist' conception of the colonized warranting analytic comparison and political solidarity between the sub-Saharan African postcolony and the living legacy of colonialism in the Middle East."[92] For Mbembe, colonial experimentation is not a relic from the past. The legacy of European colonial sovereignty persists in contemporary politics, and it is fully visible in the Palestine–Israel conflict, in Israel's neocolonial occupation of Palestine, which Mbembe considers "the most accomplished form of necropower."[93] In Palestine and elsewhere Mbembe unearths a sovereign logic characteristic of late modern colonial occupation; it works in "seizing, delimiting, and asserting control over a physical geographical area—of writing on the ground a new set of social and spatial relations."[94] Colonial sovereignty, Mbembe claims further, "define[s] who matters and who does not, who is *disposable* and who is not."[95] Palestinians, who exemplify the plight of the colonized and occupied, do not matter. Rather, they experience existence as "a permanent condition of 'being in pain,'"[96] with no respite in sight. But for Sexton this type of discourse "loses track of the *singular commodification of human existence* (not simply its labor power) under racial slavery, that structure of gratuitous violence in which a body is rendered as flesh to be accumulated and exchanged."[97] If "the lived experience of the black" has no analog, no equal, as Sexton claims, then how can blacks share a common cause with nonblacks? There is an unbridgeable gap between "contingent forms of suffering" (the lived experience of Palestinians, refugees, brown folks, etc.) and "structural forms of suffering" (the lived experience of the black population).[98]

Up to this point, Sexton is on the same page as Wilderson: whites and nonblacks of color misrecognize the fundamental and singular condition of blacks. The slogan "we're all victimized under white supremacy" flattens matters, minimizes antiblackness. Consequently, cross-racial coalitions are, at best, suspect (their penchant for analogies risks "rendering equivalent slavery and other forms of oppression"[99]) and, at worst, complicit with whiteness in their latent antiblackness, and thus readiness to betray the interest of black folks when it no longer fits their agenda. Sexton anticipates a liberal pushback. Against the charge that Afro-Pessimists are playing "Oppression Olympics" (the leftist version of "'playing the race card'"[100]) at the cost of building a solidarity movement, Sexton returns the charge by accusing his accusers of exhibiting a *"people-of-color-blindness."*[101]

And yet Sexton obliquely opens the door for a different approach to solidarity, for a solidarity grounded in *"radical* opposition"[102]—as opposed to a "decaffeinated multiracial coalition," as Žižek might say. Solidarity is possible if the "structural position of the black" is not taken as an "afterthought" but instead foregrounded in the anti-racist struggle: "the whole range of positions within the racial formation is most fully understood from this vantage point."[103] In clarifying his point, Sexton distinguishes between "the vantage of black existence" and "the views of black people."[104] He adds: "the two will likely overlap, but they are not identical. A sensibility derived from attention to the structural position of the category of blackness is likely to be produced by people designated or self-identified as black, but it will neither be exclusive to nor inherent in their intellectual practice."[105] This is not meant to be "a totalizing gesture," but is akin to the "slave" "embod[ying] what Slavoj Žižek would call the 'universal particular': not another particular group among others, but 'a singularity of the social structure' that 'relate(s) to the totality,' a point of identification with constitutive—not contingent—exclusion."[106] An anti-racist solidarity movement worthy of its name must take up the "vantage of black existence" and engage "black existence [as] the truth of the racial formation."[107] Blacks stand, in another Žižekian register, for the "part of no-part," which is "the symptomal point of universality: although it belongs to its field, it undermines its universal principle."[108] Blacks are formally citizens, but devalued by, and excluded from, civil society. Although formally included in the "set" of American society, they do not have a legitimate or respected place within it. As displayed in the Trayvon Martin tragedy, blacks live under constant suspicion, subjected to the physically and psychically devastating libidinal economy of white civil society.

Seeing the figure of the black as a candidate for the "part of no-part" de-substantializes it. It shifts the focus away from the stagnation of ontology, or what Mbembe calls "the kind of absolutization of blackness,"[109] and enables a more robust account of relationality to enter the discussion. As Žižek notes, "the figure of the 'part of no part' confronts us with the truth of our own position; and the ethico-political challenge is to recognize ourselves in this figure. In a way, we are all excluded, from nature as well as from our symbolic substance. Today, we are all potentially *homo sacer*, and the only way to avoid actually becoming so is to act preventively."[110] A quick reading of the passage might give the impression that Žižek is adopting a crudely instrumental relation to society's excluded others: What do they have to teach me? This is not the case. Žižek is acknowledging from the start an economic and political field of power, a division between the included and the excluded. What taking up the vantage point of the "part of no-part"— courageously relating and identifying with society's symptoms (as did the *refuseniks*)—discloses is the fantasy of sovereignty and wholeness. It discloses the "non-all" of white civil society (along with the structuring binary opposition of Human and antiblackness) and gives us a taste of the harshness of being (the reality of the Real—"we are all excluded, from nature as well as from our symbolic substance") but also enables the possibility of politics by revealing that social reality never coincides with the Real. Afro-Pessimists, in their desire to ontologize (anti)blackness, to make it appear as a *necessary* feature of civil society, treat the Real as outside the Symbolic, but, as Žižek argues, "the Real is not external to the Symbolic: the Real is the Symbolic itself in the modality of non-All, lacking an external Limit/Exception."[111]

Traversing the fantasy of the Human begins by acknowledging and confronting what the fundamental fantasy occludes: my virtual disposability at the hands of global capitalism. Attachment to the fantasy is an ideological ruse. It promises happiness and fulfillment, a communal and democratic existence with other fellow (nonblack) human beings. But the inexorable logic of global capital is complying less and less with this fundamental fantasy. No one is really immune from becoming global capitalism's next outsider or *homo sacer*. Afro-Pessimists, of course, argue that blacks don't have to be reminded of their existential vulnerability. And even here, Sexton avers, the problem is not so much with an "economy of disposability,"[112] but with living a life of social death.

Yet we cannot stop at juxtaposing the "contingent violence" of nonblacks with the "permanent violence" of blacks. As Sexton intimates, the lived experience of antiblackness is *not* in and of itself sufficient to propel blacks into the position of the "universal particular" or the "part of no-part." Black folks must take up the "vantage of black existence." "Black," as deployed by Afro-Pessimists like Sexton, can be read as the subjectivization of the "part of no-part"; the injustice done to blacks is staged as "the ultimate test of universality."[113] Does this move induce a crisis in civil society? Does it produce cracks and fissures in the Human armor? Is this really enough to traverse the fantasy of the Human? Does it destroy the world (in the sense of changing its very coordinates)? Does it effectively displace the socio-symbolic field and rewrite civil society's grammar of suffering?

From a Žižekian standpoint, it all depends on the bigger picture. The purity of Afro-Pessimists, their preoccupation with ontology—though it served them well in formulating bold and refreshing ideas—is now in some respects interfering with their stated collective goals: to destroy the world, to rewrite the grammar of suffering. The challenge for Afro-Pessimists is to truly see the figure of the black not as a fetish but as a candidate for the "part of no-part," which means, at the very least, to see the struggle of blacks as part of a global struggle against suffering and the destruction of lives.[114] Blacks are fighting for more than their position; it is not about "the negotiation of interests"[115] but the undoing of the racial order of things. Blacks, as the "part of no-part," would be fighting "for the universal frame of how [their] position will be perceived within this universal frame."[116] Only through such a global struggle—against the "*Becoming Black of the world*,"[117] against the voracious and intractable capitalist logic that deprives humans of rights and protection and reduces them to violable and disposable things—can blacks help to bring into existence a new "species"[118] of humanity, a humanity that would violently lay bare the fake and ideological inclusivity of the Human (again playing the "'white' egalitarian-emancipatory tradition"[119] against itself), that would touch the Real (that would render what *is* "non-all") and "redefine the very universality of what it means to be human."[120]

Many black bodies in America today (continue to) occupy a genuine proletarian position. They join Palestinians, France's blacks and *beurs*, and Europe's refugees, among others,[121] as candidates for the "part of no-part." They join them in the same internationalist anti-racist struggle and emancipatory project. Indeed, as Žižek points out, "revolutionary solidarity" happens when "it is the repressed, the exploited and suffering, the 'parts of no-part' of every culture which come together in a shared struggle"[122] This abundance of "*different proletarian positions*"[123] is and must become the stuff of revolutionary coalitions. Against toothless cross-racial coalitions that "talk as much as possible about the necessity of a radical change to make it sure that nothing will really change,"[124] the global Left must organize and coordinate its efforts, politicize or activate these *different proletarian positions* so as to make the impossible possible: to destroy the world by rewriting its grammar of suffering.

# CONCLUSION: "ALL LIVES MATTER" OR "BLACK LIVES MATTER"? YES, PLEASE!

*In a well-known Marx Brothers joke Groucho answers the standard question "Tea or coffee?" with "Yes, please!"—a refusal of choice . . . [O]ne should answer in the same way the false alternative today's critical theory seems to impose on us: either "class struggle" (the outdated problematic of class antagonism, commodity production, etc.) or "postmodernism" (the new world of dispersed multiple identities, of radical contingency, of an irreducible ludic plurality of struggles). Here, at least, we can have our cake and eat it.*

**SLAVOJ ŽIŽEK**[1]

In an age where identity politics dominates the post-political scene, where the ideology of liberal democracy still reigns, pessimism might be an all too tempting proposition. But *miracles do happen.* The current coordinates of our symbolic order are not immune to social transformation. As Žižek avers, "We should be open to this miraculous aspect: again, not a miraculous thing in the sense of God or religion, but a miraculous event in the sense that something can emerge out of nowhere. We cannot predict anything. *Political miracles give me hope.*"[2] An ongoing political miracle is arguably occurring today with the Black Lives Matter (BLM) movement. BLM constitutes what Žižek, along with Badiou, would refer to as an "Event." Akin to the rupture-inducing Lacanian act, the Event is "something shocking, out of joint that appears to happen all of a sudden and interrupts the usual flow of things; something that emerges seemingly out of nowhere, without discernible causes, an appearance without solid being as its foundation."[3] Was BLM predictable? Hardly. It emerged out of nowhere on the scene under the first black American president's tenure, when postraciality was settling in as the new ideological norm of the twenty-first century. We can say the BLM was an "*effect which exceed[ed] its causes.*"[4] It came into existence as "a contingent upheaval."[5] BLM's cofounders—Alicia Garza, Patrisse Cullors, and Opal Tometi—refused to treat Trayvon Martin as just another black death, ignored by postracialist white America. Despite, or because of, the hopelessness of their situation, they did not give up on the possibility to act. As Žižek puts it, "The situation is 'completely hopeless,' with no clear 'realistic' revolutionary perspective; but does this not give us a kind of strange freedom, a freedom to experiment? . . . One has thus to sustain a minimum of anti-determinism . . . There is always a space to be created for an act."[6] In Garza's words, the creation of this life-altering hashtag #BlackLivesMatter was "a call to action for Black people," reflecting the deadly antiblackness of civil society and a dissatisfaction with the available modes of political resistance: "It was a response to the anti-Black racism that permeates our society and also, unfortunately, our movements."[7] #BlackLivesMatter's viral circulation on social media fueled the passion of a new generation of activists. As David Theo Goldberg avers, "'Black Lives Matter' is gathering steam as the compelling human and social rights movement of our time."[8]

In concert but also in tension with calls to respect the rights of blacks as "human"—captured by one of the Ferguson protest cries, "We are human too"[9]—the formulation "Black Lives Matter" implicitly asks the simple question: why do black lives *not* matter? That is to say, why is black life in America—the bastion of democracy and human rights—lived under a cloud of suspicion, where black bodies are presumed and perceived as intrinsically dangerous, to be defended against? Against white America's pervasive indifference toward the plight of blacks, especially in its complicity with the police brutality of its minority population, the cry of "Black Lives Matter" registers and announces a problem, an ethical lacuna in today's civil society, while simultaneously seeking to rectify it by naming and insisting on *black* difference, by making black lives visible and something mournable—the object of affective investment and care rather than repulsion and dereliction.

And yet from its inception, the movement of BLM has also been met with cynical responses from the right: "White Lives Matter," "Blue Lives

Matter," and, of course, "All Lives Matter." While the first two responses try to match one difference with the like (why should black lives be privileged over police lives?), "All Lives Matter" bypasses the realm of differences and commits to an embrace of the universal—that is, the well-worn path of humanism. Counterresponses from the left have been swift and many. Putatively universal claims like "All Lives Matter" have "always bolstered racism,"[10] always perpetuated white privilege. Calls for universalism—if not deliberately obfuscating of structural inequalities—tend at the very least to forget the historical specificity of antiblackness: what *made* black lives not matter in the first place. Goldberg decries the abstraction of "All Lives Matter," its removal from the field of power and struggle:

> "All lives matter" is a universal moral principle, a Kantian categorical imperative. Other things being equal, all lives matter, equally. Except when they don't. And they don't when other things are taken not to be equal. Like racial standing in a society such as ours. The universalizing politics of "All lives matter" is one of racial dismissal, ignoring, and denial.[11]

Belonging to the universal is not the American default (as the nation's painful history makes abundantly clear); the universal was not and is not afforded to all lives: "The insistence that Black lives matter accordingly is necessary only because, unlike 'all lives,' in this society, black lives are too often taken not to matter. Black lives are presumed too readily in the U.S. not to inhabit the universal."[12] Insisting on black lives mattering is a necessary step toward inhabiting the universal.

Judith Butler for her part considers the slogan "All Lives Matter" a fundamental misapprehension of the situation, a distortion of the claim "BLM":

> When some people rejoin with "All Lives Matter" they misunderstand the problem, but not because their message is untrue. It is true that all lives matter, but it is equally true that not all lives are understood to matter which is precisely why it is most important to name the lives that have not mattered, and are struggling to matter in the way they deserve.[13]

Like Goldberg, Butler does not see "All Lives Matter" as in and of itself an illegitimate claim, only that it is misleading and somewhat premature, ignoring the structural condition of blacks, "the fact that black people have not yet been included in the idea of 'all lives.'"[14]

A Žižekian intervention into this debate begins by repeating Goldberg and Butler's charge that the proponents of "All Lives Matter" misconstrue the message of BLM. Indeed for Žižek, what BLM powerfully attests to, in its indefatigable reminder of police brutality, is a basic crisis in the *Sittlichkeit*, in society's "ethical order."[15] The law is increasingly perceived as doing the work of *in*justice: "When representatives of law commit crimes in their very enforcement of the rule of law, the rule of law is not just weakened but undermined from within—it directly appears as its own self-negation."[16] Responses to this reality, to the systemic mistreatment of blacks, follow, as we have seen, several paths. Liberal multiculturalists interpret it as a problem of intolerance with a clear pedagogical solution (more diversity training!). The partisans of difference translate black difference into another cultural identity, however fraught, vying for recognition and inclusion. Afro-Pessimism considers black difference ontologically unrecognizable within white civil society, as something marked for perpetual social death. We have the whole gamut here, from the naïve optimism of liberal multiculturalists to the blistering negativity of the Afro-Pessimists. While Žižek's sympathies arguably lie closer to Afro-Pessimism, since the existing social order must be seen as hopeless for anything to truly change, he is also adamant that no transformation to the social coordinates can take place unless there is a confrontation with the dynamics of global capitalism—a recognition that "politics is in the economy"[17]—and a proliferation of what he calls "proletarian positions." Solidarity movements (all but ruled out by Afro-Pessimism) are not an option but a necessity. So, does BLM foreclose or foster such solidarity? Is the movement myopic in its thrust—concerned only with black lives? Or, conversely, does BLM open to other racialized voices in the struggle against injustice?

Though there is always a risk in fetishizing difference whenever any difference is singled out (Afro-Pessimism's ontologization of anti-blackness, its monopolization of black suffering, only increases that risk), BLM's impact on the racial order of things was substantial. It effectively transformed the ways white civil society looks at the deaths of unarmed black bodies at the hands of the police. The framework of law and order was denaturalized, in need of more justification. It was no longer accepted by the general public as a given.

BLM as Event seized its audience. It constituted or interpellated black bodies as anti-racist subjects.[18] BLM's emergence transformed the very frame through which America perceived race and engaged it.[19] It moved the underground of the prevalent post-racial scheme. Race became less anachronistic, and racism more than exception, more than a mere social embarrassment. Antiblack violence became more than instances of subjective violence (the contingent, excessive actions of a few rotten apples). BLM made visible an objective violence experienced by blacks on a daily basis. No politician after BLM could really ignore systemic black suffering. Even the "post-Eventual" right-wing pundit who decries the reverse racism or anti-whiteness of BLM, praises the patriotic values of law and order, and considers BLM a hiccup in our post-racial and post-political era, is not the same as the "pre-Eventual" right-wing pundit, "since he is already mediated by the Event, reacting to it."[20]

What is also remarkable about BLM is the movement's refusal of the comforts of *traditional* identity politics: First, if you make enough noise, the Democratic National party (DNC) pretends to listen to you. Then, it makes superficial concessions and empty promises. Next, the DNC co-opts your message of racial and economic justice and uphold "imaginary illusions about solidarity and unity."[21] Finally, it translates your emancipatory message back into toothless demands amenable to liberal democracy—leaving you with more of the same. Malcolm X warned precisely against the co-optation and dilution of the black movement's message by white allies:

It's just like when you've got some coffee that's too black, which means it's too strong. What do you do? You integrate it with cream, you make it weak. But if you pour too much cream in it, you won't even know you ever had coffee. It used to be hot, it becomes cool. It used to be strong, it becomes weak. It used to wake you up, now it puts you to sleep.[22]

Žižek gives similar advice to the protesters of Occupy Wall Street who, he says, "should beware not only of enemies, but also of false friends who pretend to support them, but are already working hard to dilute the protest."[23] Co-optation often takes the form of a shift from politics (potential divine violence) to morality (the certitude of nonviolence). Such "friends" (i.e., pro-capitalist liberals), Žižek adds, "will try to make the protests into a harmless moralistic gesture."[24] They will "clarify" your message: the protesters are not after revolution; they only want reform—*a capitalism with a human face.*

BLM saw through the DNC's posture and declined their endorsement (i.e., their instrumentalization by the DNC).[25] As "friends" of BLM, the DNC purports to stand with BLM and its call to action *for black people*; indeed, such grassroots effort is potentially beneficial for the DNC: more registered black voters increase the winning chances of Democrat candidates. The DNC, however, feels less at ease when BLM breaks with expectations, when its call to action expands and reaches an audience outside the United States. This is what happened when BLM and Palestinian activists began working together in a shared struggle. The two groups produced a powerful short video titled "When I See Them, I See Us,"[26] in which participants hold up signs carrying messages including "Gaza Stands with Baltimore," "I Remember: Deir Yassin, Greensboro, Gaza, Charleston," and "Solidarity from Ferguson to Palestine." This video seeks to make visible the way in which

> the onslaught on Black and Palestinian lives is rife with a discourse of victim-blaming that softens the edge of systematic violence and illuminates the dehumanization process. [It] is a message to the world as much as it is a commitment among ourselves that we will struggle with and for one another. No one is free until we all are free.[27]

BLM changes the symbolic field by boldly incorporating statements into its platform condemning the ongoing Israeli genocide of the Palestinian people, describing Israel as an "apartheid state,"[28] and endorsing the BDS movement—knowing full well that it would produce a backlash at home. Charges of anti-Semitism were quickly leveled at BLM[29] (a move, as we have seen, that is consistent with the growing tendency to indiscriminately label the global left anti-Semitic whenever it is critical of Israel and its policies or actions). One wonders if there would have even been a DNC endorsement of BLM after the (re)affirmation of black-Palestinian solidarity. To the question: What is worse—the DNC tamping down the emancipatory force of BLM's energetic movement or the right-wing groups denouncing it as simultaneously playing the race card and being anti-Semitic? *Both are worse*, as Žižek would say.

The Palestinian question is clearly dividing the Democratic Party.[30] An increasing number of democratic activists—awoken from their liberal slumber by their evental encounter with BLM—no longer accept their party's blanket support for Israel.[31] If they were once "progressive except for Palestine," they now see the struggle for social justice—against "the interlinked systems of white supremacy, imperialism, capitalism, and patriarchy" (BLM's Platform)—as a global struggle, intimately connecting the plight of blacks with that of Palestinians. In this extremely important aspect, then, the Event of BLM is not restricted to blacks, to black nationalism. BLM's preoccupation with antiblack violence did not follow the predicable path of identity politics—political solidarity grounded exclusively on race—so decried by Žižek; it did not succumb to parochial politics, "lazy essentialisms,"[32] or fragmented tribalism (unlike, let's say, the white power movement). The movement kept insisting on its universal message. BLM as Event exceeded its original parameters, its assumed identity. Its call is decidedly anti-sectarian, *open to all*: "it gives rise to a commitment of the collective subject to a new universal emancipatory project, and thereby sets in motion the patient work of restructuring society."[33] BLM's universal message turns the movement into an Event.

For this reason, uttering "Palestinian Lives Matter" does not diminish BLM, or steal its energy, but attests to its critical inventiveness,[34] reinforces the emancipatory force of its message, and intensifies the life-affirming *ressentiment*—as opposed to impotent rage—that is feeding the movement. "To labor in the service of a Free Palestine" is to remain faithful to BLM.[35] Fidelity to BLM undoes the logic subtending the choice between "All Lives Matter." or "Black Lives Matter." The subject of the Event affirms the "refusal of choice," preferring not to choose between universalism and difference. Here again we get a sense of the importance of how problems are set—is a defense of universalism or difference the path for leftists? This bad question can only produce bad solutions.[36] Žižek rejects the assumptions of the question: that difference lies in a particular identity, whereas universalism is abstract and contentless. A Žižekian "Yes, Please!" to the " 'All Lives Matter' or 'Black Lives Matter'?" functions as an *answer nonanswer*. It effectively decouples difference from particularity: "the difference is not on the side of particular content (as the traditional *differentia specifica*), but on the side of the Universal."[37] What is needed is more dialectical thinking, a hermeneutic push to bring about a state where "a properly universal dimension *explodes from within a particular context and . . . is directly experienced as universal.*"[38] BLM is, I believe, such a push—in its initial request for black racial justice, it reframes the "universal dimension itself" and affirms a "new universality"[39]: the struggle for anti-racism and justice for all. It moves the stuggle outside the realm of morality (we ought to resist racism) into politics: we "cannot do otherwise."[40]

Fidelity to the Event of BLM means supporting the struggle of Palestinians and other racialized bodies. It means solidarity with the excluded of global capitalism, the "part of no-part"—the "real" neighbors—who have no proper place within culture. But, as with the Lacanian act, the Event does not come with guarantees. It offers no blueprints for an anti-racist future. An Event can even be undone. Objective violence can slip back into the background, normalizing and naturalizing its nefarious traces and marks. A postraciality 2.0 can emerge, depriving BLM of its substance, erasing its emancipatory achievements, and thus de-eventalizing the movement as a whole.[41] The struggle for racial and economic justice can also regress and produce additional setbacks: more Charlottesville-type demonstrations (in the United States and Europe), more walls and segregation, more policing and containment, more charges of terrorism, increased white paranoia, the ratcheting up of anti-immigrant sentiments, and scapegoating foreigners and Muslims for the socioeconomic ills at home and abroad. And yet for Žižek there is really no alternative. We need to remain faithful to the cause of anti-racism, to the legacy of freedom and equality: "Better a disaster of fidelity to the Event than a nonbeing of indifference to the Event."[42]

# NOTES

## THE IMPORTANCE OF THEORY: AN INTRODUCTORY NOTE

1 See https://www.thecut.com/2018/10/tarana-burke-me-too-founder-movement-has-lost-its-way.html.
2 I owe this reading to Engin Kurtay, Istanbul.

## INTRODUCTION

1 Ta-Nehisi Coates, *Between the World and Me* (New York: Spiegel and Grau, 2015), 7.
2 Slavoj Žižek, "A Leftist Plea for 'Eurocentrism,'" *Critical Inquiry* 24, 4 (1998): 997.
3 Such bold anti-Semitism—out in full public—coincides with the rise and election of Donald Trump. One simply has to recall the supporter of candidate Trump who used a Nazi salute and shouted "go to Auschwitz; go to fuckin' Auschwitz" to protesters in Cleveland during the Republican primaries.
4 Slavoj Žižek, *The Sublime Object of Ideology* (New York: Verso, 1991), 202.
5 David Theo Goldberg, *Are We All Postracial Yet?* (Cambridge: Polity, 2015), 4.
6 Slavoj Žižek, *Living in the End Times* (New York: Verso, 2010), 44. See Sara Ahmed, "'Liberal Multiculturalism is the Hegemony—It's an Empirical Fact'—A Response to Slavoj Žižek," *Darkmatter: In the Ruins of Imperial Culture* (19 February 2008). Available at http://www.darkmatter101.org/site/2008/02/19/%E2%80%98liberal-multiculturalism-is-the-hegemony-%E2%80%93-its-an-empirical-fact%E2%80%99-a-response-to-slavoj-zizek/. Accessed June 15, 2018.
7 See Žižek, "Liberal Multiculturalism Masks an Old Barbarism with a Human Face," *The Guardian* (October 3, 2010). Available at https://www.theguardian.com/commentisfree/2010/oct/03/immigration-policy-roma-rightwing-europe. Accessed June 8, 2018.

8   For example, the otherwise thorough and helpful guide, *The Žižek Dictionary* (Durham: Acumen, 2014), edited by Rex Butler, contains no entries or index references to race or racism.

9   Fredric Jameson aligns Žižek's dialectic with theory's negativity, explaining that "theory . . . has no vested interests inasmuch as it never lays claim to an absolute system, a non-ideological formulation of itself and its 'truths'; indeed, always itself complicit in the being of current language, it has only the vocation and never-finished task of undermining philosophy as such, by unravelling affirmative statements and propositions of all kinds" (Fredric Jameson, "First Impressions," *London Review of Books* 28, 17 (2016). Available at www.lrb.co.uk/v28/n17/fredric-jameson/first-impressions. Accessed February 18, 2018.

10  José Esteban Muñoz, *Disidentifications: Queers of Color and the Performance of Politics* (Minneapolis: University of Minnesota Press, 1999), 11.

11  Slavoj Žižek, "Provocations: The 1968 Revolution and Our Own," *World Policy Journal* 35, 2 (2018): 127.

12  Slavoj Žižek, *The Courage of Hopelessness: Chronicles of a Year of Acting Dangerously* (New York: Allen Lane, 2017), 11.

13  Jared Sexton, "Proprieties of Coalition: Blacks, Asians, and the Politics of Policing," *Critical Sociology* 36, 1 (2010): 95–6.

14  Slavoj Žižek, *Violence: Six Sideways Reflections* (New York: Picador, 2008), 157.

15  Sparked by high costs of living, and most recently by a measure that would raise fuel prices, the Yellow Vests (named after the fluorescent safety vests kept in vehicles for wear in emergencies) is a left populist movement that took to the streets in France on November 17, 2018.

16  Žižek, *The Courage of Hopelessness*, xiii.

17  Žižek, *Violence*, 1–2.

18  Ibid., 2.

19  Peter Hitchcock, "Revolutionary Violence: A Critique," *symplokē* 20, 1–2 (2012): 16.

20  Žižek, *Violence*, 72.

21  Frantz Fanon, *Black Skin, White Masks*, trans. Richard Philcox (New York: Grove Press, 2008), 89.

22  Achille Mbembe, "Nicolas Sarkozy's Africa," trans. Melissa Thackway, *Africultures* (August 7, 2007). Available at http://africultures.com/nicolas-sarkozys-africa-6816/. Accessed February 19, 2019.

23  The passage in question comes from Beauvoir's *America Day by Day*: "many racists, ignoring the rigors of science, insist on declaring that even if the physiological reasons haven't been established, the fact is that blacks *are* inferior to whites. You only have to travel through America

to be convinced of it" (Simone de Beauvoir, *America Day by Day*, trans. Carol Cosman [Berkeley: University of California Press, 1999], 239; qtd. Žižek, *Violence*, 71). In *The Second Sex*, Beauvoir gives a philosophical explanation of what she means by "inferior": "When an individual or a group of individuals is kept in a situation of inferiority, the fact is that he or they *are* inferior. But the scope of the verb *to be* must be understood; bad faith means giving it a substantive value, when in fact it has the sense of the Hegelian dynamic: *to be* is to have become, to have been made as one manifests oneself" (Beauvoir, *The Second Sex*, trans. Constance Borde and Sheila Malovany-Chevallier [New York: Alfred Knopf, 2010], 12).

24 Žižek, *Violence*, 72.

25 Ibid., 73.

26 Ibid., 72.

27 Žižek, *The Courage of Hopelessness*, 4. According to Camilla Fojas, Žižek's notion of systemic violence is not adequately racialized, since it only "describes the 'catastrophic consequences' of the 'smooth functioning' of the economic and political system that enacts more violence than it prevents" (Camilla Fojas, *Zombies, Migrants, and Queers: Race and Crisis Capitalism in Pop Culture* [Urbana: University of Illinois Press, 2017], 2). Fojas ignores however Žižek's point that the most impacted and disproportionally affected by capitalism's systemic violence are the racialized others of globalization, namely, the excluded of the Third World.

28 Žižek, *The Courage of Hopelessness*, 4.

29 Judith Butler, "Paris the Day After the November 13 Attacks: 'Mourning Becomes the Law,'" *Europe Solidaire Sans Frontières* (November 14, 2015). Available at http://www.europe-solidaire.org/spip.php?article36394. Accessed May 29, 2018.

30 Butler, "Paris the Day after the November 13 Attacks."

31 Žižek, *The Courage of Hopelessness*, 5. "The more capitalism gets global, the more new walls and apartheids are emerging, separating those who are IN from those who are OUT" (xix).

32 Žižek, *Demanding the Impossible*, ed. Yong-June Park (Cambridge: Polity, Press 2013), 30.

33 Žižek, *Demanding the Impossible*, 68.

34 Ibid., 26.

35 Žižek, *The Courage of Hopelessness*, 5.

36 "Our ethico-political duty is not just to become aware of the reality outside our cupola, but to fully assume our co-responsibility for the horrors outside it" (Žižek, *The Courage of Hopelessness*, 5). In sharp contrast, First World leaders shamelessly turn a blind eye to capitalism's systemic violence, preferring to " 'help' the undeveloped with aid, credits and so on, and thereby avoid the key issue, namely their complicity in and

co-responsibility for the miserable situation of the undeveloped" (Žižek, *Violence*, 22).

37  Ilan Kapoor, *Celebrity Humanitarianism: The Ideology of Global Charity* (New York: Routledge, 2013), 3.

38  Žižek, *Violence*, 46.

39  Ibid., 104.

40  Žižek, *The Parallax View* (Cambridge: MIT Press, 2006), 9.

41  Immanuel Kant, "An Answer to the Question: What Is Enlightenment?" In *What Is Enlightenment? Eighteenth-Century Answers and Twentieth-Century Questions*, ed. James Schmidt (Berkeley: University of California Press, 1996), 58–64, 60.

42  Žižek, *Violence*, 143.

43  Jacques Rancière, *Disagreement: Politics and Philosophy*, trans. J. Rose (Minneapolis: University of Minnesota Press, 1999), 11.

44  Žižek, "A Leftist Plea for 'Eurocentrism,'" 988. See Étienne Balibar, *Equaliberty: Political Essays*, trans. James Ingram (Durham: Duke University Press, 2014).

45  Paul Gilroy, *Against Race: Imagining Political Culture beyond the Color Line* (Cambridge: Harvard University Press, 2000), 43.

46  Speaking about white privilege, Sara Ahmed similarly observes: "Any project that aims to dismantle or challenge the categories that are made invisible through privilege is bound to participate in the object of its critique" (Sara Ahmed, "A Phenomenology of Whiteness," *Feminist Studies* 8, 2 (2007): 150.

47  Slavoj Žižek and Glyn Daly, *Conversations with Žižek* (Cambridge: Polity, 2004), 1.

48  Alain Badiou, *Ethics: An Essay on the Understanding of Evil*, trans. Peter Hallward (New York: Verso, 2001), 27. Badiou makes the recognition of the Same—and not difference—central to ethics: "The whole ethical predication based upon recognition of the other should be purely and simply abandoned. For the real question—and it is an extraordinarily difficult one—is much more that of *recognizing the Same* . . . The Same, in effect, is not what is (i.e. the infinite multiplicity of differences) but what *comes to be*" (Badiou, *Ethics*, 25, 27).

49  Žižek, "Philosophy, the 'Unknown Knowns' and the Public Use of Reason," *Topoi* 25, 1–2 (2006): 141.

50  The *Oxford English Dictionary* named "post-truth" its 2016 word of year, defining it as "relating to or denoting circumstances in which objective facts are less influential in shaping public opinion than appeals to emotion and personal belief." See Michael P. Lynch, "Fake News and the Internet Shell Game," *New York Times* (November 28, 2016). Available at https://www.nytimes.com/2016/11/28/opinion/

fake-news-and-the-internet-shell-game.html. Accessed November 16, 2018.

51  Jonathan Derbyshire, "Interview with Slavoj Zizek." *New Statesman* (October 29, 2009). Available at https://www.newstatesman.com/ideas/2009/10/today-interview-capitalism. Accessed October 1, 2018,

52  Žižek, "The Spectre of Ideology," in *Mapping Ideology*, ed. Slavoj Žižek (New York: Verso, 1994), 12, emphasis in original.

53  Žižek, *The Sublime Object of Ideology*, 33.

54  Jodi Dean, *Žižek's Politics* (New York: Routledge, 2006), 12.

55  Fredric Jameson, *Postmodernism; Or, the Cultural Logic of Late Capitalism* (Durham: Duke University Press, 1991), 263.

56  Žižek, "The Spectre of Ideology," 1.

57  Žižek, "Holding the Place," in *Contingency, Hegemony and Universality: Contemporary Dialogues on the Left*, ed. Judith Butler, Ernesto Laclau, and Slavoj Žižek (New York: Verso, 2000), 324, emphasis in original.

58  In the Western liberal imaginary, democracy and the free market are symbiotically interwoven; the latter could not exist without the full presence of the former in the realm of public discourse. In addition to guaranteeing a way of life at home, neoliberalism serves in this imaginary as a global antidote to the most corrupt and tyrannical governments in the world. Winning the "hearts and minds" of would-be terrorists (future agents of subjective violence) goes hand and hand with the promotion of neoliberal ideals (which, of course, means more systemic violence for the rest of the world). In 2003, for example, Paul Bremer, then head of the Iraqi Coalition Provisional Authority, observed that "rebuilding the Iraqi economy based on free market principles is central to our efforts" (Paul Bremer, "Operation Iraqi Prosperity," *Wall Street Journal* [June 20, 2003]). Available at https://www.wsj.com/articles/SB105606663932885100. Accessed June 13, 2018.

59  "An ideology is really 'holding us' only when we do not feel any opposition between it and reality—that is, when the ideology succeeds in determining the mode of our everyday experience of reality itself" (Žižek, *The Sublime Object of Ideology*, 49).

60  Žižek, "The Spectre of Ideology," 17.

61  Ibid., 16.

62  Ibid., 60.

63  Louis Althusser, "Ideology and Ideological State Apparatuses (Notes towards an Investigation)," in *Mapping Ideology*, ed. Slavoj Žižek (New York: Verso, 1994), 130, emphasis in original.

64  Žižek, *Disparities* (New York: Bloomsbury, 2016), 64. Žižek credits James R. Martel for his notion of misinterpellation. See James R. Martel, *The Misinterpellated Subject* (Durham: Duke University Press, 2017).

65   Jodi Dean, *Democracy and Other Neoliberal Fantasies* (Durham: Duke University Press, 2009), 14. For Paul Eisenstein and Todd McGowan, the Haitian revolutionaries serve as a crucial—and much needed—counterexample of resistance, forging a universal model irreducible to "the particularity of culture" (Paul Eisenstein and Todd McGowan, *Rupture: On the Emergence of the Political* [Evanston: Northwestern University Press, 2012], 80).

66   Qtd. in Žižek, *The Sublime Object of Ideology*, 32.

67   Žižek, *The Sublime Object of Ideology*, 33.

68   Ibid., 28.

69   Ibid., 31.

70   Derek Hook, *A Critical Psychology of the Postcolonial: The Mind of Apartheid* (New York: Routledge, 2012), 181.

71   See Anthony Kwame Appiah, "The Uncompleted Argument: Du Bois and the Illusions of Race," in *"Race," Writing, and Difference*, ed. Henry Louis Gates, Jr. (Chicago: University of Chicago Press, 1985), 21–37; Robert Gooding-Williams, "Outlaw, Appiah, and Du Bois's 'The Conservation of Races,'" in *W. E. B. Du Bois: On Race and Culture*, ed. Bernard R. Bell, Emily R. Grosholz, and James B. Stewart (New York: Routledge, 1996), 39–56.

72   Žižek, *Violence*, 168. Žižek is alluding to Freud's use of the following line from book 7 of the *Aeneid*: "If I cannot bend the higher powers, I will move the infernal regions [*flectere si nequeo superos, Acheronta movebo*]," quoted as the epigraph to his first edition of *The Interpretation of Dreams* (Freud, *The Interpretation of Dreams*, in *The Standard Edition of the Complete Psychological Works of Sigmund Freud*, vol. 4, ed. James Strachey (London: Hogwarth, 1953–74), ix.

73   Jacques Lacan, *On Feminine Sexuality, the Limits of Love and Knowledge, 1972–1973: Encore, The Seminar of Jacques Lacan, Book XX*, trans. Bruce Fink (New York: Norton, 1998), 95.

74   Žižek, "Avatar: Return of the Natives," *New Statesman* (March 4, 2010), emphasis added. Available at https://www.newstatesman.com/film/2010/03/avatar-reality-love-couple-sex. Accessed October 1, 2018.

75   Žižek, "Afterword: With Defenders Like These, Who Needs Attackers?" in *The Truth of Žižek*, ed. Paul Bowman and Richard Stamp (New York: Continuum, 2007), 204.

76   Žižek, "Class Struggle or Postmodernism? Yes, Please!" in *Contingency, Hegemony, Universality: Contemporary Dialogues on the Left*, ed. Judith Butler, Ernesto Laclau, and Slavoj Žižek (New York: Verso, 2000), 121.

77   Žižek, *The Ticklish Subject: The Absent Center of Political Ontology* (New York: Verso, 1999), 355.

78   Žižek, *Welcome to the Desert of the Real! Five Essays on September 11 and Related Dates* (New York: Verso, 2002), 152–3.

79  Žižek, *Enjoy Your Symptom!: Jacques Lacan in Hollywood and Out* (New York: Routledge, 1992), 44.

80  Žižek, *For They Know Not What They Do* (New York: Verso, 1991), 123.

81  Lacan, "The Signification of the Phallus," in *Écrits: The First Complete Edition in English*, trans. Bruce Fink (New York: Norton, 2006), 576.

82  Žižek, "Woman Is One of the Names-of-the-Father, or How Not to Misread Lacan's Formulas of Sexuation," *Lacanian Ink* 10 (1995). Available at http://www.lacan.com/zizwoman.htm. Accessed August 15, 2018.

83  Lacan, *On Feminine Sexuality*, 7.

84  Žižek, *Less Than Nothing: Hegel and the Shadow of Dialectical Materialism* (New York: Verso, 2012), 742.

85  I would like to thank Ilan Kapoor for his thoughts on this point.

86  Žižek, *The Parallax View*, 79.

87  Žižek, *Absolute Recoil: Towards a New Foundation of Dialectical Materialism* (New York: Verso, 2014), 1.

88  Žižek, *Less Than Nothing*, 958.

89  "What we conceal by imputing to the Other the theft of enjoyment is the traumatic fact that we never possessed what was allegedly stolen from us: the lack ('castration') is originary, enjoyment constitutes itself as 'stolen.'" (Žižek, *Tarrying with the Negative: Kant, Hegel, and the Critique of Ideology* [Durham: Duke University Press, 1993], 203–4).

90  "The position of dialectical materialism is that there is no peace even in the Void" (Žižek, *Absolute Recoil*, 415).

91  Žižek, *The Metastases of Enjoyment: Six Essays on Women and Causality* (New York: Verso, 1994), 200.

92  Žižek, "A Leftist Plea for 'Eurocentrism,'" 997.

93  Ibid.

94  George Yancy and Paul Gilroy, "What 'Black Lives' Means in Britain," *New York Times* (October 2015). Available at https://opinionator.blogs. nytimes.com/2015/10/01/paul-gilroy-what-black-means-in-britain/. Accessed October 8, 2018.

95  Žižek, *Less Than Nothing*, 452.

96  Žižek, "Holding the Place," 321.

97  Žižek, *Tarrying with the Negative*, 210.

98  Žižek, "Today's Anti-Fascist Movement Will Do Nothing to Get Rid of Right-Wing Populism—It's Just Panicky Posturing," *Independent* (December 7, 2017). Available at https://www.independent.co.uk/voices/ antifa-populism-white-nationalism-populism-brexit-donald-trump-alt-right-racism-a8097376.html. Accessed June 19, 2018.

99  Žižek, "Confessions of an Unrepentant Leninist," *International Journal of Žižek Studies* (2008). Available at http://www.lacan.com/zizbomarz.html. Accessed June 13, 2018.

100  Žižek, "Confessions of an Unrepentant Leninist."

101  Žižek, *The Ticklish Subject*, 199.

102  Žižek, "Provocations," 127.

# 1 Liberal Multiculturalism: From "Checking Your Privilege" to "Checking Our Fantasy"

1  Charles W. Mills, *The Racial Contract* (Ithaca: Cornell University Press, 1997), 127.

2  Žižek, *The Ticklish Subject*, 216, emphasis in original.

3  Žižek, "Class Struggle or Postmodernism?" 96.

4  Žižek, "Multiculturalism, or, the Cultural Logic of Multinational Capitalism," *New Left Review* 225 (1997): 40.

5  Žižek, "Multiculturalism," 46.

6  Žižek points out how Apple CEO Tim Cook can display "progressive" cultural stances, arguing for LGBTQ rights, while still engaging in systematic exploitation of its labor force in Third World countries: "Tim Cook can easily forget about hundreds of thousands of Foxconn workers in China assembling Apple products in slave conditions—he makes his big gesture of solidarity with the underprivileged by demanding the abolition of gender segregation" (Žižek, *The Courage of Hopelessness*, 204). The same can be said about Nike's "provocative" Colin Kaepernick ad campaign, featuring the line "Believe in something. Even if it means sacrificing everything." With this move, Nike purports to align itself with black athletes exercising their rights to protest the current racial injustice by kneeling during the national anthem. At the same time, do we forget about Nike's abysmal labor practices? Social justice functions here again as ideology. Nike can signal its progressive creds only by masking its cruel pursuit of profit, that is, by "export[ing] the entire working class to invisible Third World sweat shops" (Žižek, "Nobody Has to Be Vile," *London Review of Books* 28, 7 [April 6, 2006]). Available at https://www.lrb.co.uk/v28/n07/slavoj-zizek/nobody-has-to-be-vile. Accessed October 3, 2018.

7  For example, Robin DiAngelo defines "identity politics" as "the focus on the barriers specific groups face in their struggle for equality," arguing that "we have yet to achieve our founding principle, but any gains

we have made thus far have come through identity politics" (Robin DiAngelo, *White Fragility: Why It's so Hard for White People to Talk about Racism* [Boston: Beacon Press, 2018], xiii). A Žižekian rebuttal here is that identity politics works to reify the same barriers that it seeks to overcome. It is also unclear why the impetus for social change does not emanate from the desire for universality itself. Politics begins by a contestation of the status quo, the established order's positivity; it is "the space of litigation in which the excluded can protest the wrong or injustice done to them" (Žižek, "A Leftist Plea for 'Eurocentrism,'" 997)— it is the space where dialectics take place, the space that addresses the gap between abstract universality (we are all equal) and the economic reality of exploitation and domination (the exclusion of women and minorities from the protection of rights).

8   Žižek, *Did Somebody Say Totalitarian? Five Interventions in the (Mis) use of a Notion* (New York: Verso, 2001), 238. More generally, Žižek considers the struggles "against harassment, for multiculturalism, gay liberation, cultural tolerance and so on" too narrow in their focus, failing to articulate today's fundamental problem: "We shouldn't get blackmailed into accepting these struggles of upper-middle-class victimization as the horizon of our political engagement. One should simply take this risk and break the taboo—even if one gets criticized for being racist, chauvinist or whatever" (Žižek and Daly, *Conversations with Žižek*, 144). Žižek is not dismissing these struggles as false struggles (discrimination against marginalized bodies is very much real); rather, what these struggles lack is a sustained articulation of the economic situation, a direct confrontation with the realities of global capitalism.

9   We should not interpret the determination of one's enemy as a necessary lapse into political tribalism, pitting the Left against the Right, communists against capitalists, and so on. *Not all divisions are the same.* We cannot conclude, as Amy Chua does, that the logic of division or tribalism is itself the problem, and one that is hard-wired in our brains, tearing apart America's and other nations' social fabric. This is, at once, a totalizing and depoliticizing gesture; it is ideology at work. Chua's resilient optimism that America will transcend its current political tribalism as it has in the past—that it will remain faithful to the American Dream (but only by coming to terms with its "past failure instead of denying it" [Amy Chua, *Political Tribes: Group Instinct and the Fate of Nations* [New York: Penguin, 2018], 209])—must be given a Benjaminian twist: *each return to American harmony is a sign of failed revolution.*

10  Žižek and Daly, *Conversations with Žižek*, 144.

11  Žižek gives the example of today's reception of Martin Luther King Jr. as a paradigm of tolerance when the civil rights leader didn't in fact deploy the term; his focus was through and through on the economic hardship of blacks: "If you read speeches by Martin Luther King, and search for

the word tolerance, you'll find that it is practically absent. He did not perceive racism in terms of tolerance, but in terms of economics and politics" (Žižek, "Migrants, Racists and the Left," *Spike Review* [May 2016]). Available at http://www.spiked-online.com/spiked-review/article/migrants-racists-and-the-left/18395#.W0jv1RD3N54. Accessed July 13, 2018. Tolerance serves a clear ideological agenda of displacement; it is how racism is perceived in our post-political condition (Žižek, "Slavoj Žižek: The End Times," *Huck Magazine* [May 18, 2011]). Available at https://www.huckmag.com/perspectives/opinion-perspectives/slavoj-zizek/. Accessed July 13, 2018.

12   Žižek, *The Fragile Absolute; or, Why Is the Christian Legacy Worth Fighting for?* (New York: Verso, 2000), 11.

13   Ahmed, "Liberal Multiculturalism Is the Hegemony."

14   Ibid.

15   Žižek also makes the same charge against postcolonial theorist Homi Bhabha: "I don't agree with those neo-colonialists like Homi Bhabha, who said, at some point, that capitalism is universalizing and wanting to erase difference. No. Capitalism is infinitely multiculturalist and culturally pluralist" (Haseed Ahmed and Chris Cutrone, "The Occupy Movement, a Renascent Left, and Marxism Today: An Interview with Slavoj Žižek," *Platypus Review* 42 [December 2011–January 2012]. Available at https://platypus1917.org/2011/12/01/occupy-movement-interview-with-slavoj-zizek/. Accessed February 4, 2019). Yet Bhabha, while condemning the West's ubiquitous hegemonic economy of sameness, observes in the colonizers' logic of domination a perverse and ambivalent desire to sustain the otherness of the colonized, wanting the non-European to be "*almost the same, but not quite*" (Homi K. Bhabha, *The Location of Culture* [London: Routledge, 1994], 86). Today's multiculturalists are arguably producing their own version of "almost the same, but not quite."

16   The political correctness of liberal multiculturalism evacuates all of the unruliness from neighbor, the unknown other par excellence: "the Politically Correct anti-harassment stance realizes Kierkegaard's old insight that the only good neighbour is a dead neighbour" (Žižek, *How to Read Lacan* [New York: Norton, 2006], 101).

17   Žižek, *The Universal Exception* (New York: Bloomsbury, 2014), 192. Žižek describes political correctness in similar terms: "People far from the Western world are allowed to fully assert their particular ethnic identity without being proclaimed essentialist racist identitarians (native Americans, blacks, etc.). The closer one gets to the notorious white heterosexual males, the more problematic this assertion is: Asians are still OK; Italians and Irish maybe; with Germans and Scandinavians, it is already problematic. However, such a prohibition of asserting the particular identity of White Men (as the model of oppression of others), although it presents itself as the admission of their guilt, nonetheless

confers on them a central position: this very prohibition to assert their particular identity makes them into the universal-neutral medium, the place from which the truth about the others' oppression is accessible" (Žižek, "Neighbors and Other Monsters," in *The Neighbor: Three Inquiries in Political Theology*, ed. Slavoj Žižek, Eric L. Santner, and Kenneth Reinhard [Chicago: University of Chicago Press, 2006], 156). Political correctness—or the policing of white guilt—unwittingly traffics in the racist and false universalism of male whiteness, rather than decisively breaking with it.

18  Žižek, "Multiculturalism, or, the Cultural Logic of Multinational Capitalism," 46. Robert Stam and Ella Shohat object to Žižek's failure to attribute credit to radical race and postcolonial theorists' earlier critique of the abstract, Western universalist model: "The critique of the arrogant yet unmarked Western vantage point has long been a part of the larger race/colonial field" (Robert Stam and Ella Shohat, *Race in Translation: Culture Wars around the Postcolonial Atlantic* [New York: New York University Press, 2012], 120–1). Žižek however is not repeating their argument without a difference. Whereas the field of race/colonial studies (which, on Stam and Shohat's account, includes a more critical multiculturalist wing, composed not of white elite liberals but activist people of color) turns to identity politics as the remedy to universalism, Žižek insists on the negativity of the universal. When Žižek refers to the influence of universalist thought on the anti-colonial movement, he is hardly "recycl[ing] the diffusionist cliché that European ideas alone inspired the revolt against colonialism" (123). Stam and Shohat acknowledge that Žižek has more recently engaged the plight of indigenous movements in the Global South and his example of the Haitian revolution points to a rewarding archive. But they still find this new Žižek not so different from the old: "While giving credit to the Haitian revolutionaries, Žižek portrays them as more French than the French, implementing revolutionary ideology better than the French themselves did. This account prolongs Žižek's earlier portrayal of Third World revolutionaries as conceptual mimic men" (130–1). This objection misses the point. The revolutionaries' engagement with human rights discourse was never slavish parroting, but an act of invention. They creatively misinterpellated European discourse, *politicized* human rights (they do not apply only white men; nor are they limited to the French Revolution), thus disclosing to the whole world their full emancipatory potential—*they are open to all*. Stam and Shohat ask, "Must all revolutions pass through the West?" (131). The short answer is no! Žižek, for example, refers to Gandhi's work as a powerful non-Western critique of European colonialism that unsettled the capitalist order of things, and to Malcolm X's turn to Islam as a source for revolutionary universalism. Again, the point is not about the origins of ideas and values, but about

which ones are worth saving and fighting for in the ongoing global struggle for social justice.

19  Sabine Reul and Thomas Deichmann, "The One Measure of True Love Is: You Can Insult the Other," *Spiked* (November 15, 2001). Available at http://www.spiked-online.com/newsite/article/10816#. W0VMLxD3N54. Accessed July 8, 2018.

20  Ahmed, "Liberal Multiculturalism is the Hegemony." See Žižek, *Living in the End Times*, 43.

21  Žižek, *Living in the End Times*, 46.

22  Ibid.

23  Peggy McIntosh, "White Privilege and Male Privilege: A Personal Account of Coming to See Correspondences through Work in Women's Studies," in *Race, Class, and Gender*, ed. Margaret L. Andersen and Patricia Hill Collins (Belmont: Wadsworth, 2001), 94–5.

24  McIntosh, "White Privilege and Male Privilege," 95–105.

25  As Karl Gill observers, "proponents of Privilege Theory (PT) can be very different and range from the anarchist left to the liberal-dominated NGO sector" (Karl Gill, "Oppression, Intersectionality and Privilege Theory," *Irish Marxist Review* 3, 9 [2014]: 62).

26  Barbara Applebaum, *Being White, Being Good: White Complicity, White Moral Responsibility, and Social Justice Pedagogy* (Lanham: Lexington Books, 2010), 30.

27  Michael Kimmel and Abby Ferber, *Privilege: A Reader* (Boulder: Westview Press, 2010), 9.

28  Charles W. Mills maintains that today's racial system generates "an epistemology of ignorance, a particular pattern of localized and global cognitive dysfunctions (which are psychologically and socially functional), producing the ironic outcome that whites will in general be unable to understand the world they themselves have made" (Mills, *The Racial Contract*, 18).

29  Žižek defends the use of humor (particularly, dirty jokes) as an anti-racist practice because of its capacity to serve as a basis for an "obscene solidarity." For example, in an interview he relates, "To give you an extremely vulgar example, I met a big, black guy, and when we became friends, I went into it like, [assuming a naïve, awe-filled whisper] 'Is it true that you have, you know [makes gesture signifying a gigantic penis]?' and (this is a racist myth I heard in Europe) 'Is it true that you blacks can control your muscles so that when you walk with a half erection and there is a fly here you can BAM! [slaps thigh] snap it with your penis?' We became terribly close friends!" As he notes, however, the success of this kind of joking is highly context-dependent, entailing a power relation in which vulnerability is not equally distributed. Some possess the luxury of troubling stereotypes, while others—particularly the

objects or unwilling recipients of such joking—do not. The strategy thus risks failing and reproducing symbolic violence: "Now, I'm well aware of how risky these waters are, because if you do it in the wrong context, in the wrong way, I'm well aware that this is racism" (Eric Dean Rasmussen, "Liberation Hurts: An Interview with Slavoj Žižek," *Electronic Book Review* [2004]). Available at http://www.electronicbookreview.com/ thread/endconstruction/desublimation. Accessed July 8, 2018.

30  See Tobin Harshaw, "Obama's Cover Flap," *New York Times* (July 14, 2008). Available at https://opinionator.blogs.nytimes.com/2008/07/14/ obamas-cover-flap/. Accessed July 13, 2018.

31  Gary Kamiya, "Rush Limbaugh Was Right," *Salon* (July 15, 2008). Available at https://www.salon.com/2008/07/15/new_yorker_cartoon/. Accessed July 13, 2018.

32  Žižek, "Return of the Natives."

33  "Bin Laden and the Taliban emerged as part of the CIA-supported anti-Soviet guerrilla movement in Afghanistan" (Žižek, *Welcome to the Desert of the Real*, 27).

34  Žižek, "Multiculturalism," 50.

35  Žižek also importantly points out that Malcolm X, the leader of the Black Panthers, expressed his plight in universalist terms: "when he adopted X as his family name: he was not fighting on behalf of the return to some primordial African roots, but precisely on behalf of an X, an unknown new identity opened up by the very process of slavery which made the African roots forever lost" (Žižek, *Event: Philosophy in Transit* [London: Penguin Books, 2014], 48).

36  Žižek, *Tarrying with the Negative*.

37  McIntosh, "White Privilege and Male Privilege," 101, emphasis in original.

38  John Rawls, *A Theory of Justice* (Cambridge: The Belknap Press of Harvard University Press, 1971), 100.

39  Žižek, *Welcome to the Desert of the Real*, 58, 59. See also Žižek, "Happiness? No, Thanks!" *The Philosophical Salon* (April 2, 2018). Available at https://thephilosophicalsalon.com/happiness-no-thanks/. Accessed October 3, 2018.

40  For Žižek, the death drive is constitutive of the human condition (a mixture of language and automatism). There is no transcending this unruly remainder or excess, only acceptance or affirmation: "'Death drive' is not a biological fact but a notion indicating that the human psychic apparatus is subordinated to a blind automatism of repetition beyond pleasure-seeking, self-preservation, accordance between man and his milieu. Man is . . . 'an animal sick unto death,' an animal excoriated by an insatiable parasite (reason, *logos*, language). In this perspective, the 'death drive,' this dimension of radical negativity cannot be reduced

to an expression of alienated social conditions, it defines *la condition humaine* as such: there is no solution, no escape from it; the thing to do is not to 'overcome,' to 'abolish' it, but to come to terms with it, to learn to recognize it in its terrifying dimension and then, on the basis of this fundamental recognition, to try to articulate a *modus vivendi* with it. All 'culture' is in a way a reaction-formation, an attempt to limit, canalize—to *cultivate* this imbalance, this traumatic kernel, this radical antagonism through which man cuts his umbilical cord with nature, with animal homeostasis" (Žižek, *The Sublime Object of Ideology*, 4–5).

41   Available at http://challengingmalesupremacy.org/wp-content/ uploads/2015/04/privilege101.pdf. Accessed July 19, 2017.

42   See Judith Butler, *Precarious Life: The Powers of Mourning and Violence* (New York: Verso, 2004) and *Parting Ways: Jewishness and the Critique of Zionism* (New York: Columbia University Press, 2012).

43   David Theo Goldberg, *The Threat of Race: Reflections on Racial Neoliberalism* (Malden: Wiley-Blackwell, 2009), 117. To be sure, white supremacists in America would hardly view Jews as whites. The Charlottesville episode is a case in point. The anti-Semitic chant "Jews will not replace us" makes clear the protesters' perception of an ontological difference between whites and Jews. And yet Alt-Right leader Richard Spencer could not deny the affinities between white supremacy and Zionism, even describing himself as a "white Zionist" to Israel's Channel 2 News: "As an Israeli citizen, someone who understands your identity, who has a sense of nationhood and peoplehood, and the history and experience of the Jewish people, you should respect someone like me, who has analogous feelings about whites. You could say that I am a white Zionist—in the sense that I care about my people, I want us to have a secure homeland for us and ourselves. Just like you want a secure homeland in Israel" (see "Richard Spencer Tells Israelis They 'Should Respect' Him: 'I'm a White Zionist,'" *Haaretz* [August 16, 2017]). Available at https://www.haaretz.com/israel-news/richard-spencer-to-israelis-i-m-a-white-zionist-respect-me-1.5443480. Accessed November 2, 2018. Whiteness and Zionism here are synonymous with rootedness and exclusive/exclusionary claims to sovereignty.

44   Herbert Marcuse, "The End of Utopia," in *Marxism, Revolution, and Utopia: Collected Papers, volume 6*, ed. Douglas Kellner and Clayton Pierce (New York: Routledge, 2014), 252–3.

45   Marcuse, "The End of Utopia," 254.

46   "We designate it [the reality principle] as the *performance principle* in order to emphasize that under its rule society is stratified according to the competitive economic performances of its members" (Marcuse, *Eros and Civilization: A Philosophical Inquiry into Freud* [Boston: Beacon Press, 1955], 44).

47   Marcuse, "The End of Utopia," 251.

48    Marcuse, "The End of Utopia," 254.

49    Robert T. Tally, *Utopia in the Age of Globalization: Space, Representation, and the World-System* (New York: Palgrave Macmillan, 2013), 100.

50    Marcuse, "A Revolution in Values," in *Towards a Critical Theory of Society: Collected Papers, volume 2*, ed. Douglas Kellner (New York: Routledge, 2014), 197.

51    "Man is evaluated according to his ability to make, augment, and improve socially useful things" (Marcuse, *Eros and Civilization*, 155). See also Marcuse, Five Lectures: Psychoanalysis, Politics and Utopia (London: Allen Lane, 1970), 35.

52    Marcuse, *One-Dimensional Man: Studies in the Ideology of Advanced Industrial Society* (Boston: Beacon Press, 1964), 72.

53    Žižek, *How to Read Lacan*, 92.

54    Žižek's classic example is how the postmodern father disciplines his son's freedom and desires. The father does not order his son to visit his grandmother but leaves to him to make the final decision only after setting the manipulative affective scene: " 'You know how much your grandmother loves you! But, nonetheless, I do not want to force you to visit her—go there only if you really want to!' Every child who is not stupid . . . will immediately recognize the trap of this permissive attitude: beneath the appearance of a free choice there is an even more oppressive demand than the one formulated by the traditional authoritarian father, namely an implicit injunction not only to visit the grandmother, but to do it voluntarily, out of the child's own free will. Such a false free choice is the obscene superego injunction: it deprives the child even of his inner freedom, ordering him not only what to do, but what to want to do" (Žižek, *How to Read Lacan*, 92–3).

55    Žižek, *How to Read Lacan*, 79.

56    Žižek, *Trouble in Paradise: From the End of History to the End of Capitalism* (Brooklyn: Melville House, 2014), 98.

57    Žižek, *Trouble in Paradise*, 98.

58    Žižek approvingly quotes Nikki Johnson-Huston on white Liberals' fake progressiveness, exposing how they seem more invested in disciplining the discourse of others than in changing society's structural inequalities, more invested in diversity as an abstract or exotic idea than in fully confronting its challenges at home: "My problem with Liberalism is that it's more concerned with policing people's language and thoughts without requiring them to do anything to fix the problem. White liberal college students speak of 'safe spaces,' 'trigger words,' 'micro aggressions' and 'white privilege' while not having to do anything or, more importantly, give up anything. They can't even have a conversation with someone who sees the world differently without resorting to calling someone a racist, homophobic, misogynistic, bigot and trying to have them banned from campus, or ruin them and

their reputation. They say they feel black peoples' pain because they took a trip to Africa to help the disadvantaged, but are unwilling to go to a black neighbourhood in the city in which they live. These same college students will espouse the joys of diversity, but will in the same breath assume you are only on campus because of affirmative action or that all black people grew up in poverty" (qtd. in Žižek, *The Courage of Hopelessness*, 186). See Nikki Johnson-Huston, "The Culture Of The Smug White Liberal," *Huffington Post Online* (August 17, 2016). Available at https://www.huffingtonpost.com/ nikki-johnsonhuston-esq/the-culture-of-the-smug-w_b_11537306.html. Accessed December 17, 2018.

59  Žižek, *The Ticklish Subject*, 204.

60  Žižek, *The Plague of Fantasies* (New York: Verso, 1997), 47.

61  Judith Butler, "Collected and Fractured: Response to Identities," in *Identities*, ed. Kwame Anthony Appiah and Henry Louis Gates, Jr. (Chicago: University of Chicago Press, 1995), 443.

62  Žižek, *The Courage of Hopelessness*, 186.

63  Žižek's observation dovetails nicely with Pierre Bourdieu and Loïc Wacquant's analysis of American multiculturalism. "Cut off from the public sphere," US academics invest their political libido in the endless practice of privilege-checking, elevating and mystifying what they do: "US professors have nowhere to invest their political libido but in campus squabbles dressed up as conceptual battles royal" (Pierre Bourdieu and Loïc Wacquant, "NewLiberalSpeak: Notes on the Planetary Vulgate," *Radical Philosophy* 105 [2001]: 4).

64  It is in some ways an idealist approach—if you change individual consciences, the structures will then change. It appears to acknowledge on some level the problem to be a materialist one, but it doesn't take the next step of acting in accordance with a materialist critique. It takes structural inequality as the object of thought but ultimately assumes those structures to be the additive result and problem of individual behaviors and thoughts.

65  Žižek, "Holding the Place," 326. Žižek also points to the ways the same slogan can be read cynically as reinforcing the status quo: "Let's be realists: we, the academic Left, want to appear critical, while fully enjoying the privileges the system offers us. So let's bombard the system with impossible demands: we all know that these demands won't be met, so we can be sure that nothing will actually change, and we'll maintain our privileged status!" (Žižek, *Welcome to the Desert of the Real*, 61). The happiness of the academic Left is protected and rejuvenated, their "progressive" *bone fides* secured, without anything actually changing— without any change really being desired.

66  Žižek, "The Yellow Vest Protesters Revolting against Centrism Mean Well—But Their Left Wing Populism Won't Change French Politics," *Independent* (December 17, 2018). Available at https://www.independent.

co.uk/voices/yellow-vest-protests-france-paris-gilets-jaunes-macron-fuel-tax-minimum-wage-populism-a8686586.html. Accessed December 20, 2018.

67   Žižek, *Revolution at the Gates: Selected Writings of Lenin from 1917* (New York: Verso, 2002), 170.

68   Žižek, *Revolution at the Gates*, 172.

69   Mills, *The Racial Contract*, 127.

70   Žižek, *Living in the End Times*, 363.

71   Žižek, *Violence*, 87.

72   Andrea Smith similarly remarks: "as the rituals of confessing privilege have evolved, they have shifted our focus from building social movements for global transformation to individual self-improvement" (Andrea Smith, "Unsettling the Privilege of Self-Reflexivity," in *Geographies of Privilege*, ed. France Winddance Twine and Bradley Gardener [New York: Routledge, 2013], 278).

73   Sigmund Freud, *Group Psychology and the Analysis of the Ego*, trans. James Strachey (New York: Norton, 1959), 67.

74   Žižek, "The Revolt of the Salaried Bourgeoisie," *London Review of Books* 34, 2 (January 26, 2012). Available at https://www.lrb.co.uk/v34/n02/slavoj-zizek/the-revolt-of-the-salaried-bourgeoisie. Accessed July 17, 2017, emphasis in original.

75   Žižek, "The Revolt of the Salaried Bourgeoisie." Žižek praises Fredric Jameson's *An American Utopia* for its insistence on envy in any imaginings of post-capitalism: "He totally rejects the predominant optimistic view according to which, in communism, envy will be left behind as a remainder of capitalist competition, to be replaced by solidary collaboration and pleasure in other's pleasures. Dismissing this myth, Jameson emphasizes that in communism, precisely insofar as it will be a more just society, envy and resentment will explode" (Žižek, "The Seeds of Imagination," in *An American Utopia: Dual Power and the Universal Army*, ed. Slavoj Žižek [New York: Verso, 2016], 285–6).

76   Derbyshire, "Interview with Slavoj Zizek."

77   Jameson, *An American Utopia*, 88–89.

78   Friedrich Nietzsche, *On the Genealogy of Morals*, trans. Walter Kaufmann (New York: Vintage, 1989), I, 14, 48.

79   Žižek, *Violence*, 190.

80   "Contrary to what Nietzsche attacked as the prevailing 'slave morality' of his time," Victoria Fareld writes, "Améry's victim morality is an expression of individuality and non-conformity. It is articulated as a moral call directed toward contemporary society; far from representing a herd mentality, it entails a fundamental critique directed against the latter" (Victoria Fareld, "*Ressentiment* as Moral Imperative: Jean

Améry's Nietzschean Revaluation of Victim Morality," in *Re-thinking Ressentiment: On the Limits of Criticism and the Limits of Its Critics*, ed. Jeanne Riou and Mary Gallagher [Bielefeld: Transcript Verlag, 2016], 65).

81  Jean Améry, *At the Mind's Limits: Contemplations by a Survivor on Auschwitz and Its Realities*, trans. Sidney Rosenfeld and Stella P. Rosenfeld (Bloomington: Indiana University Press, 1980), 72.

82  Améry, *At the Mind's Limits*, 72.

83  Žižek, *Violence*, 189–90.

84  Žižek, *Violence*, 190.

85  Žižek, "Class Struggle or Postmodernism?" 123.

86  Žižek, *Event*, 181. The Event as such is "a traumatic intrusion of something New which remains unacceptable for the predominant view" (Žižek, *Event*, 78).

87  Žižek, *On Belief* (New York: Routledge, 2001), 85.

88  As Eisenstein and McGowan insightfully observe, "The universal is forged from the rupture with the ruling system . . . . Universality resides in negating the oppression of what is" (Eisenstein and McGowan, *Rupture*, 82).

89  Žižek, *The Ticklish Subject*, 169.

90  Žižek, "Happiness? No, Thanks!"

91  Žižek, *Living in the End of Times*, 53.

# 2 Deconstruction: Hospitality, Hostility, and the "Real" Neighbor

1  Jacques Derrida, *Of Hospitality: Anne Dufourmantelle Invites Jacques Derrida to Respond* (Stanford: Stanford University Press, 2000), 77, emphasis in original.

2  Žižek, "The Non-Existence of Norway," *London Review of Books* (September 9, 2015). Available at https://www.lrb.co.uk/2015/09/09/slavoj-zizek/the-non-existence-of-norway. Accessed July 17, 2018.

3  Emmanuel Levinas, "The Trace of the Other," in *Deconstruction in Context: Literature and Philosophy*, ed. Mark C. Taylor, trans. Alphonso Lingis (Chicago: University of Chicago Press, 1986), 346.

4  Levinas, *Totality and Infinity: An Essay on Exteriority*, trans. Alphonso Lingis (Pittsburgh: Duquesne University Press, 1969), 78. See also Levinas's powerful dedication of *Otherwise than Being* "to the memory of those who were closest among the six million assassinated by the National Socialists, and of the millions on millions of all confessions and nations, victims of the same hatred of the other man, the same anti-semitism," which attests to

the status of the Jew as a paradigmatic figure of the excluded other—of the timeless Victim.

5  Levinas, *Totality and Infinity*, 50.

6  Levinas, *Otherwise than Being, or, Beyond Essence*, trans. Alphonso Lingis (The Hague: Martinus Nijhoff, 1981), 195n.12.

7  Derrida, *Aporias*, trans. Thomas Dutoit (Stanford: Stanford University Press, 1993), 22.

8  Derrida, *Negotiations: Interventions and Interviews 1971–2001*, ed. and trans. Elizabeth Rottenberg (Stanford: Stanford University Press, 2002), 102.

9  Derrida, "Autoimmunity: Real and Symbolic Suicides—A Dialogue with Jacques Derrida," in *Philosophy in a Time of Terror: Dialogues with Jürgen Habermas and Jacques Derrida*, ed. Giovanna Borradori (Chicago: University of Chicago Press, 2004), 127–8.

10  Derrida, *Of Hospitality*, 27.

11  Derrida, " 'Eating Well,' or the Calculation of the Subject," trans. Peter Connor and Avital Ronell, in *Points …: Interviews, 1974–1994*, ed. Elisabeth Weber (Stanford: Stanford University Press, 1995), 282.

12  Following Levinas, as well as Maurice Blanchot, Derrida deploys the formulation of "*rapport sans rapport*," or its multiple variations such as "community without community," "sovereign without sovereignty," "messianity without messianism," for its paradoxical logic.

13  See, for example, Nicholas De Genova, "The 'Migrant Crisis' as Racial Crisis: Do *Black Lives Matter* in Europe," *Ethnic and Racial Studies* 41, 10 (2018): 1765–82; Nick Riemer, "How to Justify a Crisis," *Jacobin* (October 5, 2015). Available at https://www.jacobinmag.com/2015/10/refugee-crisis-europe-zizek-habermas-singer-greece-syria-academia/. Accessed October 15, 2018; Sam Kriss," Building Norway: A Critique of Slavoj Žižek," *Idiot Joy Showland* (September 11, 2015). Available at https://samkriss.com/2015/09/11/building-norway-a-critique-of-slavoj-zizek/. Accessed October 15, 2018.

14  Žižek, *Against the Double Blackmail: Refugees, Terror and Other Troubles with the Neighbors* (London: Penguin Random House, 2016), 99.

15  Derrida, "Some Statements and Truisms about Neologisms, Newisms, Postisms, Parasitisms, and Other Small Seismisms," in *The States of "Theory,"* ed. David Carroll (New York: Columbia University Press, 1989), 63–94, 80.

16  Derrida, "A Europe of Hope," *Epoché* 10, 2 (2006): 410.

17  Žižek, *Against the Double Blackmail*, 79.

18  Žižek, "Love Thy Neighbor? No, Thanks!" in *The Psychoanalysis of Race*, ed. Christopher Lane (New York: Columbia University Press, 1998), 155.

19  Žižek, *Like a Thief in Broad Daylight: Power in the Era of Post-Humanity*. New York: Allen Lane, 2018, 98.

20  Žižek, " 'OMG Some Leftists Would Lynch Me for That'—Part I," *Doxa Journal* (November 16, 2017). Available at http://doxajournal.ru/en/texts/zizek1. Accessed December 5, 2018.

21  Slavoj Žižek, Eric L. Santner, and Kenneth Reinhard, *The Neighbor: Three Inquiries in Political Theology, with a New Preface* (Chicago: University of Chicago Press, 2013), ix.

22  Žižek, *The Parallax View*, 341, 11. See also Žižek, "Preface: Burning the Bridges," in *The Žižek Reader*, ed. Elizabeth Wright and Edmond Wright (Oxford: Blackwell, 1999), ix.

23  Žižek, Eric L. Santner, and Kenneth Reinhard, "Preface, 2013," in *The Neighbor: Three Inquiries in Political Theology, with a New Preface* (Chicago: University of Chicago Press, 2013), ix.

24  Levinas, *Entre Nous: On Thinking-of-the Other*, trans. Michael B. Smith and Barbara Harshav (New York: Columbia University Press, 1998), 101.

25  George Yancy, *Black Bodies, White Gazes: The Continuing Significance of Race in America* (Lanham: Rowman & Littlefield, 2008), xxxv.

26  Achille Mbembe, "Raceless Futures in Critical Black Thought," *Archives of the Nonracial* (June 30, 2014). Available at https://www.youtube.com/watch?v=VkqmAi1yEpo. Accessed July 19, 2018.

27  Luce Irigaray, *This Sex Which Is Not One*, trans. Catherine Porter (Ithaca: Cornell University Press, 1985), 74.

28  Badiou, *Ethics*, 20.

29  Ibid., 25.

30  Levinas, "The *I* and the Totality," in *Entre Nous: Thinking of the Other*, trans. Michael B. Smith and Barbara Harshav (New York: Columbia University Press, 1998), 28.

31  Žižek, *In Defense of Lost Causes* (New York: Verso, 2008), 165.

32  Žižek, "Neighbors and Other Monsters," 161.

33  Ibid., 162.

34  Ibid.

35  Ibid., 140–1.

36  Žižek, *In Defense of Lost Causes*, 16.

37  Qtd. in "Introduction," in *The Neighbor: Three Inquiries in Political Theology*, ed. Slavoj Žižek, Eric L. Santner, and Kenneth Reinhard (Chicago: University of Chicago Press, 2006), 4.

38  Žižek, "Neighbors and Other Monsters," 162.

39  Ibid., 140.

40  Žižek and Daly, *Conversations with Žižek*, 71.

41   Fanon, *Black Skin, White Masks*, 202, translation modified.

42   Žižek, *In Defense of Lost Causes*, 16–17. See also Žižek, *Less Than Nothing*, 831.

43   Žižek, *Less Than Nothing*, 831.

44   A generalized Levinasian thought informs multiculturalism which systematically "suspends the traumatic kernel of the Other reducing it to an aseptic folklorist entity" (Žižek, "Love Thy Neighbor? No, Thanks!" 168).

45   Alexander G. Weheliye, *Habeas Viscus: Racializing Assemblages, Biopolitics, and Black Feminist Theories of the Human* (Durham: Duke University Press, 2014), 3.

46   Levinas, "Ethics and Politics," in *The Levinas Reader*, ed. Seán Hand (Oxford: Blackwell, 1989), 294.

47   Levinas, "Ethics and Politics," 294.

48   Levinas, *Ethics and Infinity: Conversations with Philippe Nemo*, trans. Richard A. Cohen (Pittsburgh: Duquesne University Press, 1985), 85.

49   Žižek, *Organs without Bodies: On Deleuze and Consequences* (New York: Routledge, 2004), 106.

50   Žižek, "Neighbors and Other Monsters," 183.

51   Žižek, *The Fragile Absolute*, 11, emphasis in original.

52   Amanda Loumansky, "Israel and the Palestinians: the Challenge to Levinasian Ethics," *SCTIW Review: Journal of the Society for Contemporary Thought of the Islamicate World* (February 21, 2019). Available at https://sctiw.org/wp-content/uploads/2019/02/175-Continental-Philosophy-and-the-Palestinian-Question-Amanda-Loumansky.pdf. Accessed February 21, 2019.

53   Michael L. Morgan, *The Cambridge Introduction to Emmanuel Levinas* (Cambridge: Cambridge University Press, 2011), 228.

54   Levinas, "Ethics and Politics," 297. This comment comes quite late in the interview with Malka.

55   Amanda Loumansky, "Israel and the Palestinians."

56   See Zahi Zalloua, *Continental Philosophy and the Palestinian Question: Beyond the Jew and the Greek* (New York: Bloomsbury, 2017).

57   Loumansky, "Israel and the Palestinians."

58   Levinas, *Difficult Freedom: Essays on Judaism*, trans. Seán Hand (Baltimore: Johns Hopkins University Press, 1990), 5.

59   Edward Said, *The Politics of Dispossession: The Struggle for Palestinian Self-Determination 1969–1994* (New York: Vintage, 1994), 101.

60   *Terra nullius* is an eighteenth-century legal concept, which literally means "a land of no one," used to justify or legitimize the dispossession of indigenous peoples' lands by European colonizers.

61   Mbembe, "Necropolitics," trans. Libby Meintjes, *Public Culture* 15, 1 (2003): 39.

62   For the more fervent Zionists, calling the West Bank Occupied Territories is itself "factually" inaccurate. They emphatically dispute Palestinian claims to indigeneity, preferring the biblical designation of Judea and Samaria. As they see it, Israeli Jews are not *occupying* the land, but are *liberating* it from the Palestinian usurpers (Ilan Pappé, *Ten Myths About Israel* [New York: Verso, 2017], 32, 41). They are the "true" indigenous population, insisting that the existence of Israel is biblically guaranteed, immune to the whims of the United Nations, or to any effort at curtailing Zionist privilege.

63   Levinas, "Zionisms," in *The Levinas Reader*, ed. Seán Hand (Oxford: Blackwell, 1989), 277–8.

64   As Elias Sanbar points out, "Never will you hear [Zionists] say, 'the Palestinian people have no right to anything,' no amount of force can support such a position and they know it very well. On the contrary you will certainly hear them affirm that 'there is no Palestinian people'" (Gilles Deleuze and Elias Sanbar, "The Indians of Palestine," trans. Timothy S. Murphy, *Discourse* 20, 3 [1998]: 29).

65   Shahid Alam, *Israeli Exceptionalism: The Destabilizing Logic of Zionism* (New York: Palgrave Macmillan, 2009), 14.

66   Žižek, *Violence*, 117.

67   See Pappé, *The Ethnic Cleansing of Palestine* (Oxford: Oneworld, 2006).

68   For Zionists, the Palestinians are first and foremost a "demographic problem"; they must be "transferred"—a euphemism for forced expulsion (of course, if the Israeli occupation becomes sufficiently unbearable, there is always the Zionist hope for the "voluntary transfer" of Palestinians). Saree Makdisi, *Palestine Inside Out: An Everyday Occupation* (New York: Norton, 2008), 9–10.

69   Emma Green, "Israel's New Law Inflames the Core Tension in Its Identity," *The Atlantic* (July 21, 2018). Available at https://www.theatlantic.com/international/archive/2018/07/israel-nation-state-law/565712/. Accessed August 2, 2018.

70   See the website of Adalah (The Legal Center for Arab Minority Rights in Israel). Adalah has "compris[ed] a list of over 65 Israeli laws that discriminate directly or indirectly against Palestinian citizens in Israel and/or Palestinian residents of the Occupied Palestinian Territory (OPT) on the basis of their national belonging. The discrimination in these laws is either explicit—'discrimination on its face'—or, more often, the laws are worded in a seemingly neutral manner, but have or will likely have a disparate impact on Palestinians in their implementation." Available at http://www.adalah.org/en/content/view/7771. Accessed November 22, 2018.

71  "By isolating being apart in some sort of essence or hypostasis, the word corrupts it into a quasi-ontological segregation. At every point, like all racisms, [apartheid] tends to pass segregation off as natural—and as the very law of the origin" (Derrida, "Racism's Last Word," trans. Peggy Kamuf, *Critical Inquiry* 12, 1 [1985]: 292).

72  Qtd. in Omri Boehm, "Did Israel Just Stop Trying to Be a Democracy?" *New York Times* (July 26, 2018). Available at https://www.nytimes.com/2018/07/26/opinion/israel-law-jewish-democracy-apartheid-palestinian.html. Accessed August 2, 2018.

73  Žižek, "Whither Zionism?" *In These Times* (March 2, 2015). Available at http://inthesetimes.com/article/17702/slavoj_zizek_zionism. Accessed August 2, 2018. Louis Nayman objects to Žižek's call to jettison the mythical rhetoric of creation, seeing it as resulting in a "might makes right" doctrine: "By delegitimizing reliance on a 'mythic past' as a claim to peoplehood and land, Zizek validates conquest, force of arms, and perpetual occupation. In this construct, appeals for justice and redress lose their justification over time, so that all that counts is the power and means for imposing hegemony, either by Arabs or Jews" (Louis Nayman, "Whither Žižek?: On Zionism and Jews," *In These Times* [March 18, 2015]). Available at http://inthesetimes.com/article/17745/whither-zizek-on-zionism-and-jews. Accessed August 4, 2018. Nayman's reasoning does not hold up to scrutiny: the existence of a mythical framework is precisely what gives justification to all kinds of conquest and domination; indeed, the rhetoric of Manifest Destiny has often had a genocidal legacy. Nayman sees nothing objectionable to the nation-state of Israel being ontologized and abstracted from the material, historical, and dynamic field of power. But what are Palestinians rights? What do international laws mean if the land of Palestine was promised to the Jews by God? A resolution to the Israeli-Palestinian impasse begins by demythification of Zionism, which, in turn, reveals Israel's actions and policies not as irreproachable (realizing God's plans), but as an instance of a "land grab," reflecting not a higher religious mission but a systematic plan to dispossess the indigenous Palestinians, emblematic of a settler colonial ideology.

74  Gianni Vattimo and Michael Marder, "Introduction: 'If Not Now, When?'" in *Deconstructing Zionism: A Critique of Political Metaphysics*, ed. Gianni Vattimo and Michael Marder (New York: Bloomsbury, 2013), xiii.

75  See Pappé, "Zionism as Colonialism: A Comparative View of Diluted Colonialism in Asia and Africa," *South Atlantic Quarterly* 107, 4 (2008): 611–33; Adam Rovner, *In the Shadow of Zion: Promised Lands before Israel* (New York: New York University Press, 2014).

76  Vattimo and Michael Marder, "Introduction: 'If Not Now, When?'" xii.

77  Goldberg, *The Threat of Race*, 139, emphasis in original.

78  As Pappé observes, Zionist discourse demonizes Palestinians from birth: "When an Israeli soldier sees a Palestinian baby he does not see an

infant—he sees the enemy" (Pappé, "The Old and New Conservations," in Noam Chomsky and Ilan Pappé, *On Palestine*, ed. Frank Barat [Chicago: Haymarket Books, 2015], 31).

79   Deleuze and Sanbar, "The Indians of Palestine," 28.

80   See Jacqueline Rose, *The Question of Zion* (Princeton: Princeton University Press, 2005).

81   For Badiou, such disproportionality characterizes the barbarism of the West: "The proportion of Western deaths in explicitly declared wars, such as Iraq or Palestine, is around one in twenty. The West have gone so far as to claim that the aim is zero deaths on their side and all deaths on the other side, which is a very particular mode of warfare. They haven't quite got there yet. But nearly, if we count the deaths in the Iraq, Afghan, Palestinian and other conflicts, which average one death on one side against twenty on the other. And people notice this fantastic disproportionality: those who live in this type of situation see very well that this is how it works, and for them, the greatest barbarian is the West" (Alain Badiou, *Our Wound is Not So Recent*, trans. Robin Mackay [Cambridge: Polity, 2016], 61). Whose life matters more was obscenely made apparent in the exchange release of IDF tank gunner Gilad Shalit, negotiated between Hamas and Israel through back channels (namely, Egypt). On October 18, 2011, Shalit, who was captured by Hamas in 2006, was released in exchange for 1027 Palestinian prisoners held in Israel. This forced choice makes Palestinians complicit in their own dehumanization, naturalizing further an unmistakable hierarchization of racialized lives. See Barak Ravid, Avi Issacharoff and Jack Khoury, "Israel, Hamas Reach Gilad Shalit Prisoner Exchange Deal, Officials Say," *Haaretz* (October 11, 2011). Available at http://www.haaretz.com/israel-news/israel-hamas-reach-gilad-shalit-prisoner-exchange-deal-officials-say-1.389404. Accessed October 8, 2018.

82   Peretz Kidron, *Refusenik!: Israel's Soldiers of Conscience* (New York: Zed Books, 2004), 76.

83   Žižek, *Welcome to the Desert of the Real*, 116, emphasis in original. Similarly, Žižek observes: "In the electoral campaign, President Bush named as the most important person in his life Jesus Christ. Now he has a unique chance to prove that he meant it seriously: for him, as for all Americans today, 'Love thy neighbor!' means 'Love the Muslims!' OR IT MEANS NOTHING AT ALL." (Žižek, "Welcome to the Desert of the Real," *Lacanian Ink* 2 (2002). Available at http://www.lacan.com/desertsymf.htm . Accessed May 13, 2018.

84   Žižek, *Welcome to the Desert of the Real*, 116.

85   Ibid.

86   Dominick LaCapra, *History and Its Limits: Human, Animal, Violence* (Ithaca: Cornell University Press, 2009), 43.

87   While Žižek's reliance on a Judeo-Christian framework can indeed arguably be read as unnecessarily exclusionary—it would also be accurate to say "Abrahamic" here in recognition of Islam's place within this tradition—his focus is on the tensions or contradictions internal to a discourse aligning Jewish tradition with the Christian West, tensions that serve as openings for rereading and redeploying revolutionary potentials.

88   Žižek, "Neighbors and Other Monsters," 161.

89   Weheliye, *Habeas Viscus*, 3.

90   Mbembe, "Necropolitics," 27.

91   Žižek, "Anti-Semitism and Its Transformations," in *Deconstructing Zionism: A Critique of Political Metaphysics*, ed. Gianni Vattimo and Michael Marder (New York: Bloomsbury, 2013), 6.

92   Žižek, "A Leftist Plea for 'Eurocentrism,' " 988.

93   Žižek, "Anti-Semitism and Its Transformations," 6.

94   This is how Richard Landes and Benjamin Weinthal labeled Judith Butler after her publication of *Parting Ways* (Richard Landes and Benjamin Weinthal, "The Post-Self-Destructivism of Judith Butler," *Wall Street Journal* (September 9, 2012).

95   Žižek, "Anti-Semitism and Its Transformations," 6.

96   Ibid.

97   Bruno Chaouat, *Is Theory Good for the Jews? French Thought and the Challenge of the New Antisemitism* (Liverpool: Liverpool University Press, 2016), 66, 8–9.

98   See Neve Gordon, "The 'New Anti-Semitism,' " *London Review of Books* 40, 1 (January 4, 2018). Available at https://www.lrb.co.uk/v40/n01/neve-gordon/the-new-anti-semitism. Accessed October 1, 2018.

99   Along with Chaouat, Alain Finkielkraut, Bernard-Henri Lévy, and Pierre-André Taguieff have argued for the emergence of a "new anti-Semitism" emerging from the political Left which no longer expresses its hatred of Jews in biological terms but "speaks the idiom of anti-racism" (Alain Finkielkraut, "Interview: Simon Schama and Alain Finkielkraut Discuss a Perceived Resurgence of Anti-Semitism in the US and Europe," *NPR. All Things Considered* [May 13, 2004]). Available at http://www.npr.org/programs/atc/transcripts/2003/may/030513.finkielkraut.html. Accessed August 4, 2018. See also Bernard-Henri Lévy, *Left in Dark Times: A Stand Against the New Barbarism* (New York: Random House, 2008); Pierre-André Taguieff, *Rising from the Muck: The New Anti-Semitism in Europe*, trans. Patrick Camiller (Chicago: Ivan R. Dee, 2004). For a decisive critique of this new label, see Alain Badiou, Eric Hazan, and Ivan Segré, *Reflections on Anti-Semitism*, trans. David Fernbach (New York: Verso, 2013).

100  Judith Butler, "Foreword," in *On Anti-Semitism: Solidarity and the Struggle for Justice* (Chicago: Haymarket Books, 2017), x.

101  Žižek, *The Parallax View*, 30. In the earlier *The Puppet and the Dwarf*, Žižek makes a similar observation: "I am tempted to suggest a return to the earlier Derrida of *différance*: what if . . . Derrida's turn to 'postsecular' messianism is not a necessary outcome of his initial 'deconstructionist' impetus? What if the idea of infinite messianic Justice which operates in an indefinite suspension, always to come, as the undeconstructible horizon of deconstruction, already obfuscates 'pure' *différance*, the pure gap which separates an entity from itself" (Žižek, *The Puppet and the Dwarf: The Perverse Core of Christianity* [Cambridge: MIT Press, 2003], 141).

102  Žižek, *The Parallax View*, 30.

103  Derrida, *Of Hospitality*, 77, emphasis in original.

104  Jacques Derrida, "Violence and Metaphysics," *Writing and Difference*, trans. Alan Bass (Chicago: University of Chicago Press, 1978), 151.

105  Derrida, "Violence and Metaphysics," 84.

106  Derrida, *Aporias*, 22.

107  Derrida, *Rogues: Two Essays on Reason*, trans. Pascale-Anne Brault and Michael Naas (Stanford: Stanford University Press, 2005), 60, emphasis in original.

108  Žižek, *Welcome to the Desert of the Real*, 11.

109  Žižek, *Against the Double Blackmail*, 101.

110  Ibid., 46.

111  Ibid., 46–7.

112  Žižek, "The Need to Traverse the Fantasy," *In These Times* (December 28, 2015). Available at http://inthesetimes.com/article/18722/Slavoj-Zizek-on-Syria-refugees-Eurocentrism-Western-Values-Lacan-Islam. Accessed August 8, 2018.

113  John Caputo and Gianni Vattimo, *After the Death of God*, ed. Jeffrey W. Robbins (New York: Columbia University Press, 2007), 124–5. Qtd. in Žižek's *First as Tragedy, Then as Farce* (New York: Verso, 2009), 77–8.

114  Žižek, *First as Tragedy*, 77–78.

115  Žižek, "Nobody Has to Be Vile."

116  Karl Marx, "Letters from the *Deutsch-Französische Jahrbucher*," in *Collected Works of Marx and Engels*, Vol. 3 (New York: International Publishers, 1975), 142.

117  "It is easy to make fun of Fukuyama's notion of the End of History, but the dominant ethos today is 'Fukuyamaian': liberal-democratic capitalism is accepted as the finally found formula of the best possible society, all

that one can do is render it more just, tolerant, and so forth" (Žižek, *In Defense of Lost Causes*, 421).

118 Kelly Oliver, *Carceral Humanitarianism: Logics of Refugee Detention* (Minneapolis: University of Minnesota Press, 2017), 15.

119 Žižek, *Against the Double Blackmail*, 7–8.

120 "The 'impossible' (an openness to immigrants) has to happen in reality— this would be a true political event" (Žižek, *First as Tragedy*, 120).

121 Žižek, *Against the Double Blackmail*, 62–3.

122 Žižek, "Migrants, Racists and the Left."

123 There are documented instances of racist behavior from the Yellow Vests. One egregious example is when some Yellow Vests threw six immigrants (asylum-seekers) into their truck, shouting, "Throw them on a giant barbecue" and "They cost us too much in taxes," before handing them over to a police patrol. (Nabila Ramdani, "It's Not Surprising That Fuel Protests in Paris Turned Violent—The French Establishment Has Long Ignored Social Inequality," *Independent* [November 25, 2018]). Available at https://www.independent.co.uk/voices/paris-protests-fuel-tax-france-police-emmanuel-macron-yellow-vests-immigrants-a8650901.html. Accessed December 21, 2018. The Yellow Vests make contrary demands with respect to immigrants. A document they issued demands, on the one hand, that "immigrants better 'integrate' into French society," that is, that they conform to French majority norms, while also demanding "that the government improve its treatment of asylum seekers" (Cole Stangler, "What's Really Behind France's Yellow Vest Protest? It's Not Just About the Fuel Tax; It's about Anger at Ever-Increasing Burdens on the Working Class," *The Nation* [December 7, 2018]). Available at https://www.thenation.com/article/france-yellow-vest-protest-macron/. Accessed December 21, 2018.

124 Žižek, "The Yellow Vest Protesters."

125 Ibid.

126 Ibid.

127 Ibid.

128 Žižek, *Against the Double Blackmail*, 9.

129 Ibid., 100, 110.

130 Žižek, Santner, and Reinhard, "Preface, 2013," ix.

131 I explore the interpretive and ethico-political potential of autoimmunity in *Theory's Autoimmunity: Skepticism, Literature, and Philosophy* (Evanston: Northwestern University Press, 2018).

132 Derrida, "Autoimmunity," 94.

133 Derrida, "Faith and Knowledge," in *Acts of Religion*, ed. Gil Anidjar (New York: Routledge, 2002), 87.

134 Roberto Esposito, *Terms of the Political: Community, Immunity, Biopolitics* (New York: Fordham University Press, 2013), 59.

135 Kapoor, *Celebrity Humanitarianism*, 4.

136 Žižek, *Against the Double Blackmail*, 10.

137 Derrida, *Rogues*, 34.

138 Ibid., 123.

139 Žižek, "Neighbors and Other Monsters," 144.

140 Žižek, *Against the Double Blackmail*, 82.

141 Žižek, *Disparities*, 181.

142 Žižek, *Against the Double Blackmail*, 82.

143 Žižek, *Disparities*, 181. Failing to confront the logic of our own *jouissance*, we turn to the other's *jouissance* as a means to resolve our impasse: "the [Western] subject projects the core of its *jouissance* onto an Other, attributing to this Other full access to a consistent *jouissance*. Such a constellation cannot but give rise to jealousy: in jealousy, the subject *creates/imagines a paradise* (a utopia of full *jouissance*) *from which he is excluded*" (Žižek, *Disparities*, 181).

144 "The true clash is the clash within each civilization" (Žižek, *Welcome to the Desert of the Real*, 44).

145 Žižek, *Against the Double Blackmail*, 79. On the strangeness of foreigners, Žižek refers to Hegel's insight that "the secrets of the ancient Egyptians were secret also for the Egyptians themselves" (Žižek, *Against the Double Blackmail*, 79).

146 Similarly, Žižek objects to the liberal left's immediate condemnation of any critique of the non-Western world even when that critique comes from within. Discussing Udi Aloni's film *Junction 48*, which addresses the difficulties of growing up as "Israeli Palestinians" caught up in "a continuous struggle on two fronts: against both Israeli state oppression and the fundamentalist pressures from within their own community" (Žižek, *The Courage of Hopelessness*, 197)—Žižek highlights the comments of the film's main actor Tamer Nafar, a famous Israeli-Palestinian rapper, whose music ridicules the tradition of the "honor killing" of Palestinian girls by their Palestinian families. The comments took place at Columbia University after Nafar performed his song protesting the practice. The reaction of some anti-Zionist students was critical, reproaching him for playing into the Zionist narrative of Palestinians as "barbaric primitives" (Žižek, *The Courage of Hopelessness*, 198). Moreover, they explained away the problem of "honor killing" by blaming Israel for creating the conditions for Palestinian primitivity. Nafar's response redirects our attention: "When you criticize me you criticize my own community in English to impress your radical professors. I sing in Arabic to protect the women in my own 'hood' "

(Žižek, *The Courage of Hopelessness*, 198). Žižek praises Nafar's position for its refusal to play the liberal game of political correctness, which consists of policing what people says at the cost of perpetuating rather than changing the existing oppressive conditions. It also reveals the extent to which the Palestinian way of life is divided within itself: what should matter for the Left is not a bland respect for Palestinian culture but an attentiveness to that culture's inner struggles—wherein lies the hope of a "solidarity of struggles" (Žižek, "The Need to Traverse the Fantasy"). A more nuanced objection to the critique of "honor killing" is the way it has been used to promote "homonationalism," or the portrayal of the Arab and Muslim world as backward and intolerant, morally, culturally, and politically inferior in order to legitimize, in turn, targets of military domination by the West. Israel's Prime Minister Benjamin Netanyahu is fond of evoking Israel's progressive sexual policies when trying to deflect criticism from his government's treatment of Palestinians (a phenomenon known as "pinkwashing"). See Jasbir Puar, *Terrorist Assemblages: Homonationalism in Queer Times* (Durham: Duke University Press, 2007). Žižek recognizes at some level the validity of that objection, pointing out how Western feminism was used ideologically to justify the War on Terror and the invasion of Iraq (Žižek, *Against the Double Blackmail*, 7; see also Žižek, *Welcome to the Desert of the Real*, 67). Still, Žižek insists that the Left must be able to condemn the ideological manipulation of human rights discourse, without giving up on its radical-emancipatory tradition, a tradition invested not in a "dialogue of cultures" but a "solidarity of struggles."

147   Kapoor, *Celebrity Humanitarianism*, 3.

148   Žižek, *Against the Double Blackmail*, 110.

149   Edward Said, *Representations of the Intellectual* (New York: Vintage, 1996), 32.

# 3 Postcolonialism: From the Culturalization of Politics to the Politicization of Culture

1   Peter Hallward, *Absolutely Postcolonial: Writing between the Singular and the Specific* (New York: Palgrave, 2001), 64, emphasis in original.

2   Žižek, "Afterword: Lenin's Choice," in V. I. Lenin, *Revolution at the Gates: Selected Writings of Lenin from 1917*, ed. Slavoj Žižek (New York: Verso, 2002), 271.

3   Žižek, "Class Struggle or Postmodernism?" 127.

4   Žižek, *The Year of Dreaming Dangerously*, 78.

5   Jameson, "First Impressions."

6   See Žižek, *Violence*, 140–4.

7   "By 'economism' I do not mean . . . to neglect the powerful role which the economic foundations of a social order or the dominant economic relations of a society play in shaping and structuring the whole edifice of social life. I mean, rather, a specific theoretical approach which tends to read the economic foundations of society as the only determining structure. This approach tends to see all other dimensions of the social formation as simply mirroring 'the economic' on another level of articulation, and as having no other determining or structuring force in their own right. The approach, to put it simply, reduces everything in a social formation to the economic level, and conceptualizes all other types of social relations as directly and immediately 'corresponding' to the economic" (Stuart Hall, "Gramsci's Relevance for the Study of Race and Ethnicity," *Journal of Communication Inquiry* 10, 5 [1986]: 10).

8   Bill Ashcroft, "Future Thinking: Postcolonial Utopianism," in *The Future of Postcolonial Studies*, ed. Chantal Zabus (New York: Routledge, 2015), 235.

9   Likewise, Chris Bongie expresses serious doubt about the viability of a cultural politics, pointing out its "disastrous confusion of spheres," which, in turn, results in mistaking cultural performances for "an incisive political action" (Chris Bongie, *Friends and Enemies: The Scribal Politics of Post/ Colonial Literature* [Liverpool: Liverpool University Press, 2008], 351). For a lucid account of the fault lines in the debate over postcolonial critique, see Nicole Simek, "The Criticism of Postcolonial Critique," in *Criticism after Critique: Aesthetics, Literature, and the Political*, ed. Jeffrey R. Di Leo (New York: Palgrave, 2014), 113–26.

10  Žižek, "Entretien avec Slavoj Zizek–Le nouveau philosophe," *Nouvel Observateur* (November 11, 2004). Available at http://www.lacan.com/ nouvob.htm. Accessed August 8, 2018.

11  Žižek, *The Universal Exception*, 239. Ian Almond questions Žižek's evacuation of the sociopolitical register in his ontologizing of the monster within and without: "In situations where the Other is already demonized—such as the Muslim or the Mexican/Latino—a call to recognize the monstrous Other not only appears redundant but, more importantly, ironically overlooks imbalances of power or income in order to make a psychoanalytical/ontological point about the 'Monster in Ourselves'" (Ian Almond, "Anti-Capitalist Objections to the Postcolonial: Some Conciliatory Remarks on Žižek and Context," *Ariel* 43, 1 [2012]: 10). As we saw in Chapter 2, though there is always a danger of repeating their dehumanization by referring to them as "monsters" (i.e., ironically playing into the hands of political Zionists and anti-immigrant populists), Žižek never simply ontologizes or fully removes the "real" Palestinians and the refugees from the economic and political field of ideological struggle. They are historically situated as global capitalism's

desubjectivized others, its symptoms, making them today's candidates for the "part of no-part."

12  As Ilan Kapoor insightfully observes, "Mignolo . . . seems to equate non-European particularity with a certain authenticity, as though a distinct or pristine non-European identity can be retrieved in the wake of colonialism and the globalization of capital" (Ilan Kapoor, "Žižek, Antagonism and Politics Now: Three Recent Controversies," *International Journal of Žižek Studies* 12, 1 [2018]: 6). I am reminded here of Gayatri Chakravorty Spivak's perspicacious observation about the festishizing impulse of the Western self toward the non-Western other: "the person who *knows* has all of the problems of selfhood. The person who is *known*, somehow seems not to have a problematic self. These days . . . only the dominant self can be problematic; the self of the Other is authentic without problem . . . This is frightening" (Gayatri Chakravorty Spivak, *The Post-Colonial Critic: Interviews, Strategies, Dialogues*, ed. Sarah Harasym [New York: Routledge, 1990], 66). Authenticity (of the non-Western other) comes at a hermeneutic cost: a flattening of depth and complexity. If Mignolo expresses his distance from the idealization of the Western self, he nevertheless duplicates some of the latter fantasies when it comes to the non-Western other.

13  See Walter D. Mignolo, *The Darker Side of Western Modernity: Global Futures, Decolonial Options* (Durham: Duke University Press, 2011).

14  José Medina, "Varieties of Hermeneutical Injustice," in *The Routledge Handbook of Epistemic Injustice*, ed. Ian James Kidd, José Medina and Gaile Pohlhaus (New York: Routledge, 2017), 49.

15  Žižek, *Trouble in Paradise*, 183.

16  Žižek often draws on the example of the Dalits or "untouchables," members of the lowest caste in India, in order to complicate the colonized's attitude toward colonialism. For the Dalits, the antagonism was not only between Indians and the British, but within their culture as well. They did not conceive "true victory over colonization" as a "the return to any 'authentic' pre-colonial existence, even less any 'synthesis' between modern civilization and pre-modern origins." Quite the contrary, the Dalits sought "the *fully accomplished loss of these pre-modern origins*." What British colonialism and its dissemination of the English language paradoxically opened up was a way to denaturalize their positionality in society and to break free from their culturally ontologized inferiority: "a large proportion of Dalits welcomed English and in fact even the colonial encounter as a whole. For Ambedkar (the foremost political figure of the Dalit caste) and his legatees, British colonialism—unwittingly and incidentally—gives scope for the so-called rule of law and formal equality for all Indians" (Žižek, *The Trouble in Paradise*, 192).

17  Jameson, "Third-World Literature in the Era of Multinational Capitalism," *Social Text* 15 (1986): 69.

18  R. Radhakrishnan, "Poststructuralist Politics: Towards a Theory of Coalition," in *Postmodernism/Jameson/Critique* (Washington: Maisonneuve Press, 1989), 329. Edward Said makes a similar argument against Marxist theorists more generally denouncing their "blithe universalism" (Edward Said, *Culture and Imperialism* [New York: Vintage, 1994], 277), pointing to their bad record when it came to questions of race and representation.

19  This depiction of Jameson's work is quite widespread, reaching almost a state of consensus. This critique of Jameson's approach to postcolonial or Third-World affairs has not however gone uncontested. Ian Buchanan and Imre Szeman mount a compelling defense of Jameson's reading of "national allegory," pointing out the ways the essay has been systematically misread. What is meant by "national allegory" is from the start distorted. Buchanan argues that Jameson's critics dubiously conflate "national allegory" with "nationalist allegory." Jameson never argues that nationalism is the dominant ethos of Third-World literary writers, only that they are "obsessively concerned with the 'national situation'— nationalism would be but one part of this vastly more complex problem" (Ian Buchanan, "National Allegory Today: A Return to Jameson," in *On Jameson: From Postmodernism to Globalism*, ed. Caren Irr and Ian Buchanan [New York: State University of New York Press, 2006], 174). Literature is an avenue for Third-World writers because, unlike their First World counterparts, literature for them continues to embody a political dimension. Whereas, in the First World, literary production is about "the private rather than the public sphere . . . individual tastes and solitary meditations rather than public debate and deliberation," in the Third World, such an opposition simply does not exist (Imre Szeman, "Who's Afraid of National Allegory? Jameson, Literary Criticism, Globalization," in *On Jameson: From Postmodernism to Globalism*, ed. Caren Irr and Ian Buchanan [New York: State University of New York Press, 2006], 192). "National allegory" is really then "political allegory" (Szeman, "Who's Afraid of National Allegory?" 200).

20  Jameson, "Third-World Literature," 68.

21  For a nuanced reading of the place of the postcolonial in Žižek's political thought, see Jamil Khader, "Concrete Universality and the End of Revolutionary Politics: A Žižekian Approach to Postcolonial Women's Writings," in *Everything You Always Wanted to Know about Literature but Were Afraid to Ask Žižek*, ed. Russell Sbriglia (Durham: Duke University Press, 2017), 137–68.

22  Angela Y. Davis, *Freedom Is a Constant Struggle: Ferguson, Palestine, and the Foundations of a Movement* (Chicago: Haymarket Books, 2016), 87.

23  Žižek, *The Parallax View*, 35.

24  Qtd. in Fanon, *Black Skin, White Masks*, 112.

25  James Penney, "Passing into the Universal: Fanon, Sartre, and the Colonial Dialectic," *Paragraph* 27, 3 (2004): 54.

26   Jean-Paul Sartre, "Black Orpheus," in *What Is Literature? And Other Essays*, trans. John McCombie (Cambridge: Harvard University Press, 1988), 296.

27   Fanon, *Black Skin, White Masks*, 163.

28   Ibid., 114.

29   Ibid., 118.

30   Ibid., 113.

31   Ibid., 111.

32   Ibid., 116. As James Penney puts it, "Fanon held firmly to the view that racially based identity claims on the part of non-European subjects in colonized situations carried an irreducible, cathartic importance" (Penney, "Passing into the Universal," 56).

33   Žižek, "A Leftist Plea for 'Eurocentrism,'" 988.

34   Mignolo, "Yes, We Can: Non-European Thinkers and Philosophers" (February 19, 2013). Available at http://www.aljazeera.com/indepth/opin ion/2013/02/20132672747320891.html. Accessed 26 March 2018.

35   Mignolo approvingly cites Sartre's prologue to Fanon's *The Wretched of the Earth* (originally published in 1961), when he observes that Fanon's audience, importantly, has shifted: "listen, pay attention, Fanon is no longer talking to us" (Mignolo, "Yes, We Can"; Jean-Paul Sartre, "Preface," in *The Wretched of the Earth*, trans. Richard Philcox [New York: Grove Press, 2004], lvii). To see Sartre's observation as definitive, to accept that Fanon's addressee is now exclusively non-European, simplifies to the point of distortion. Mignolo ignores Fanon's continued engagement with Sartre, and how the former discussed the latter's *Critique de la raison dialectique*, which came out in 1960, with the Armée de Libération Nationale, the military wing of the National Liberation Front. The anti-colonial struggle, as Fanon conceived it, did not jettison European thought but sought to harness its critical force. While we don't know what Fanon talked about with the ALN fighters, Robert Bernasconi speculates with good reason that Fanon introduced them to Sartre's work because "it was not enough . . . that these fighters were committed to their particular struggle. He wanted them in addition to think about the struggle in more global terms" (Robert Bernasconi, "Fanon's *the Wretched of the Earth* as the Fulfillment of Sartre's *Critique of Dialectical Reason*," *Sartre Studies International* 16, 2 [2010]: 36). The least we can say is that Sartre and Mignolo overstate Fanon's new audience, especially given the fact that Fanon ends *The Wretched of the Earth* with an inclusive gesture, soliciting solidarity rather than sectarianism: "For Europe, for ourselves, and for humanity, comrades, we must turn over a new leaf, we must work out new concepts, and try to set afoot a new man" (Fanon, *The Wretched of the Earth*, trans. Richard Philcox [New York: Grove Press, 2004], 239).

36   Žižek, *Trouble in Paradise*, 184.

37   Hamid Dabashi, *Can Non-Europeans Think?* (London: Zed Books, 2015), 7.

38   Dabashi, *Can Non-Europeans Think?* 8. Unfortunately, Dabashi also
     undermines his case against the West as the sole measure of truth, by
     misattributing to Žižek a quotation that is actually from Fanon: "I am
     a man and what I have to recapture is the whole past of the world, I am
     not responsible only for the slavery involved in Santo Domingo, every
     time man has contributed to the victory of the dignity of the spirit, every
     time a man has said no to an attempt to subjugate his fellows, I have
     felt solidarity with his act. In no way does my basic vocation have to be
     drawn from the past of peoples of color. In no way do I have to dedicate
     myself to reviving some black civilization unjustly ignored. I will not
     make myself the man of any past. My black skin is not a repository
     for specific values. Haven't I got better things to do on this earth than
     avenge the blacks of the 17th century?" While Dabashi misreads this as
     a symptom of Žižek's assimilative Western logic, what Fanon resists here
     is another form of reductionism: namely, his interpellation as a *black*
     intellectual, one who could only be responsible for and responsive to
     black matters. Fanon insists that his fellows include not only blacks but
     others as well.

39   For Mignolo, "identity in politics" is preferable to "identity politics" since,
     unlike the latter, the former is always already denaturalized, lacking any
     intrinsic properties or force. Identity in politics acknowledges that one's
     identity has been constructed and allocated by European colonial powers.
     See Mignolo, "The Decolonial Option and the Meaning of Identity in
     Politics," *Anales Nueva Época* 9, 10 (2007): 43–72. Even so, the investment
     in any form of identity carries with it the risk of fetishization, opening the
     partisan up to the lure of authenticity.

40   Žižek, "A Leftist Plea for 'Eurocentrism,'" 1002.

41   Fanon, *Black Skin, White Masks*, 205–6.

42   See Fanon, *A Dying Colonialism*, trans. Haakon Chevalier (New York:
     Grove Press, 1965). "It is inadequate only to affirm that a people was
     dispossessed, oppressed or slaughtered, denied its rights and its political
     existence, without at the same time doing what Fanon did during the
     Algerian war, affiliating those horrors with the similar afflictions of other
     people. This does not at all mean a loss in historical specificity, but rather
     it guards against the possibility that a lesson learnt about oppression in
     one place will be forgotten or violated in another place or time" (Said,
     *Representations of the Intellectual*, 44).

43   Mignolo, "Decolonizing the Nation-State: Zionism in the Colonial
     Horizon of Modernity," in *Deconstructing Zionism: A Critique of Political
     Metaphysics*, ed. Gianni Vattimo and Michael Marder (New York:
     Bloomsbury, 2013), 57.

44   Mignolo, "Decolonizing the Nation-State," 60.

45   Ibid., 63.

46  Aluf Benn, "The Jewish Majority in Israel Still See Their Country as 'a Villa in the Jungle,'" *The Guardian* (August 20, 2013). Available at https://www.theguardian.com/commentisfree/2013/aug/20/jewish-majority-israel-villa-in-the-jungle. Accessed January 19, 2019. Žižek alludes to a 2016 scandelous episode involving Rabbi Colonel Eyal Karim, the nominee for the role of chief military rabbi, who came under fire over his previous remarks on rape (though his appointment was ultimately confirmed), claiming that the Torah gave the right to Jewish soldiers, during wartime, "to satisfy the evil urge . . . for the purpose of the success of the whole" (qtd. in Peter Beaumont, "Women's Groups Denounce Israeli Military over Nominee for Chief Rabbi," *Guardian* [July 12, 2016]). Available at https://www.theguardian.com/world/2016/jul/12/womens-groups-and-mps-denounce-appointment-of-idfs-chief-rabbi. Accessed December 5, 2018. Extrapolating from the rabbi's comments, the IDF are apparently permitted on this view to rape local Palestinian women in the Occupied Territories. Žižek uses this example not to highlight to need to modernize religious beliefs and make them conform to contemporary norms but to undermine the neat opposition between the civilized and the barbarians that Israel and its Western allies are fond of promoting: "The lesson of this scandal is not just that religious authorities should apply today's moral standards in their effort to make traditional religious sources relevant—we all know that ancient sacred texts are monuments to barbarian brutality. A much more important lesson concerns the unexpected (perhaps) proximity of 'civilized' Israeli hardliners and 'barbarian' Muslim fundamentalists" (Žižek, *The Courage of Hopelessness*, 154).

47  Mignolo, "Decolonizing the Nation-State," 61.

48  Ibid., 60.

49  Ibid., 65.

50  Ibid., 72.

51  Ibid., 71.

52  "The One State Declaration" (November 29, 2007). Available at https://electronicintifada.net/content/one-state-declaration/793.

53  Edward W. Said, "My Right of Return," in *Power, Politics, and Culture: Interviews with Edward W. Said*, ed. Gauri Viswanathan (New York: Vintage, 2001), 458.

54  A difference deployed for the sole purpose of the "rigidly enforced and policed separation of populations into different groups" (Said, "An Ideology of Difference," *Critical Inquiry* 12, 1 [1985]: 40).

55  Žižek, "Anti-Semitism and Its Transformations," in *Deconstructing Zionism: A Critique of Political Metaphysics*, ed. Gianni Vattimo and Michael Marder (New York: Bloomsbury, 2013), 6.

56  Žižek, *The Puppet and the Dwarf*, 109.

57  Žižek, "A Leftist Plea for 'Eurocentrism,'" 988.

58  Žižek, *The Metastases of Enjoyment*, 200.

59  Žižek points to a meeting between Adolf Eichmann and Feivel Polkes, a member of Haganah (a Zionist paramilitary organization in British Mandate Palestine): "Both Germans and Zionists wanted as many Jews as possible to move to Palestine: Germans preferred them out of Western Europe, and Zionists themselves wanted the Jews in Palestine to outnumber the Arabs as fast as possible . . . .. Is this strange incident not the supreme case of how the Nazis and the radical Zionists did share a common interest? In both cases, the purpose was a kind of 'ethnic cleansing,' i.e., to violently change the ratio of ethnic groups in the population" (Žižek, "Whither Zionism?"). The 1917 Balfour Declaration, the British support for establishing "a national home for the Jewish people" in Palestine, must also be read from this perspective: the anti-Semitic dream of a Europe free of Jews and Jewish control. Anti-Semitism also taints the support of Christian Zionists whose commitment to Israel is purely instrumental, since their reason for returning the Jews to Palestine is to bring about the apocalyptic second coming of the Messiah (Pappé, *Ten Myths about Israel*, 17).

60  Žižek, "Multitude, Surplus, and Envy," *Rethinking Marxism* 19, 1 (2006): 56.

61  Jamil Khader, "The Living Dead in Palestine and the Failure of International Humanitarian Intervention," *Truthout* (November 8, 2015). Available at https://truthout.org/articles/the-living-dead-in-palestine-and-the-failure-of-international-humanitarian-intervention/. Accessed June 23, 2018.

62  As Journalist Patrick Strickland notes: "Many Israeli Facebook users have posted violent and disturbing content on their personal accounts. Talya Shilok Edry, who has more than one thousand followers, posted the following 'status': 'What an orgasm to see the Israeli Defense Forces bomb buildings in Gaza with children and families at the same time. Boom boom'" (Patrick Strickland, "Bombing of Gaza Children Gives Me 'Orgasm': Israelis Celebrate Slaughter on Facebook," *Electronic Intifada* [July 13, 2014]. Available at https://electronicintifada.net/blogs/patrick-strickland/bombing-gaza-children-gives-me-orgasm-israelis-celebrate-slaughter-facebook. Accessed May 15, 2018.

63  Ronit Lentin, *Traces of Racial Exception: Racializing Israeli Settler Colonialism* (New York: Bloomsbury, 2018), 88.

64  Judith Butler, "Versions of Binationalism in Said and Buber," in *Conflicting Humanities*, ed. Rosi Braidotti and Paul Gilroy (New York: Bloomsbury, 2016), 185.

65  Judith Butler, "Versions of Binationalism," 187.

66  Said, "My Right of Return," 451. Said always hesitated to equate Zionism with racism, arguing that Jews "not sloppily be tarnished with the

sweeping rhetorical denunciation associated with 'racism' . . .. *Racism* is too vague a term: Zionism is Zionism" (Said, *The Question of Palestine* [New York: Vintage Books, 1992], 111–12). It is arguably when Zionism adopts the divinely ordained perspective of exclusivity that it slides into racism, that it betrays or overshadows its emancipatory goals, its fully justified yearning to escape from European anti-Semitism.

67  Žižek, *The Void of Incontinence: Economico-Philosophical Spandrels* (Cambridge: MIT Press, 2017), 160.

68  Lauren Berlant, *Cruel Optimism* (Durham: Duke University Press, 2011), 102.

69  Žižek, "Anti-Semitism and Its Transformations," 9. Butler insists that it is a "wretched fact" that is "being lived out as a specific historical form of settler colonialism" (Butler, *Parting Ways*, 30).

70  Žižek, "Anti-Semitism and Its Transformations," 10. On the question of Israel's apartheid logic, see Jon Soske and Sean Jacobs, eds., *Apartheid Israel: The Politics of an Analogy* (Chicago: Haymarket Books, 2015).

71  Žižek, *Violence*, 127.

72  Ibid., 126.

73  Žižek, "What Does a Jew Want? On the Film *Local Angel*," in *What Does a Jew Want?: On Binationalism and Other Specters* (New York: Columbia University Press, 2011), 178.

74  Žižek, *Violence*, 127, 126.

75  I pursue these questions in greater detail in *Continental Philosophy and the Palestinian Question*.

76  Mahmoud Darwish, *Memory for Forgetfulness*, trans. Ibrahim Muhawi (Berkeley: University of California Press, 1995), 125-6.

77  Butler, *Parting Ways*, 53.

78  Ibid.

79  Ibid.

80  Jameson, "Third-World Literature," 65.

81  Žižek, *How to Read Lacan*, 49.

82  Žižek, *The Metastases of Enjoyment*, 159–60, emphasis in original.

83  Žižek, "Beyond Discourse Analysis," in *Interrogating the Real*, ed. Butler Rex and Scott Stephens (London: Continuum, 2005), 252.

84  Tim Dean and Christopher Lane, "Homosexuality and Psychoanalysis: An Introduction," in *Homosexuality and Psychoanalysis*, ed. Tim Dean and Christopher Lane (Chicago: University of Chicago Press, 2001), 26.

85  Jacques Lacan, *On Feminine Sexuality*, 45.

86  See for example Salim Tamari, "The Dubious Lure of Binationalism," *Journal of Palestine Studies* 30, 1 (2000): 83-7.

87  Adrian Johnston, "Nothing Is Not Always No-One: (A)voiding Love," *Filozofski Vestnik* 26, 2 (2005): 75.

88  Anna Kornbluh, "Romancing the Capital: Choice, Love, and Contradiction in *The Family Man* and *Memento*," in *Lacan and Contemporary Film*, ed. Todd McGowan and Sheila Kunkle (New York: Other Press, 2004), 128.

89  Žižek, *Looking Awry: An Introduction to Jacques Lacan through Popular Culture* (Cambridge: MIT Press, 1992), 168.

90  Said, *The World, the Text and the Critic* (Cambridge: Harvard University Press, 1983), 20.

91  Darwish, *Memory for Forgetfulness*, 126.

92  Mignolo, *Local Histories/Global Designs: Coloniality, Subaltern Knowledges, and Border Thinking* (Princeton: Princeton University Press, 2000), 23.

93  Mignolo, "I Am Where I Think: Remapping the Order of Knowing," in *The Creolization of Theory*, ed. Françoise Lionnet and Shu-mei Shi (Durham: Duke University Press, 2011), 161.

94  Mignolo, "I Am Where I Think," 174.

95  Lacan, *Anxiety: The Seminar of Jacques Lacan. Book X*, ed. Jacques-Alain Miller (Cambridge: Polity, 2014), 82.

96  Žižek, *Welcome to the Desert of the Real*, 142.

97  Žižek, "Da Capo senza Fine," in *Contingency, Hegemony, Universality: Contemporary Dialogues on the Left*, ed. Judith Butler, Ernesto Laclau, and Slavoj Žižek (New York: Verso, 2000), 258.

98  This is akin to Gayatri Chakravorty Spivak's formulation of the double bind as "a persistent critique of what we cannot not want" (Gayatri Chakravorty Spivak, *Critique of Postcolonial Reason: Toward a History of the Vanishing Present* [Cambridge: Harvard University Press, 1999], 110).

99  The cowardice of pragmatism—ramped up by the dubious saying that the Palestinians have never missed an opportunity to miss an opportunity—captures the ethos that informed the peace process. The Palestinian Authority acquiesced time and time again to the will of Israel and the international community: make compromises (give up more of your land), be a peace partner (don't behave like Hamas), renounce terrorism (don't put up any resistance to Israel's will), and so on. The peace process is currently stalled (with the US punishing the moderate Palestinian leadership by withholding vital financial aid); the next "breakthrough" (through some maneuvering to get the Palestinians back to negotiations) will most likely return to an earlier horizon of possibilities, which will do little to redress Israel's historic wrongs and current mistreatment of Palestinians. The two-state solution is itself part of the problem. More "peace process" and "two-state solution" rhetoric can only prolong the violence of the conflict, failing to touch its causes, and lead to the election of even stauncher Israeli hardliners, running on a racist platform to resolve the demographic problem and put an end to the Palestinian threat.

100  See "Thought Is the Courage of Hopelessness: An Interview with Philosopher Giorgio Agamben," Interview by Jordan Skinner. Verso Books (June 17, 2014). Available at https://www.versobooks.com/blogs/1612-thought-is-the-courage-of-hopelessness-an-interview-with-philosopher-giorgio-agamben. Accessed May 17, 2018.

101  Žižek, *Event*, 30.

102  As Žižek puts it, "the true courage is to admit that the light at the end of the tunnel is most likely the headlight of another train approaching us from the opposite direction" (Žižek, *The Courage of Hopelessness*, xi–xii).

103  Terry Eagleton, *Ideology: An Introduction* (New York: Verso, 1991), 80.

104  Žižek, *The Parallax View* (Cambridge: MIT Press, 2006), 320, emphasis in original.

105  Žižek, *The Parallax View*, 4.

106  Ibid., 17.

107  Ibid., 315.

108  Žižek, "Afterword: Lenin's Choice," 271.

109  Jameson, "First Impressions."

110  Ernesto Laclau, "Constructing Universality," in *Contingency, Hegemony, Universality*, ed. Judith Butler, Ernesto Laclau, and Slavoj Žižek (New York: Verso, 2000), 291.

111  Žižek, "The Palestinian Question: The Couple Symptom/Fetish," *Lacan. com* (2009). Available at http://www.lacan.com/essays/?page_id=261. Assessed May 13, 2018.

112  Žižek, *Tarrying with the Negative*, 210.

113  Žižek, *The Parallax View*, 255.

114  Žižek, *Disparities*, 183.

115  Žižek, "The Palestinian Question."

116  Jameson, *Representing Capital: A Reading of Volume One* (New York: Verso, 2011), 150. Qtd. Žižek, *Less Than Nothing*, 1003. Žižek repeatedly returns to four antagonisms that are unresolvable by today's capitalism: "The looming threat of ecological catastrophe; the inappropriateness of private property for so-called intellectual property; the socio-ethical implications of new techno scientific developments, especially in biogenetics; and last, but not least, new forms of social apartheid—new walls and slums" (Žižek, "How to Begin from the Beginning," *New Left Review* 57 [2009]: 53). The last antagonism produces the Included and the Excluded. Without addressing it—without directly confronting the exploitive logic of global capitalism—the three other antagonisms lose their emancipatory potential: "Ecology turns into a problem of sustainable development; intellectual property into a complex legal challenge; biogenetics into an ethical issue. One

can sincerely fight for ecology, defend a broader notion of intellectual property, oppose the copyrighting of genes, without confronting the antagonism between the Included and the Excluded" (Žižek, *Against the Double Blackmail*, 105).

117  Israel's necropolitics took the form of a spectacle on May 14, 2018, the day of the US embassy opening in Jerusalem. The world watched on split screen the jubilant celebration of mostly white bodies on one side, and the defiant brown bodies of teenagers shrouded by tear gas and subjected to live fire on the other. Israeli Brigadier General Zvika Fogel gave a remarkable justification for the practice of shooting at unarmed civilians, deeming this violence a preemptive measure justified by the future guilt of the victims: "Anyone who could be a future threat to the border of the State of Israel and its residents, should bear a price for that violation." And the price borne is unambiguous: "His punishment is death" (qtd. in Phyllis Bennis's "Palestinians Are Forcing the World to See Their Humanity: The Gaza Massacre Is a War Crime. And the United States Is Complicit Alongside Israel," *In These Times* (May 19, 2018). Available at http://inthesetimes.com/article/21148/palestinians-gaza-israel-massacre-jerusalem-embassy-donald-trump. Accessed October 1, 2018.

118  In 2006, Dov Weisglass, an adviser to the Israeli Prime minister, said: "The idea is to put the Palestinians on a diet, but not to make them die of hunger" (qtd. in Mouin Rabbani, "Israel Mows the Lawn," *London Review of Books* [July 31, 2014]. Available at https://www.lrb.co.uk/v36/n15/mouin-rabbani/israel-mows-the-lawn. Accessed December 15, 2018. As Max Blumenthal notes, Israeli military analysis demonstrates this biopolitical calculus: "A January 2008 Israeli military study called 'Food Consumption in the Gaza Strip—The Red Lines,' estimated the required daily calorie intake in Gaza at 2,279 per person 'in order to maintain the basic fabric of life' " (Max Blumenthal, *The 51 Day War: Ruin and Resistance in Gaza* [New York: Nation Books, 2015], 6).

119  MaxBlumenthal, "Waiting for the Next Israeli Assault in Gaza," *In These Times* (July 16, 2015). Available at http://inthesetimes.com/article/18208/israel-gaza-max-blumenthal. Accessed May 13, 2018.

120  Žižek, *The Parallax View*, 255. Žižek flatly rejects the argument that ontologizes the Jews' *objet petit a* status, which would entitle them the status of timeless Victims, irreproachable in the eyes of the West: "If—as Lacanian Zionists like to claim—Jews are the *objet petit a* among nations, if they represent the troubling excess of Western history, how can one resist them with impunity? Is it possible to be the *objet a* of *objet a* itself? It is precisely this ethical blackmail that we should reject" (Žižek, *The Universal Exception*, 251n25).

121  Ali Abinumah, *The Battle for Justice in Palestine* (Chicago: Haymarket Book, 2014), 78–9.

122 For Žižek, the "true enemy" of the Palestinians lies in "those Arab regimes that themselves manipulate their plight in order, precisely, to prevent that shift, i.e., a political radicalisation in their own midst" (Žižek, *The Courage of Hopelessness*, 159–60). The Arab regimes use the Palestinian cause to expose Western hypocrisy—how the West supports Israel despite its brutal domination of Palestinians—but only to the extent that nothing happens. There is no real incentive to resolve the Israel-Palestine conflict in a just fashion, where the outcome would lead to secular and egalitarian democracy (as you would with binationalism) since such a realization would be detrimental to the socioeconomic structures of these Arab regimes themselves. A neoliberal Palestine satisfies the status quo: it depoliticizes the Palestinian people while sustaining their status as abject victims, the object of control and ideological manipulation.

123 Abinumah, "Economic Exploitation of Palestinians Flourishes under Occupation," *Al Jazeera* (September 13, 2012). Available at https://www.aljazeera.com/indepth/opinion/2012/09/20129128052624254.html. Accessed May 13, 2018. See also Toufic Haddad, *Palestine Ltd.: Neoliberalism and Nationalism in the Occupied Territories* (London: I.B. Tauris, 2016).

124 Jameson, "First Impressions."

125 David Harvey, *Seventeen Contradictions and the End of Capitalism* (New York: Oxford University Press, 2014), 203. See also Pappé, "The Old and New Conservations," 45–6.

126 Unlike black workers under apartheid South Africa, Palestinian workers are not as necessary to Israel's labor force as they once were—cheap labor is increasingly imported from the Philippines, Romania and Thailand (Goldberg, *The Threat of Race*, 114). So if the Afrikaners sought to masterfully incorporate its black population inside its territory, political Zionists want to purge Palestinian labor from Israel. To take up binationalism as a universal project is to undercut Zionism's investment in the socioeconomic status quo, countering its vision of Israel's common enemy—the demonized Palestinian—with a plea for solidarity that cuts across national, cultural, and religious lines.

127 Žižek, *Less Than Nothing*, 831.

128 Žižek, *Trouble in Paradise*, 108.

# 4 Critical Race Theory: The Subject Supposed to Loot, Rape, and Terrorize

1 Claudia Rankine, *Citizen: An American Lyric* (Minneapolis: Graywolf, 2014), 15. Copyright © 2014 by Claudia Rankine. Reprinted with the

permission of The Permissions Company, LLC on behalf of Graywolf Press, www.graywolfpress.org.

2   Žižek, "Are We in a War? Do We Have an Enemy?" *London Review of Books* 24, 10 (May 23, 2002). Available at https://www.lrb.co.uk/v24/n10/slavoj-zizek/are-we-in-a-war-do-we-have-an-enemy. Accessed August 16, 2018.

3   "What do critical race theorists believe? . . . First, racism is ordinary, not aberrational—'normal science', the usual way a society does business, the common, everyday experience of most people of color in this country" (Richard Delgado and Jean Stefanic, *Critical Race Theory: An Introduction* [New York: New York University Press, 2017], 8).

4   Derrick Bell, "Racial Realism," *Connecticut Law Review* 24, 2 (1992): 373–4.

5   Bell, "Learning the Three 'I's' of America's Slave Heritage," in *Slavery and the Law*, ed. Paul Finkelman (Madison: Madison House Publishers, 1997), 38.

6   Bell, "Racial Realism," 377.

7   Ibid., 379.

8   See Glenn E. Bracey, II, "Toward a Critical Race Theory of State," *Critical Sociology* 41, 3 (2015): 553–72.

9   See Josiah Ryan, "'This Was a Whitelash': Van Jones' Take on the Election Results," *CNN* (November 9, 2016). Available at https://www.cnn.com/2016/11/09/politics/van-jones-results-disappointment-cnntv/index.html. Accessed August 16, 2018.

10  Žižek, *The Courage of Hopelessness*, 170.

11  Ibid., 169.

12  Žižek, *The Sublime Object of Ideology*, 49.

13  Žižek, *Disparities*, 375.

14  Those who charge that Zionism is a form of settler colonialism are frequently met with a problematic, but not any less effective, countercharge of anti-Semitism. For a discussion foregrounding settler colonialism as an interpretive framework for analyzing Israel, see the special issue of *Settler Colonial Studies* 2, 1 (2012), "Past is Present: Settler Colonialism in Palestine," edited by Omar Jabary Salamanca et al.; Lorenzo Veracini, *Israel and Settler Society* (London: Pluto Press, 2006); Patrick Wolfe, "Settler Colonialism and the Elimination of the Native," *Journal of Genocide Research* 8 (2006): 387–409.

15  Alain Finkielkraut, *L'identité malheureuse* (Paris: Stock, 2013), 23.

16  Tommy J. Curry, "Please Don't Make Me Touch 'Em: Towards a Critical Race Fanonianism as a Possible Justification for Violence against Whiteness," in *Democracy, Racism, and Prisons*, ed. Harry van der Linden (Charlottesville: Philosophy Documentation Center, 2007), 138.

17  Jon Hanson and Kathleen Hanson, "The Blame Frame: Justifying (Racial) Injustice in America," *Harvard Civil Right-Civil Liberties Review* 41 (2006): 457.

18  Hanson and Hanson, "The Blame Frame," 456. Shannon Winnubst similarly comments: "From the apocryphal but self-fulfilling stories of raping and pillaging at the Superdome to the iconic, blackface images of Aunt Jemima and the Coon, the long-standing reservoir of racism gave us the language we needed to explain and absolve: 'savages live in nature and so die of nature' " (Shannon Winnubst, *Way Too Cool: Selling Out Race and Ethics* [New York: Columbian University Press, 2015], 195).

19  The chaos was naturalized in yet another way: "for all of the criticisms made of the Bush Government for acting too slowly in response to the crisis, this is again to assume that the problem was only natural, that everything could be made right by the timely intervention of the State, when in fact it is the State itself that is the problem" (Rex Butler and Scott Stephens, "Play Fuckin' Loud: Žižek Versus the Left," *The Symptom* 7 [2007]). Available at http://www.lacan.com/symptom7_articles/butler.html. Accessed September 1, 2018. Here blaming the state for not doing its job is to tacitly assume the state as non-racist, which only obfuscates the causes of the catastrophe.

20  Žižek, "The Subject Supposed to Loot and Rape: Reality and Fantasy in New Orleans." *In These Times* (October 20, 2005). Available at http://inthesetimes.com/article/2361. Accessed August 28, 2018.

21  Žižek, "The Subject Supposed to Loot and Rape." Candidate Donald Trump's description of Mexican undocumented immigrants as criminals and rapists successful tapped into the fear of brown bodies, feeding a similar white hysteria about the threatening other/enemy living among us.

22  Žižek, "The Subject Supposed to Loot and Rape," emphasis in original.

23  Wendy Brown, *Edgework: Critical Essays on Knowledge and Politics* (Princeton: Princeton University Press, 2005), 42.

24  Hanson and Hanson, "The Blame Frame," 472.

25  See Charles W. Mills, *Black Rights/White Wrongs: The Critique of Racial Liberalism* (Oxford: Oxford University Press, 2017); Cedric J. Robinson, *Black Marxism: The Making of the Black Radical Tradition* (Chapel Hill: University of North Carolina Press, 2000).

26  Mills, *The Racial Contract*, 127.

27  Delgado and Stefanic, *Critical Race Theory*, 115.

28  Bell, *Faces at the Bottom of the Well: The Permanence of Racism* (New York: Basic Books, 1992), 7.

29  While such antiblack violence recalls a pre-Civil Rights Era, Cedric Robinson and Elizabeth Robinson caution against adopting "a familiar, manageable and seductive narrative" of the Civil Rights movement of the 1960s and 1970s as the antidote to today's racism. What is needed is an account of racism in the age of postraciality, attentiveness to a

racism "submerged in a 'post racial' nation where reversing the freedom movement's achievements is masqueraded in race projects like the war on drugs which disproportionally impact communities of color" (Cedric Robinson and Elizabeth Robinson, "Ferguson, Gaza, Iraq: An Outline on the Official Narrative in 'Post-Racial' America," *Commonware* [September 4, 2013]). Available at https://www.commonware.org/index.php/cartografia/452-ferguson-gaza-iraq-outline. Accessed October 15, 2018.

30  Žižek, *Demanding the Impossible*, 58, emphasis in original.

31  Ibid.

32  Henry Giroux, "The Militarization of Racism and Neoliberal Violence," *Truthout* (August 18, 2014). Available at https://truthout.org/articles/the-militarization-of-racism-and-neoliberal-violence/. Accessed August 28, 2018. See also Giroux, *Stormy Weather: Katrina and the Politics of Disposability* (Boulder: Paradigm, 2006).

33  Giroux, "The Militarization of Racism and Neoliberal Violence."

34  Žižek, "Divine Violence in Ferguson," *The European* (March 9, 2015). Available at https://www.theeuropean-magazine.com/slavoj-zizek/9774-slavoj-zizek-on-ferguson-and-violence. Accessed August 26, 2018.

35  Žižek, *Against the Double Blackmail*, 35.

36  Žižek, *Demanding the Impossible*, 72.

37  Ellen Wulfhorst, Daniel Wallis, Edward McAllister, "More Than 400 Arrested as Ferguson Protests Spread to Other U.S. Cities," *Reuters* (November 25, 2014). Available at https://www.reuters.com/article/us-usa-missouri-shooting/more-than-400-arrested-as-ferguson-protests-spread-to-other-u-s-cities-idUSKCN0J80PR20141126. Accessed August 26, 2018.

38  Žižek, "Divine Violence in Ferguson."

39  Žižek, "Divine Violence in Ferguson." See also Žižek, *Less Than Nothing*, 452.

40  Žižek, *Against the Double Blackmail*, 36.

41  The untying harnessed by the Tea Party is at odds with the traditional wing of the Republican Party who tends to be far more invested in order.

42  Žižek, "Divine Violence in Ferguson."

43  Žižek, *Violence*, 185.

44  Ibid., 201, emphasis in original.

45  Žižek, "Divine Violence and Liberated Territories: SOFT TARGETS Talks with Slavoj Žižek," *Soft Targets* (March 14, 2007). Available at http://www.softtargetsjournal.com/web/zizek.php. Accessed August 26, 2018.

46  Žižek, "Robespierre, or, the 'Divine Violence' of Terror," in Maximilien Robespierre, *Virtue and Terror*, ed. Jean Ducange, trans. John Howe (New York: Verso, 2007), x–xi, emphasis in original.

47  Žižek, *Against the Double Blackmail*, 40.

48  Žižek, *Violence*, 199.

49 "*Argue*, as much as you want and about what you want, *but obey!*" (Immanuel Kant, "What Is Enlightenment?" 59). See Žižek, *Enjoy Your Symptom!*, ix–x.

50 Žižek, *Against the Double Blackmail*, 41.

51 Žižek, *Violence*, 202.

52 Ibid.

53 Žižek, "Shoplifters of the World Unite," *London Review of Books* (August 19, 2011). Available at https://www.lrb.co.uk/2011/08/19/slavoj-zizek/shoplifters-of-the-world-unite. Accessed August 26, 2018.

54 Žižek, *Demanding the Impossible*, 7–8, emphasis in original.

55 Ibid., 7, emphasis in original.

56 Žižek, "Shoplifters of the World Unite."

57 Qtd. in Žižek, *Violence*, 77.

58 Žižek, *Violence*, 3–4.

59 Paul A. Taylor, *Žižek and the Media* (Cambridge: Polity, 2010), 179, emphasis in original.

60 Žižek, *Violence*, 76

61 Ibid., 75.

62 Butler and Stephens, "Play Fuckin' Loud."

63 Žižek, "Shoplifters of the World Unite."

64 Ibid.

65 Žižek, *Violence*, 76.

66 Žižek, "Robespierre, or, the 'Divine Violence' of Terror," xxvi. To act/riot with a guarantee of success is to riot, for instance, only when the polls say that the majority of the French people support your cause.

67 Žižek, "Shoplifters of the World Unite."

68 Žižek, *Violence*, 212–13, emphasis in original.

69 Butler and Stephens, "Play Fuckin' Loud."

70 Žižek, *Violence,* 75, 76.

71 Beauvoir, *The Second Sex*, 16, emphasis added.

72 Žižek says something similar about the Yellow Vest protesters: "One should be clear here: in all the explosion of demands and expression of dissatisfaction, it is clear the protesters don't really know what they want, they don't have a vision of a society they want, just a mixture of demands that are impossible to meet within the system although they address them at the system. This feature is crucial: their demands express their interests rooted in the existing system" (Žižek, "The Yellow Vest Protesters").

73 Žižek, *Against the Double Blackmail*, 37.

74 Žižek, *Violence*, 78.

75 Ibid.

76  Fanon, *The Wretched of the Earth*, 169.

77  Ibid.

78  Qtd. Žižek, *First as Tragedy*, 120.

79  Žižek, "The Audacity of Rhetoric," *In These Times* (September 2, 2008). Available at http://inthesetimes.com/article/3862/the_audacity_of_rhetoric/. Accessed September 1, 2018.

80  Žižek, *Welcome to the Desert of the Real*, 2.

81  Stokely Carmichael and Stanley Hamilton distinguish institutional racism (the covert kind) from individual racism (the overt kind): "Racism is both overt and covert. It takes two, closely related forms: individual whites acting against individual blacks, and acts by the total white community against the black community. We call these individual racism and institutional racism. The first consists of overt acts by individuals, which cause death, injury or the violent destruction of property. This type can be recorded by television cameras; it can frequently be observed in the process of commission. The second type is less overt, far more subtle, less identifiable in terms of specific individuals committing the acts. But it is no less destructive of human life. The second type originates in the operation of established and respected forces in the society, and thus receives far less public condemnation than the first type" (Stokely Carmichael and Charles Hamilton, *Black Power: The Politics of Liberation in America* [New York: Vintage Books, 1992, 4). From Žižek's vantage point, the overt racism is a type of subjective violence, whereas convert racism is a type of objective violence, and as such, naturalized and rendered invisible in the everyday practices of most white Americans.

82  Žižek, *First as Tragedy*, 120.

83  Ibid.

84  Fanon, *Toward the African Revolution*, trans. Haakon Chevalier (New York: Grove Press, 1967), 25.

85  Fanon, *Toward the African Revolution*, 27.

86  Nick Nesbitt, *Caribbean Critique: Antillean Critical Theory from Toussaint to Glissant* (Liverpool: Liverpool University Press 2013), 20.

87  Aimé Césaire, *A Tempest*, trans. Richard Miller (New York: TCG Translations, 2002), 27.

88  Žižek, *Event*, 48.

89  Jamil Khader, "Class Struggle for the 21st Century: Racial Inequality, International Solidarity, and the New Apartheid Politics," *Journal of World-Systems Research* 23, 2 (2017): 479.

90  Žižek, "Disputations: Who Are You Calling Anti-Semitic?" *New Republic* (January 6, 2009). Available at https://newrepublic.com/article/62376/disputations-who-are-you-calling-anti-semitic. Accessed August 26, 2018.

91  Žižek, "Disputations."

92  Žižek, *Trouble in Paradise*, 119. In *Hind Swaraj*, Gandhi formulates the problem of the colonized in India as follows: "We want the English rule without the Englishman. You want the tiger's nature but not the tiger" (M. K. Gandhi, *Hind Swaraj and Other Writings*, ed. Anthony J. Parel [Cambridge: Cambridge University Press, 2009], 27).

93  Žižek, *First as Tragedy*, 38.

94  Tommy Curry underscores the politically neutralizing effects of liberal non-violence: "Dogmatic allegiance to non-violence is a price that African descended people in America can no longer afford to pay" (Curry, "Please Don't Make Me Touch 'Em," 134).

95  Žižek, "The Fear of Four Words: A Modest Plea for the Hegelian Reading of Christianity," in Slavoj Žižek and John Milbank, *The Monstrosity of Christ: Paradox or Dialectic?*, ed. Creston Davis (Cambridge: MIT Press, 2009), 66.

96  Makdisi, *Palestine Inside Out*, 6.

97  Ibid.

98  Žižek, *Demanding the Impossible*, 118, emphasis in original.

99  I am alluding here to Lacan's seminar, *The Ethics of Psychoanalysis*, where, in his discussion of Sophocles' *Antigone*, Lacan formulates an ethics grounded in the injunction: "do not give way on your desire" (*ne pas céder sur son désir*). "Lacan's ethical imperative," as Joan Copjec perceptively notes, "proposes itself as anything but an insistence that one stubbornly conform to one's personal history. In short, the ethics of psychoanalysis filiates itself with Kant's argument that ethical progress has nothing to do with that form of progress promoted by modern industry, or the 'service of good,' but is rather a matter of personal conversion, of the subjective necessity of going beyond oneself" (Joan Copjec, *Imagine There's No Woman: Ethics and Sublimation* [Cambridge: MIT Press, 2002], 44).

100  See Victoria Mason and Richard Falk, "Assessing Nonviolence in the Palestinian Rights Struggle," *State Crime Journal* 5, 1 (2016): 163–86; Zaha Hassan, "Still Waiting for a Palestinian Gandhi? S/he's Already Here," *Haaretz* (July 30, 2017). Available at https://www.haaretz.com/opinion/still-waiting-for-a-palestinian-gandhi-s-he-s-already-here-1.5437153. Accessed September 2, 2018.

101  Žižek, *The Courage of Hopelessness*, 114.

102  Žižek, *Demanding the Impossible*, 117.

103  Ibid., 113.

104  For Rancière, politics is the struggle for "a new landscape of the possible" (Jacques Rancière, *The Emancipated Spectator*, trans. G. Elliott [New York, Verso, 2009], 103)—the unsettling of what he calls *le partage du sensible*, "the distribution/partition/sharing of the sensible" (Rancière, *The Politics*

*of Aesthetics: Distribution of the Sensible*, trans. G. Rockhill [New York, Continuum, 2004]). Palestinian resistance, as witnessed in the first Intifada, he says, seeks to alter the existing "field of experience" (Rancière, *Disagreement*, 35), to trouble the unjust "distribution of places and roles," Israel's "order of the visible and the sayable" (Rancière, *Disagreement*, 28–9).

105  Said, *The Politics of Dispossession*, 88.

106  Feldman, *A Shadow Over Palestine: The Imperial Life of Race in America* (Minneapolis: University of Minnesota Press, 2015), 223.

107  Pappé, "The Inevitable War on Terror: De-terrorising the Palestinians," in *States of War since 9/11 Terrorism, Sovereignty and The War on Terror*, ed. Alex Houen (New York: Routledge, 2014), 86.

108  Žižek, "Divine Violence and Liberated Territories."

109  Žižek, *Against the Double Blackmail*, 41. See Udi Aloni, "Divine Violence?" *Mondoweiss* (October 16, 2015). Available at https://mondoweiss.net/2015/10/divine-violence/. Accessed September 1, 2018.

110  Žižek, *Demanding the Impossible*, 119.

111  Ibid., 23.

112  Ibid., 63.

113  See Patrisse Khan-Cullors and Asha Bandele, *When They Call You a Terrorist: A Black Lives Matter Memoir* (New York: St. Martin's Press, 2018).

114  Žižek, *Demanding the Impossible*, 54.

115  Gilroy, *Against Race*, 52.

116  Gilroy, *Darker than Blue: On the Moral Economies of Black Atlantic Culture* (Cambridge: Harvard University Press, 2010), 157.

117  Žižek, *Demanding the Impossible*, 56–61.

118  Žižek, *In the Incontinence of the Void*, 23.

119  Žižek, *Demanding the Impossible*, 60.

120  Žižek, *In Defense of Lost Causes*, 289.

121  Žižek, *Demanding the Impossible*, 60.

# 5 Afro-Pessimism: Traversing the Fantasy of the Human, or Rewriting the Grammar of Suffering

1  From *Red, White and Black*, Frank Wilderson B. (c) 2010, Frank Wilderson. All rights reserved. Republished by permission.

2  Žižek, *Violence*, 157.

3   Saidiya V. Hartman, *Scenes of Subjection: Terror, Slavery, and Self-Making in Nineteenth-Century America* (Oxford: Oxford University Press, 1997), 234 n.8.

4   Wilderson, *Red, White, and Black*, 58.

5   Ibid., 38.

6   Ibid.

7   Agamben, *Means without End*, trans. Vincenzo Binetti and Cesare Casarino (Minneapolis: University of Minnesota Press, 2000), 39.

8   Fanon, *Black Skin, White Masks*, xii.

9   Orlando Patterson, *Slavery and Social Death: A Comparative Study* (Cambridge: Harvard University Press, 1982), 38.

10  Jared Sexton, "The Social Life of Social Death: On Afro-Pessimism and Black Optimism," *In Tensions* 5 (2011): 28.

11  Wilderson, *Red, White, and Black*, 18. See also Stephanie Smallwood, *Saltwater Slavery: A Middle Passage from Africa to American Diaspora* (Cambridge: Harvard University Press, 2007).

12  Wilderson, *Red, White, and Black*, 18.

13  Cedric Robinson argues against the evacuation of all culture and agency from the side of the slave. Despite the brutality of slavery, Robinson insists that it was not an absolutely seamless system: (a desire for) black sovereignty persisted. "African labor" smuggled culture—albeit in a hybridized form—back to the lives of blacks, serving as a source of resistance, as "the embryo of the demon that would be visited on the whole entreprise of primitive accumulation" (Robinson, *Black Marxism*, 122).

14  Mbembe, *Critique of Black Reason*, trans. Laurent Dubois (Durham: Duke University Press, 2017), 6, translation modified.

15  Mbembe, "Conversation: Achille Mbembe and David Theo Goldberg on *Critique of Black Reason*," *Theory, Culture, and Society* (July 3, 2018). Available at https://www.theoryculturesociety.org/conversation-achille-mbembe-and-david-theo-goldberg-on-critique-of-black-reason/. Accessed September 19, 2018.

16  Hartman, *Scenes of Subjection*, 62.

17  "Slavery was the condition of possibility for defining the content of 'free' labour of the propertyless proletariat. To be 'free' and to be a worker was negatively defined in relation to the slave" (R. L. "Wanderings of the Slave: Black Life and Social Death," *Mute* [June 5, 2013]). Available at http://www.metamute.org/editorial/articles/wanderings-slave-black-life-and-social-death. Accessed September 10, 2018.

18  Marx, *Capital: A Critique of Political Economy*, vol. 1, trans. Ben Fowkes (New York: Penguin Books, 1976), 874; Wilderson, *Red, White, and Black*, 12–13. See also Nikhil Pal Singh, "On Race, Violence, and 'So-Called

Primitive Accumulation,'" in *Futures of Black Radicalism*, ed. Gaye Theresa Johnson and Alex Lubin (New York: Verso, 2017), 39–58.

19  Wilderson, "The Prison Slave as Hegemony's (Silent) Scandal," *Social Justice* 30, 2 (2003): 22.

20  "Not all free persons are white (nor are they equal or equally free), but slaves are paradigmatically black. And because blackness serves as the basis of enslavement in the logic of a transnational political and legal culture, it permanently destabilizes the position of any nominally free black population" (Jared Sexton, "People-of-Color-Blindness: Notes on the Afterlife of Slavery," *Social Text* 28, 2 103 [2010]: 36).

21  Saidiya Hartman and Frank B. Wilderson III, "The Position of the Unthought," *Qui Parle* 13, 2 (2003): 188.

22  Hartman, *Lose Your Mother: A Journey along the Atlantic Slave Route* (New York: Farrar, Straus and Giroux, 2007), 68, 133.

23  Frank B. Wilderson III, Saidya Hartman, Steve Martinot, Jared Sexton, Hortense J. Spillers, "Editors' Introduction," in *Afro-Pessimism: An Introduction*, ed. Frank B. Wilderson III, Saidya Hartman, Steve Martinot, Jared Sexton, and Hortense J. Spillers (Minneapolis: Racked & Dispatched, 2017), 7n.1. Mbembe describes slavery in similarly libidinal terms: "slavery is not only about capturing, selling and shipping human cargoes across the Atlantic. It is also about remodeling the structures of *jouissance*, reconfiguring the psychic world of the matter, unleashing new forms of voracity and greed" (Mbembe, "Conversation").

24  Žižek discusses *Time* magazine's 2006 cover story "The Deadliest War in the World," detailing how around 4 million people died in the Democratic Republic of Congo due to political violence over the last decade. Žižek draws attention to the lack of attention that this story received, failing to alter the "symbolic space" of its readership: "To put it cynically, *Time* picked the wrong victim in the struggle for hegemony in suffering. It should have stuck to the list of usual suspects: Muslim women and their plight, or the families of 9/11 victims and how they have coped with their losses. The Congo today has effectively re-emerged as a Conradean 'heart of darkness.' No one dares to confront it head on. The death of a West Bank Palestinian child, not to mention an Israeli or an American, is mediatically worth thousands of times more than the death of a nameless Congolese" (Žižek, *Violence*, 3). What explains, at least in part, Western blindness to the naturalization of violence in the Congo is an antiblackness that considers the life of a Congolese incomparable to the life of a Westerner.

25  Sexton, "People-of-Color-Blindness," 36.

26  "In short, White (Human) capacity, in advance of the event of discrimination or oppression, is parasitic on Black incapacity: Without the Negro, capacity itself is incoherent, uncertain at best" (Wilderson, *Red, White, and Black*, 45).

27  Žižek, *The Courage of Hopelessness*, xi. To be clear, Žižek is not ruling out hope *tout court* but only rejecting an ideological vision of hope where people believe that transformative change is actually possible *within* the confines of the existing system. In his endorsement of Badiou's *I Know There Are So Many of You*, Žižek gestures toward a more radical sense of hope, a hope that declines the blackmail of the moderates: "The main function of ideology today is not to crush actual resistance—this is the job of repressive state apparatuses—but to crush hope, to immediately denounce every critical project as opening a path at the end of which is something like the Gulag. At this precise point, Badiou's wonderful short book intervenes: it brings hope, especially to the young whose situation is often without any prospects."

28  Žižek, *The Courage of Hopelessness*, xi–xii. Žižek's dismissal of mainstream political candidates such as Hillary Clinton—along with his unsettling "endorsement" of candidate Trump—is not a reflection of some commitment to accelerationism, a "leftist" view that encourages the intensification and exacerbation of capitalism's self-destructive processes so as to hasten its ultimate demise (the notion, e.g., that Trump will get us there faster than Clinton). For Žižek, this Deleuzian-inspired anarchic Left simplifies and distorts the political situation: "to solve the problems of ecology and so on we need very strong large organizations, the problem is precisely how to do it not in the old totalitarian way." A truly progressive democracy cannot afford fetishizing the absence of order, the local, and nonhierarchical decision-making but must "reinvent power structures" in order to successfully deal with the overwhelming challenges of global capitalism (Žižek, "'Pornography No Longer Has Any Charm'—Part II," *Doxa Journal* [January 19, 2018]. Available at http://doxajournal.ru/en/texts/zizek2. Accessed December 5, 2018; see also Žižek, *The Parallax View*, 261–7). Žižek's hope, his wager, is that the Trump presidency will energize the Left (Clinton would have only further blinded us to the upcoming disasters ["the headlight of another train approaching"]) and compel it to confront fully the wide-ranging and ceaseless violence of global capitalism, not to bring about chaos, but rather to spur the Left to take on that work of reinvention.

29  Decca Aitkenhead, "Slavoj Žižek: 'Humanity is OK, but 99% of People Are Boring Idiots,'" *Guardian* (June 10, 2012). Available at https://www.theguardian.com/culture/2012/jun/10/slavoj-zizek-humanity-ok-people-boring. Accessed September 18, 2018.

30  While generally critical of Ryan Coogler's *Black Panther* for its de-politicization of black struggle—for making "African aesthetics . . . seamlessly compatible with global capitalism," "tradition and ultra-modernity blend together"—Žižek does point to moments in the film that hold more promise, ones that take Erik Killmonger as the film's "true hero." Unlike its purported hero, the king T'Challa, the benevolent ruler who envisions "a gradual and peaceful globalism that would act within

the coordinates of the existing world order and its institutions, spreading education and technological help—and simultaneously maintaining the unique Wakandan culture and way of life," his cousin Killmonger champions "militant global solidarity," pushing Wakanda (Africa's El Dorado) to make its secret and unmatchable resources available to "the oppressed all around the world so that they can overthrow the existing world order." When Killmonger's plans falter, T'Challa offers his wounded cousin a chance to save his life. Killmonger declines the peace offer, preferring "to die free than to be healed and survive in the false abundance of Wakanda." Žižek and Afro-Pessimists can appreciate in Killmonger's refusal, a staunch rejection of the liberal multicultural vision of slow and non-violent progress (Žižek, "*Quasi Duo Fantasias*: A Straussian Reading of 'Black Panther,'" *The Los Angeles Review of Books* (March 3, 2018). Available at https://lareviewofbooks.org/article/quasi-duo-fantasias-straussian-reading-black-panther/#!). Accessed September 19, 2018.

31   Wilderson, *Red, White, and Black*, 38.

32   As Mbembe cautions, "the argument about the turning of human beings into things or about social death has its limits. Wherever African slaves happened to be settled, no death of social life actually occurred. The work of producing symbols and rituals, language, memory and meaning— and therefore the substance necessary to sustain life—never stopped" (Mbembe, "Conversation").

33   Asad Haider, *Mistaken Identity: Race and Class in the Age of Trump* (New York: Verso, 2018), 37. Keeanga-Yamahtta Taylor also observes: "It is one thing to respect the organizing that has gone into the movement against police violence and brutality, but quite another to conceive of Black oppression and anti-Black racism as so wholly unique that they are beyond the realm of understanding and, potentially, solidarity from others who are oppressed" (Keeanga-Yamahtta Taylor, *From #BlackLivesMatter to Black Liberation* [Chicago: Haymarket Books, 2016], 187).

34   Wilderson, "Irreconcilable Anti-Blackness and Police Violence," *IMIXWHATILIKE!* (October 1, 2014). Available at http://imixwhatilike. org/2014/10/01/frankwildersonandantiblackness-2/. Accessed September 10, 2018.

35   Afro-Pessimism's insistence on the ontological alterity of blacknesss, of course, recalls Žižek's critical engagement with Levinas. Žižek had opposed the faceless *Muslemann* to the Levinasian ethics of the face. Would Afro-Pessimists also accuse Žižek of relying too heavily on a European narrative? Perhaps. But to do so would misconstrue what Žižek is after in his example of the *Muslemann*. Unlike Agamben, Žižek is not meditating on the Shoah as the ultimate paradigm for the making of "bare life," for understanding the separation of biological existence (*zoē*) from political existence (*bios*). (Giorgio Agamben, *Homo Sacer: Sovereign Power and Bare Life*, trans. Daniel Heller-Roazen [Stanford: Stanford University Press, 1998], 28).

His example serves to interrogate the gentrification of other in Levinasian ethical thought.

36 Hortense J. Spillers, "Mama's Baby, Papa's Maybe: An American Grammar Book," *Diacritics* 17, 2 (1987): 64–81.

37 Wilderson, *Red, White, and Black*, 28.

38 Wilderson, "The Prison Slave," 25.

39 Wilderson, "Irreconcilable Anti-Blackness."

40 Wilderson, *Red, White, and Black*, 82, emphasis in original.

41 Safiya Umoja Noble, "Teaching Trayvon: Race, Media, and the Politics of Spectacle," *Black Scholar* 44, 1 (2014): 15.

42 Jelani Cobb, "Trayvon Martin and the Parameters of Hope," *New Yorker* (March 21, 2012). Available at https://www.newyorker.com/news/news-desk/trayvon-martin-and-the-parameters-of-hope. Accessed September 10, 2018.

43 Wilderson, "The Prison Slave," 18.

44 Michelle Alexander, *The New Jim Crow: Mass Incarceration in the Age of Colorblindness* (New York: The New Press, 2010), 16. America's criminal justice institutions structurally disadvantage blacks, crippling if not foreclosing their possibilities for social and economic mobility: "What is completely missed in the rare public debates today about the plight of African Americans is that a huge percentage of them are not free to move up at all. It is not just that they lack opportunity, attend poor schools, or are plagued by poverty. They are barred by law from doing so . . . To put the matter starkly: The current system of control permanently locks a huge percentage of the African American community out of the mainstream society and economy. The system operates through our criminal justice institutions, but it functions more like a caste system than a system of crime control . . .. Although this new system of racialized social control purports to be colorblind, it creates and maintains racial hierarchy much as earlier systems of control did. Like Jim Crow (and slavery), mass incarceration operates as a tightly networked system of laws, policies, customs, and institutions that operate collectively to ensure the subordinate status of a group defined largely by race" (Alexander, *The New Jim Crow*, 13). See also Loïc Wacquant, "From Slavery to Mass Incarceration: Rethinking the 'Race Question in the US," *New Left Review* 13 (2002): 41–60; Angela Davis, *Are Prisons Obsolete?* (New York: Seven Stories Press, 2003); Douglas Blackmon, *Slavery by Another Name: The Re-Enslavement of Black Americans from the Civil War to World War II* (New York: Anchor Books, 2008).

45 Calvin Warren, "Black Time: Slavery, Metaphysics, and the Logic of Wellness," in *The Psychic Hold of Slavery: Legacies in American Expressive Culture*, ed. Soyica Diggs Colbert, Robert J. Patterson, and Aida Levy-Hussen (New Brunswick: Rutgers University Press, 2016), 65.

46 Wacquant, "From Slavery to Mass Incarceration," 52, emphasis in original.

47 Noble perceptively observes how the liberal pro-Martin coverage led to an overinvestment in Martin the innocent victim (as the victim of subjective violence) at the expense of a much needed structural analysis of society's systemic antiblackness (of Martin as the victim of objective violence): "Liberal commentators on stations like MSNBC and BET were heavily invested in defending Trayvon from being portrayed as a criminal, while deflecting attention from larger systemic and structural critiques, which ultimately served to derail needed conversations about race, power, and privilege" (Noble, "Teaching Trayvon," 16). Against the backdrop of liberal coverage of these issues, candidate Trump, in a regressive gesture, ran on a law and order platform that positioned blacks, in particular, as a priori menacing subjects, requiring preemptive control.

48 Noble documents the economic commodification of the Trayvon Martin case: "media spectacle was used to bring about news ratings, increased advertising, and social media traffic at the expense of a national conversation about racial justice, ending racial violence, and stopping gun proliferation" (Noble, "Teaching Trayvon," 12).

49 Bryan J. McCann, "On Whose Ground? Racialized Violence and the Prerogative of 'Self-Defense' in the Trayvon Martin Case," *Western Journal of Communication* 78, 4 (2014): 493.

50 McCann, "On Whose Ground?" 481.

51 The idea that a violent Martin may have been acting in self-defense against Zimmerman's aggressive racial profiling did not fit the liberal narrative, too hesitant to associate justified violence and blackness. On this topic, see McCann, "On Whose Ground?"

52 Robin D. G. Kelley pointedly notes, "it was Trayvon Martin, not George Zimmerman, who was put on trial. He was tried for the crimes he may have committed and the ones he would have committed had he lived" (Robin D. G. Kelley, "The U.S. v. Trayvon Martin: How the System Worked," *Huffington Post Online* [July 15, 2013]). Available at https://www.huffingtonpost.com/robin-d-g-kelley/nra-stand-your-ground-trayvon-martin_b_3599843.html. Accessed September 14, 2018.

53 "The Daily Caller Obtains Trayvon Martin's Tweets." Available at http://dailycaller.com/2012/03/26/the-daily-caller-obtains-trayvon-martins-tweets/. Accessed September 14, 2018; "Second Trayvon Martin Twitter Feed Identified." Available at http://dailycaller.com/2012/03/29/second-trayvon-martin-twitter-feed-identified/. Accessed September 14, 2018.

54 "Fox's Geraldo Rivera: 'You Dress Like a Thug, People Are Going to Treat You Like a Thug. That's True. I Stand by That.'" Available at https://www.mediamatters.org/video/2013/07/14/foxs-geraldo-rivera-you-dress-like-a-thug-peopl/194866. Accessed September 10, 2018.

55  Ben Adler, "Conservative Media Smears Trayvon Martin," *Nation* (March 27, 2012). Available at https://www.thenation.com/article/conservative-media-smears-trayvon-martin/. Accessed September 12, 2018. Also from *Nation*, Patricia Williams exposes the ways the defense's narrative transformed Martin into a vicious active subject while depicting Zimmerman as pathetically passive, a recipient of black rage: "By the end of the trial, the 200-pound Zimmerman, despite martial arts training and a history of assaulting others, was transformed into a 'soft,' retiring marshmallow of a weakling. The 158-pound Martin had been reimagined as an immense, athletically endowed, drug-addled 'thug'" (Patricia J. Williams, "The Monsterization of Trayvon Martin," *Nation* [July 31, 2013]). Available at https://www.thenation.com/article/monsterization-trayvon-martin/. Accessed September 10, 2018.

56  Hartman and Wilderson, "The Position of the Unthought," 189.

57  Ibid.

58  Marcuse, "The End of Utopia," 253.

59  To be sure, white conservatives can also experience imaginary identification with blacks. 2016 Republican presidential candidate Ben Carson and the fascination he inspires on the Right is a case in point. Žižek exposes the ways Carson perversely insisted on his delinquent black youth (against journalist charges to the contrary) in order to portray himself as a reformed, Christianized, and "unblackened" subject: "Wouldn't it have been better for Carson to come across in the eyes of his supporters (mostly white Christian conservatives) as a good boy from the beginning? No: his delinquent past perfectly fitted his image, that of the usual black boy, caught up in crime and other vices, who found strength in hard work, discipline and Christianity. This is what his supporters wanted to see: not simply a good black boy (as such he would have to be recognized as one of us, fully equal to us), but somebody who first fully enjoyed being black in its transgressive aspects (the sins of 'lower' races always fascinate white conservatives and are clearly an object of ambiguous envy), and then found strength to castigate his black wildness and become a moral Christian like them" (Žižek, *Like a Thief in Broad Daylight*, 83). Liberals and conservatives alike, then, only view blacks as desirable on condition that they present themselves, or are presented, as through and through decaffeinated, nonviolent, and unthreatening to their respective white audiences.

60  Žižek, *The Courage of Hopelessness*, 170.

61  Jack Kerwick, "Trayvon Martin: A Child, or a Thug Wannabe?" *New American* (July 15, 2013). Available at https://www.thenewamerican.com/reviews/opinion/item/15986-trayvon-martin-a-child-or-a-thug-wannabe. Accessed September 13, 2018.

62  Wilderson, "The Black Liberation Army and the Paradox of Political Engagement," in *Postcoloniality-Decoloniality-Black Critique: Joints and*

*Fissures*, ed. Sabine Broeck and Carsten Junker (Frankfurt: Campus Verlag, 2014), 177.

63   Wilderson, *Red, White, and Black*, 55.

64   Mbembe, "Raceless Futures."

65   Ibid.

66   Léopold Sédar Senghor, "De la négritude," in *Liberté V: Le Dialogue des cultures* (Paris: Seuil, 1993), 17.

67   R. L., "Wanderings of the Slave."

68   See Calvin L. Warren, "Black Nihilism and the Politics of Hope," *CR: The New Centennial Review* 15, 1 (2015): 237.

69   Wilderson, "The Black Liberation Army," 178.

70   Wilderson, *Red, White, and Black*, 338.

71   Ibid., 337. For Wilderson, "the liberation of Black people is tantamount to moving into an epistemology that we cannot imagine. Once Blacks become incorporated and recognized I don't think we have the language or the concepts to think of what that is. It's not like moving from Capitalism to Communism, it's like the end of the world" (Frank Wilderson, "Wallowing in the Contradictions, Part 2 with Percy Howard" [July 14, 2010]). Available at https://percy3.wordpress.com/2010/07/14/frank-wilderson-wallowing-in-the-contradictions-part-2/. Accessed October 8, 2018. Wilderson here understands communism to be one totalizing system simply replacing another. But for Žižek communism means something else completely. To be a communist is precisely not to subscribe to "the system which deservedly collapsed in 1990" but instead "to care for the commons—the commons of nature, of knowledge—which are threatened by the [capitalist] system" (Žižek, "Actual Politics," *Theory & Event* 14, 4 [2011]). The desire for communism and the desire to end of the world are by no means mutually exclusive.

72   Wilderson, "The Black Liberation Army," 203.

73   "The blind spots which critical theorists have when thinking relations of power through the figure of the Black, the Slave: the end of the chattel technologies of slavery is often transposed as the end of slavery itself; which, in turn, permits the facile drawing of political analogies between Blacks and workers, and between Blacks and postcolonial subjects" (Wilderson, "The Black Liberation Army," 177).

74   Wilderson, "The Black Liberation Army," 178.

75   Wilderson, "Irreconcilable Anti-Blackness." Another form of remedy explored by Afro-Pessimists is economic reparations. Though in general supportive of the idea, Hartman is also skeptical of its realizability and its emancipatory value: "The reparations movement puts itself in this contradictory or impossible position, because reparations are not going to solve the systemic ongoing production of racial inequality, in material

or any other terms. And like inequality, racial domination and racial abjection are produced across generations. In that sense, reparations seem like a very limited reform: a liberal scheme based upon certain notions of commensurability that reinscribe the power of the law and of the state to make right a certain situation, when, clearly, it cannot" (Hartman and Wilderson, "The Position of the Unthought," 198). See also Wilderson, "Reparations . . . Now." Available at https://vimeo.com/73991006; Ta-Nehisi Coates, *We Were Eight Years in Power: An American Tragedy* (New York: One World, 2017). Not unlike Hartman, Žižek cautions that the demand for reparations repeats the status quo and its structure of compensation: "it is not too radical, but not radical enough. The true task is not to get compensation from those responsible, but to deprive them of the position which makes them responsible" (Žižek and Daly, *Conversations with Žižek*, 134).

76  Wilderson, *Red, White, and Black*, 338, emphasis in original.

77  Wilderson, "Irreconcilable Anti-Blackness." Žižek echoes Wilderson's stress on the necessity for analysis, on the need to resist easy answers, but he finds his inspiration in Lenin's own emphasis on patient deliberation, on his call to "learn, learn, learn" (Žižek, *Violence*, 8). Moreover, whereas Wilderson treats "What is to be done?" as a programmatic mode of action, pointing to answers available within society's existing coordinates—thus treating the symbolic order as a totalizing space—Žižek aligns Lenin's deliberative mode of revolutionary thinking with the Lacanian act: "[Lenin's] idea is simply that there is no big Other; you never get the guarantee; you must act" (Žižek and Daly, *Conversations with Žižek*, 164).

78  Wilderson, "Irreconcilable Anti-Blackness."

79  Ibid. Wilderson is not just singling out Palestinians but objecting to a long list of leftist movements that have sought to coopt and neutralize the demands of blacks: "In its critique of social movements, Afro-Pessimism argues that Blacks do not function as political subjects; instead, our flesh and energies are instrumentalized for postcolonial, immigrant, feminist, LGBT, and workers' agendas. These so-called allies are never *authorized* by Black agendas predicated on Black ethical dilemmas. A Black radical agenda is terrifying to most people on the Left because it emanates from a condition of suffering for which there is no imaginable strategy for redress—no narrative of redemption" (Wilderson, "Afro-Pessimism and the End of Redemption," *Humanities Futures. Franklin Humanities Institute: Duke University* [October 20, 2015]). Available at https://humanitiesfutures.org/papers/afro-pessimism-end-redemption/. Accessed September 18, 2018.

80  And if blacks are going to support the Palestinian cause, if blacks are going to participate in a global Left resistance, Wilderson urges them to maintain something of an ironic distance: "what we have to do is remind each other, to know our history in terms of slavery and our resistance to it, but also to

be able to have x-ray vision, and say that just because we're walking around in suits and ties and are professors and journalists doesn't mean we're not slaves. That is, to understand things diachronically. And that will allow us to be in a coalition with people of color, moving on the system with them, but ridiculing them at the same time for the paucity—the *lameness*—of their desire and demand. And for the fact that we know, once they get over [their own hurdles], the anti-Blackness that sustains them will rear its ugly head again against us" (Wilderson, "Irreconcilable Anti-Blackness," emphasis in original). Wilderson's "knowledge" that nonblacks will betray blacks is more than pessimistic; it is fatalistic in its outlook.

81  Wilderson, "Irreconcilable Anti-Blackness."

82  Žižek, *Disparities*, 375.

83  See Alice Speri, "Israel Security Forces Are Training American Cops Despite History of Rights Abuses," *The Intercept* (September 15, 2017). Available at https://theintercept.com/2017/09/15/police-israel-cops-training-adl-human-rights-abuses-dc-washington/. Accessed September 18, 2018.

84  Wilderson would undoubtedly not take too kindly to an analogy between Israel and Apartheid South Africa, such as the one offered by Israeli political geographer Oren Yiftachel for whom Israel's citizenship discourse recalls the political situation in apartheid South Africa: "Jews between the Jordan and the sea are 'white' citizens, Arabs in Israel have 'colored' (in other words, partial) citizenship, and Palestinians in the territories have 'black' citizenship, without political rights" (Oren Yiftachel, "Call Apartheid in Israel by Its Name," *Haaretz* [February 11, 2016]). Available at https://www.haaretz.com/opinion/.premium-call-apartheid-in-israel-by-its-name-1.5402831. Accessed September 14, 2018. This is another example of the ruse of analogy. Yet Wilderson and others who object this type of analogy mistake analogy with straightforward identification, similarity with sameness. A more justified objection might be Ronit Lentin's charge that Yiftachel's account homogenizes the Palestinian situation, displaying a lack of specificity in accounting for the various Palestinian positions and subcategories: "Palestinians under occupation in areas A, B, and C of the West Bank, besieged Palestinians in the Gaza enclave, Palestinians with residency rights but without citizenship in occupied Jerusalem, Syrians in the annexed Golan, exiled and diasporic Palestinians without the right of return," and so on (Lentin, *Traces of Racial Exception*, 86).

85  Wilderson, "Irreconcilable Anti-Blackness."

86  Ibid.

87  Haider, *Mistaken Identity*, 38.

88  In a different piece, Wilderson does offer an anecdote about his disillusionment with black-Palestinian solidarity: "I was living in Minneapolis, doing work around the First Palestinian Intifada

(1988–89). I was sitting on a grassy knoll trying to console a Palestinian friend of mine whose cousin had blown himself up (accidentally) while making a bomb in the West Bank. My friend was speaking openly and without his internal censors at work, which was fine—he was grieving. At one point, he said that it was really shameful and humiliating the way Israeli men ran their hands over your body when they stop you at a checkpoint. Then he said that the deepest sense of humiliation was felt when the Israeli soldier was an Ethiopian Jew" (Wilderson, "Afro-Pessimism and the End of Redemption"). The Palestinian friend's comment understandably disappoints. For Wilderson, his friend's comment exemplifies Palestinian antiblackness. He asks: "How was it that people who stole his land and slaughtered his relatives were somehow less of a threat than the speaking implements (the Black Jews) White Israelis got to do their dirty work? What was it about Blacks that made us so fungible . . . we could be tossed like salad in the minds of oppressors *and* of the oppressed who were not Black?" (Wilderson, "Afro-Pessimism and the End of Redemption"). Wilderson expresses here legitimate concerns about who belongs to Palestine: Ethiopian Jews should not be a priori excluded—again remembering Said's words, it is the exclusionary claims of political Zionism that are most objectionable. At the same time, there are additional elements that are worth considering. What might be provoking his friend's outrage is the Ethiopian Jew's status as a newcomer, an outsider, who is in a position of absolute control over the land's indigenous population. Wilderson frames the Ethiopian Jew as a passive subject, even a victim—white Israelis enticed Ethiopian Jews to come to Israel to do their "dirty work"—who happens to be an IDF soldier. Without minimizing the economic coercion that may have brought them to Israel, Ethiopian Jews, who serve in the IDF, and thus decline the *refusenik* option, are not immune from reproach. Finally, is blackness in the service of occupation any less deplorable than whiteness in the service of occupation?

89  For thoughtful accounts of black-Palestinian solidarity, see, for example, Angela Davis, *Freedom Is a Constant Struggle*; Feldman, *A Shadow Over Palestine*; Greg Burris, "Birth of a 'Zionist' Nation: Black Radicalism and the Future of Palestine," in *Futures of Black Radicalism*, ed. Gaye Theresa Johnson and Alex Lubin (New York: Verso, 2017), 120–32; Robin D. G. Kelley, "Yes, I Said, 'National Liberation,'" in *Letters to Palestine: Writers Respond to War and Occupation*, ed. Vijay Prashad (New York: Verso, 2015), 139–53; Kristian Davis Bailey, "Black-Palestinian Solidarity in the Ferguson-Gaza Era," *American Quarterly* 67, 4 (2015): 1017–26; Michael R. Fischbach, *Black Power and Palestine: Transnational Countries of Color* (Stanford: Stanford University Press, 2018); Michelle Alexander, "Time to Break the Silence on Palestine," *New York Times* (January 19, 2019). Available at https://www.nytimes.com/2019/01/19/opinion/sunday/martin-luther-king-palestine-israel.html. Accessed February 5, 2019.

90 Étienne Balibar, "A Complex Urgent Universal Political Cause," *Address before the Conference of Faculty for Israeli–Palestinian Peace (FFIPP)*. *Université Libre de Bruxelles* (July 3–4, 2004). Available at http://users. resist.ca/~elkilombo/documents/%20BalibarBrusseBD480.pdf. Accessed September 18, 2018.

91 Žižek, *Less Than Nothing*, 831.

92 Sexton, "People-of-Color-Blindness," 37.

93 Mbembe, "Necropolitics," 27.

94 Ibid., 25–6.

95 Ibid., 27, emphasis in original.

96 Ibid., 39.

97 Sexton, "People-of-Color-Blindness," 38.

98 Ibid., 44.

99 Sexton, *Amalgamation Schemes: Antiblackness and the Critique of Multiracialism* (Minneapolis: University of Minnesota Press, 2008), 293n.9.

100 Sexton, "People-of-Color-Blindness," 47.

101 Ibid., 48, emphasis in original.

102 Ibid., 48, emphasis in original.

103 Ibid., 48.

104 Ibid., 56n.75.

105 Ibid.

106 Ibid.

107 Ibid., 56n.75. A cross-racial coalition might take mass incarceration as a fundamental problem and challenge the ways black bodies are treated as socially and legally as insignificant, "meant to be warehoused and die" (Wilderson, "Gramsci's Black Marx: Whither the Slave in Civil Society?," *Social Identities* 9, 2 [2003]: 238).

108 Žižek, "Learn to Live without Masters," *Naked Punch* (October 3, 2009). Available at http://www.nakedpunch.com/articles/34. Accessed September 14, 2018.

109 Mbembe, "Conversation."

110 Žižek, *Demanding the Impossible*, 106.

111 Žižek, *The Puppet and the Dwarf*, 69. Again, Žižek insists that "*there is no ontology of the Real*: the very field of ontology, of the positive order of Being, emerges through the subtraction of the Real. The order of Being and the Real are mutually exclusive: The Real is the immanent blockage or impediment of the order of Being, what makes the order of Being inconsistent" (Žižek, *Less Than Nothing*, 958).

112 Sexton, "Unbearable Blackness," *Cultural Critique* 90 (2015): 168.

113  Žižek, "A Leftist Plea for 'Eurocentrism,'" 989.

114  Haider, *Mistaken Identity*, 38.

115  Žižek, *The Ticklish Subject*, 208.

116  Žižek, "Human Rights and Its Discontents," Lecture at Bard College (November 15, 1999). Available at http://www.lacan.com/zizek-human.htm. Accessed September 14, 2018. Žižek is praising here modern feminism for its refusal to limit its demands to personal ones, for its desire to change the existing coordinates of universality itself.

117  Mbembe, *Critique of Black Reason*, 6, emphasis in original.

118  Fanon, *The Wretched of the Earth*, 1.

119  Žižek, *First as Tragedy*, 120.

120  Žižek, "Human Rights and Its Discontents."

121  Žižek also turns to the "slum-dwellers"—the "'living dead' of global capitalism"—as candidates for the "part of no-part" (Žižek, *The Parallax View*, 269). These "slum-dwellers" are not merely a "redundant surplus," an "unfortunate accident" of global capitalism, "but a necessary product" of its "innermost logic" (Žižek, *In Defense of Lost Causes*, 424). Žižek describes the slum-dwellers, residing more often than not in racialized enclaves, as "the counter-class to the other newly emerging class, the so-called symbolic class (managers, journalists, and public relations people, academics, artists, etc.), which is also uprooted and perceives itself as directly universal," and not tied to its organic or given community. Yet rather than simply accepting this juxtaposition as "the new axis of class struggle," Žižek proceeds to complicate the homogeneity of the "symbolic class," envisioning the possibility of a non-identitarian coalition between the two classes. He asks us to see the "symbolic class" as "inherently split so that one can make the emancipatory wager of coalition between slum-dwellers and the 'progressive' part of the symbolic class? What we should be looking for are signs of the new forms of social awareness that will emerge from the slum collectives: they will be the germs of the future" (Žižek, *In Defense of Lost Causes*, 425). On the global phenomena of the slum-dwellers, see Mike Davis, *Planet of Slums* (New York: Verso, 2006).

122  Žižek, *Violence*, 157.

123  Žižek, *Demanding the Impossible*, 60, emphasis in original.

124  Žižek, "Afterword: Lenin's Choice," 172.

# Conclusion

1  Žižek, "Class Struggle or Postmodernism?" 90.

2  Žižek, *Demanding the Impossible*, 99, emphasis in original.

3   Žižek, *Event*, 2.

4   Ibid., 3, emphasis in original.

5   Ibid., 180.

6   Žižek, *In Defense of Lost Causes*, 361.

7   Alicia Garza, 'A Herstory of the #BlackLivesMatter Movement,' *Feminist Wire* (October 7, 2014). Available at https://thefeministwire.com/2014/10/blacklivesmatter-2. Accessed September 24, 2018.

8   David Theo Goldberg, "Why 'Black Lives Matter' Because All Lives Don't Matter in America," *Huffington Post* (September 25, 2015). Available at https://www.huffingtonpost.com/david-theo-goldberg/why-black-lives-matter_b_8191424.html. Accessed September 24, 2018.

9   Nadine Bloch, "The Art of #BlackLivesMatter," *OpenDemocracy* (February 3, 2015). Available at https://www.opendemocracy.net/transformation/nadine-bloch/art-of-blacklivesmatter. Accessed September 28, 2018.

10  Davis, *Freedom Is a Constant Struggle*, 87.

11  Goldberg, "Why 'Black Lives Matter.'"

12  Ibid.

13  George Yancy and Judith Butler, "What's Wrong with 'All Lives Matter'?" *New York Times* (January 12, 2015). Available at http://opinionator.blogs.nytimes.com/2015/01/12/whats-wrong-with-all-lives-matter/. Accessed September 24, 2018.

14  Yancy and Butler, "What's Wrong with 'All Lives Matter'?"

15  Žižek, *The Courage of Hopelessness*, 246.

16  Ibid., 247.

17  Derbyshire, "Interview with Slavoj Zizek."

18  For Badiou, "to be really faithful to the event, I must completely rework my ordinary way of living my situation" (Badiou, *Ethics*, 41–2). Receptivity and response to the Event are inextricably linked for Badiou. The disorganizing and derailing newness of the event reveals a "void" in the order of being, involving an interpellation (the becoming-subject of the Event) and an unending task of responsibility (fidelity to the Event).

19  Žižek, *Event*, 13.

20  Žižek, *Absolute Recoil*, 75.

21  Žižek, *Trouble in Paradise*, 119.

22  Malcolm X, "Message to the Grassroots" (1963). Available at http://www.blackpast.org/1963-malcolm-x-message-grassroots. Accessed July 14, 2018.

23  Žižek, "Occupy Wall Street: What Is to Be Done Next?" *Guardian* (April 24, 2012). Available at https://www.theguardian.com/commentisfree/cifamerica/2012/apr/24/occupy-wall-street-what-is-to-be-done-next. Accessed July 14, 2018.

24 Žižek, "Occupy Wall Street."

25 Amanda Terkel, 'Black Lives Matter Disavows Democratic Party's Show of Support,' *Huffington Post* (August 31, 2015). Available at https://www.huffingtonpost.com/entry/black-lives-matter-dnc_ us_55e48104e4b0c818f6188cab. Accessed September 26, 2018.

26 The video is available at https://www.washingtonpost.com/video/world/ when-i-see-them-i-see-us/2015/10/15/c8f8aa40-72c2-11e5-ba14- 318f8e87a2fc_video.html?utm_term=.499d8ed0ff17. Accessed September 27, 2018. The script is available at http://www.blackpalestiniansolidarity. com/script.html. Accessed September 27, 2018.

27 "Statement of Black Palestinian Solidarity." Available at http://www. blackpalestiniansolidarity.com/about.html. Accessed September 26, 2018. Black and Palestinian activists also extended their solidarity to the Standing Rock Sioux in their protest over the Dakota access pipeline. See M. Shadee Malaklou, 'DAPL and the Matter/ing of Black Life,' *Feminist Wire* (November 30, 2016). Available at https://thefeministwire. com/2016/11/dapl-mattering-black-life/. Accessed September 26, 2018. Nadya Raja Tannous, "Palestinians Join Standing Rock Sioux to Protest Dakota Access Pipeline," *Mondoweiss* (October 24, 2016). Available at http://mondoweiss.net/2016/10/palestinians-standing-pipeline/. Accessed September 26, 2018.

28 Available at https://policy.m4bl.org/invest-divest/. Accessed September 26, 2018.

29 Alan Dershowitz blames BLM for "singling Israel out and falsely accusing it of 'genocide,'" which, he contends, "can be explained in no other way than blatant hatred of Jews and their state" (Alan Dershowitz, 'Black Lives Matter Must Rescind Anti-Israel Declaration,' *Boston Globe* [August 12, 2016]). Available at https://www.bostonglobe.com/ opinion/columns/2016/08/12/black-lives-matter-must-rescind-anti-israel-declaration/EHDYV3gNLwrTTwfp0JA8QN/story.html. Accessed September 27, 2018. Because BLM is not critical of Syria, Saudi Arabia, Turkey, Hamas, China, and others for dismal human right record, Dershowitz, like many other defenders of Israel, maintains that their interest in Israel stems from anti-Semitism. What is of course missed by Dershowitz is that none of these countries pretend to be democratic, nor are they seen as such by the rest of the world. If the State of Israel wants to pass itself off as "democratic," it must be held to a higher standard. See also Jonathan A. Greenblatt, 'ADL Statement on Black Lives Matter,' *Jewish Week* (July 28, 2016). Available at https://heartland.adl.org/news/adl-statement-on-black-lives-matter. Accessed September 26, 2018. For critical responses to the dubious charge of anti-Semitism, see Rania Khalek, 'Black Activists Slam Israel Lobby Attack on Movement for Black Lives,' *Electronic Intifada* (August 6, 2016). Available at https://electronicintifada.net/blogs/rania-khalek/black-activists-slam-israel-lobby-attack-movement-black-lives.

Accessed September 26, 2018; Thomas S. Harrington, "Alan Dershowitz's 'Advice' to Black Lives Matter," *Counterpunch* (August 16, 2016). Available at https://www.counterpunch.org/2016/08/16/alan-dershowitzs-advice-to-black-lives-matter/. Accessed September 27, 2018.

30  Jonathan S. Tobin, from the conservative journal *The National Review*, observes: "The problem for pro-Israel Democrats is that their party, increasingly dependent on minority voters, has become vulnerable to intersectional arguments in which the Palestinian war on Israel is a Third World parallel to the Black Lives Matter movement" (Jonathan S. Tobin, 'Democrats Reach a Tipping Point on Israel,' *National Review* [May 18, 2018]). Available at https://www.nationalreview.com/2018/05/democrats-israel-tipping-point/. Accessed September 26, 2018.

31  As the 2018 national survey by Pew Research Center shows, "currently, 79% of Republicans say they sympathize more with Israel than the Palestinians, compared with just 27% of Democrats" ("Republicans and Democrats Grow Even Further Apart in Views of Israel, Palestinians," *Pew Research Center* [January 23, 2018]). Available at http://www.people-press.org/2018/01/23/republicans-and-democrats-grow-even-further-apart-in-views-of-israel-palestinians/. Accessed September 27, 2018.

32  Gilroy, *Against Race*, 53.

33  Žižek, *Event*, 180.

34  As Greg Burris puts it, "Those who participate in the imagining of Black-Palestinian ties are not simply describing the world as it already exists; they are creating something new, giving flesh to a potential that had previously been hidden" (Burris, "Birth of a (Zionist) Nation," 130).

35  Jasbir Puar, *The Right to Maim: Debility, Capacity, Disability* (Durham: Duke University Press, 2017), 154.

36  Hannah Arendt, for example, sides with difference, which she sets in opposition to universality: "If one is attacked as a Jew, one must defend oneself as a Jew. Not as a German, not as a world-citizen, not as an upholder of the Rights of Man, or whatever" (Hannah Arendt, *Essays in Understanding 1930–1954: Formation, Exile and Totalitarianism*, ed. Jerome Kohn [New York: Shocken Books, 1994], 12).

37  Žižek, *The Parallax View*, 34.

38  Žižek, *Violence*, 152, emphasis in original.

39  Žižek, *Event*, 184.

40  Žižek, *The Parallax View*, 334.

41  Žižek, *Event*, 161–78.

42  Žižek, *In Defense of Lost Causes*, 7.

# BIBLIOGRAPHY

Abinumah, Ali. *The Battle for Justice in Palestine*. Chicago: Haymarket Books, 2014.

Abinumah, Ali. "Economic Exploitation of Palestinians Flourishes under Occupation." *Al Jazeera* (September 13, 2012). https://www.aljazeera.com/indepth/opinion/2012/09/20129128052624254.html.

Adler, Ben. "Conservative Media Smears Trayvon Martin." *Nation* (March 27, 2012). https://www.thenation.com/article/conservative-media-smears-trayvon-martin/.

Agamben, Giorgio. *Homo Sacer: Sovereign Power and Bare Life*. Trans. Daniel Heller-Roazen. Stanford: Stanford University Press, 1998.

Agamben, Giorgio. *Means without End*. Trans. Vincenzo Binetti and Cesare Casarino. Minneapolis: University of Minnesota Press, 2000.

Ahmed, Haseed and Chris Cutrone. "The Occupy Movement, a Renascent Left, and Marxism Today: An Interview with Slavoj Žižek." *Platypus Review* 42 (December 2011–January 2012). https://platypus1917.org/2011/12/01/occupy-movement-interview-with-slavoj-zizek/.

Ahmed, Sara. "'Liberal Multiculturalism Is the Hegemony—It's an Empirical Fact'—A Response to Slavoj Žižek." *Darkmatter: In the Ruins of Imperial Culture* (February 19, 2008). http://www.darkmatter101.org/site/2008/02/19/%E2%80%98liberal-multiculturalism-is-the-hegemony-%E2%80%93-its-an-empirical-fact%E2%80%99-a-response-to-slavoj-zizek/.

Ahmed, Sara. "A Phenomenology of Whiteness." *Feminist Studies* 8, 2 (2007): 149–68.

Aitkenhead, Decca. "Slavoj Žižek: 'Humanity Is OK, but 99% of People Are Boring Idiots.'" *Guardian* (June 10, 2012). www.theguardian.com/culture/2012/jun/10/slavoj-zizek-humanity-ok-people-boring.

Alam, Shahid. *Israeli Exceptionalism: The Destabilizing Logic of Zionism*. New York: Palgrave Macmillan, 2009.

Alexander, Michelle. *The New Jim Crow: Mass Incarceration in the Age of Colorblindness*. New York: The New Press, 2010.

Alexander, Michelle. "Time to Break the Silence on Palestine." *New York Times* (January 19, 2019). https://www.nytimes.com/2019/01/19/opinion/sunday/martin-luther-king-palestine-israel.html.

Almond, Ian. "Anti-Capitalist Objections to the Postcolonial: Some Conciliatory Remarks on Žižek and Context." *Ariel* 43, 1 (2012): 1–21.

Aloni, Udi. "Divine Violence?" *Mondoweiss* (October 16, 2015). https://mondoweiss.net/2015/10/divine-violence/.

Althusser, Louis. "Ideology and Ideological State Apparatuses (Notes towards an Investigation)." In *Mapping Ideology*. Ed. Slavoj Žižek. New York: Verso, 1994: 100–40.

Améry, Jean. *At the Mind's Limits: Contemplations by a Survivor on Auschwitz and Its Realities*. Trans. Sidney Rosenfeld and Stella P. Rosenfeld. Bloomington: Indiana University Press, 1980.

Appiah, Anthony Kwame. "The Uncompleted Argument: Du Bois and the Illusions of Race." In *"Race" Writing, and Difference*. Ed. Henry Louis Gates, Jr. Chicago: University of Chicago Press, 1985: 21–37.

Applebaum, Barbara. *Being White, Being Good: White Complicity, White Moral Responsibility, and Social Justice Pedagogy*. Lanham: Lexington Books, 2010.

Arendt, Hannah. *Essays in Understanding 1930–1954: Formation, Exile and Totalitarianism*. Ed. Jerome Kohn. New York: Shocken Books, 1994.

Ashcroft, Bill. "Future Thinking: Postcolonial Utopianism." In *The Future of Postcolonial Studies*. Ed. Chantal Zabus. New York: Routledge, 2015: 235–53.

Badiou, Alain. *Ethics: An Essay on the Understanding of Evil*. Trans. Peter Hallward. New York: Verso, 2001.

Badiou, Alain. *I Know There Are so Many of You*. Trans. Susan Spitzer. Cambridge: Polity, 2018.

Badiou, Alain. *Our Wound Is Not so Recent*. Trans. Robin Mackay. Cambridge: Polity, 2016.

Badiou, Alain, Eric Hazan, and Ivan Segré, *Reflections on Anti-Semitism*. Trans. David Fernbach. New York: Verso, 2013.

Bailey, Kristian Davis. "Black-Palestinian Solidarity in the Ferguson-Gaza Era." *American Quarterly* 67, 4 (2015): 1017–26.

Balibar, Étienne. "A Complex Urgent Universal Political Cause." *Address Before the Conference of Faculty for Israeli–Palestinian Peace (FFIPP)*. Université Libre de Bruxelles (July 3–4, 2004). http://users.resist.ca/~elkilombo/documents/%20 BalibarBrusseBD480.pdf.

Balibar, Étienne. *Equaliberty: Political Essays*. Trans. James Ingram. Durham: Duke University Press, 2014.

Beaumont, Peter. "Women's Groups Denounce Israeli Military over Nominee for Chief Rabbi." *Guardian* (July 12, 2016). https://www.theguardian.com/ world/2016/jul/12/womens-groups-and-mps-denounce-appointment- of-idfs-chief-rabbi.

Beauvoir, Simone de. *America Day by Day*. Trans. Carol Cosman. Berkeley: University of California Press, 1999.

Beauvoir, Simone de. *The Second Sex*. Trans. Constance Borde and Sheila Malovany-Chevallier. New York: Alfred Knopf, 2010.

Bell, Derrick. *Faces at the Bottom of the Well: The Permanence of Racism*. New York: Basic Books, 1992.

Bell, Derrick. "Learning the Three 'I's' of America's Slave Heritage." In *Slavery and the Law*, Ed. Paul Finkelman. Madison: Madison House Publishers, 1997: 29–41.

Bell, Derrick. "Racial Realism." *Connecticut Law Review* 24, 2 (1992): 363–79.

Benn, Aluf. "The Jewish Majority in Israel Still See Their Country as 'a Villa in the Jungle.'" *Guardian* (August 20, 2013). https://www.theguardian.com/commentisfree/2013/aug/20/jewish-majority-israel-villa-in-the-jungle.

Bennis, Phyllis. "Palestinians Are Forcing the World to See Their Humanity: The Gaza Massacre Is a War Crime. And the United States Is Complicit Alongside Israel." *In These Times* (May 19, 2018). http://inthesetimes.com/article/21148/palestinians-gaza-israel-massacre-jerusalem-embassy-donald-trump.

Bernasconi, Robert. "Fanon's *the Wretched of the Earth* as the Fulfillment of Sartre's *Critique of Dialectical Reason.*" *Sartre Studies International* 16, 2 (2010): 36–47.

Berlant, Lauren. *Cruel Optimism*. Durham: Duke University Press, 2011.

Bhabha, Homi K. "Democracy De-Realized." *Diogenes* 50, 1 (2003): 27–35.

Bhabha, Homi K. *The Location of Culture*. London: Routledge, 1994.

Blackmon, Douglas. *Slavery by Another Name: The Re-Enslavement of Black Americans from the Civil War to World War II*. New York: Anchor Books, 2008.

Bloch, Nadine. "The Art of #BlackLivesMatter." *Open Democracy* (February 3, 2015). https://www.opendemocracy.net/transformation/nadine-bloch/art-of-blacklivesmatter.

Blumenthal, Max. *The 51 Day War: Ruin and Resistance in Gaza*. New York: Nation Books, 2015.

Blumenthal, Max. "Waiting for the Next Israeli Assault in Gaza." *In These Times* (July 16, 2015). http://inthesetimes.com/article/18208/israel-gaza-max-blumenthal.

Bongie, Chris. *Friends and Enemies: The Scribal Politics of Post/Colonial Literature*. Liverpool: Liverpool University Press, 2008.

Bourdieu, Pierre and Loïc Wacquant, "NewLiberalSpeak: Notes on the Planetary Vulgate." *Radical Philosophy* 105 (2001): 2–5.

Bracey, Glenn E. II, "Toward a Critical Race Theory of State." *Critical Sociology* 41, 3 (2015): 553–72.

Bremer, Paul. "Operation Iraqi Prosperity." *Wall Street Journal* (June 20, 2003). https://www.wsj.com/articles/SB105606663932885100.

Brown, Wendy. *Edgework: Critical Essays on Knowledge and Politics*. Princeton: Princeton University Press, 2005.

Buchanan, Ian. "National Allegory Today: A Return to Jameson." In *On Jameson: From Postmodernism to Globalism*. Ed. Caren Irr and Ian Buchanan. New York: State University of New York Press, 2006: 173–88.

Burris, Greg. "Birth of a 'Zionist' Nation: Black Radicalism and the Future of Palestine." In *Futures of Black Radicalism*. Ed. Gaye Theresa Johnson and Alex Lubin. New York: Verso, 2017: 120–32.

Butler, Judith. "Collected and Fractured: Response to Identities." In *Identities*. Ed. Kwame Anthony Appiah and Henry Louis Gates, Jr. Chicago: University of Chicago Press, 1995: 439–47.

Butler, Judith. "Foreword." In *On Anti-Semitism: Solidarity and the Struggle for Justice*. Chicago: Haymarket Books, 2017: vii–xiii.

Butler, Judith. "Paris the Day after the November 13 Attacks: 'Mourning Becomes the Law.'" *Europe Solidaire Sans Frontières* (November 14, 2015). http://www.europe-solidaire.org/spip. php?article36394.

Butler, Judith. *Parting Ways: Jewishness and the Critique of Zionism*. New York: Columbia University Press, 2012.

Butler, Judith. *Precarious Life: The Powers of Mourning and Violence*. New York: Verso, 2004.

Butler, Judith. "Versions of Binationalism in Said and Buber." In *Conflicting Humanities*. Ed. Rosi Braidotti and Paul Gilroy. New York: Bloomsbury, 2016: 185–210.

Butler, Rex, Ed. *The Žižek Dictionary*. Durham: Acumen, 2014.

Butler, Rex and Scott Stephens. "Play Fuckin' Loud: Žižek Versus the Left." *Symptom* 7 (2007). http://www.lacan.com/symptom7_articles/butler.html.

Caputo, John and Gianni Vattimo. *After the Death of God*. Ed. Jeffrey W. Robbins. New York: Columbia University Press, 2007.

Carmichael, Stokely and Charles Hamilton. *Black Power: The Politics of Liberation in America*. New York: Vintage Books, 1992.

Césaire, Aimé. *A Tempest*. Trans. Richard Miller. New York: TCG Translations, 2002.

Chaouat, Bruno. *Is Theory Good for the Jews? French Thought and the Challenge of the New Antisemitism*. Liverpool: Liverpool University Press, 2016.

Chua, Amy. *Political Tribes: Group Instinct and the Fate of Nations*. New York: Penguin, 2018.

Coates, Ta-Nehisi. *Between the World and Me*. New York: Spiegel and Grau, 2015.

Coates, Ta-Nehisi. *We Were Eight Years in Power: An American Tragedy*. New York: One World, 2017.

Cobb, Jelani. "Trayvon Martin and the Parameters of Hope." *New Yorker* (March 21, 2012). https://www.newyorker.com/news/news-desk/trayvon-martin-and-the-parameters-of-hope.

Copjec, Joan. *Imagine There's No Woman: Ethics and Sublimation*. Cambridge: MIT Press, 2002.

Curry, Tommy J. "Please Don't Make Me Touch 'Em: Towards a Critical Race Fanonianism as a Possible Justification for Violence against Whiteness." In *Democracy, Racism, and Prisons*. Ed. Harry van der Linden. Charlottesville: Philosophy Documentation Center, 2007: 133–58.

Dabashi, Hamid. *Can Non-Europeans Think?* London: Zed Books, 2015.

Darwish, Mahmoud. *Memory for Forgetfulness*. Trans. Ibrahim Muhawi. Berkeley: University of California Press, 1995.

Davis, Angela Y. *Are Prisons Obsolete?* New York: Seven Stories Press, 2003.

Davis, Angela Y. *Freedom Is a Constant Struggle: Ferguson, Palestine, and the Foundations of a Movement*. Chicago: Haymarket Books, 2016.

Davis, Mike. *Planet of Slums*. New York: Verso, 2006.

Dean, Jodi. *Democracy and Other Neoliberal Fantasies*. Durham: Duke University Press, 2009.

Dean, Jodi. *Žižek's Politics*. New York: Routledge, 2006.

Dean, Tim and Christopher Lane. "Homosexuality and Psychoanalysis: An Introduction." In *Homosexuality and Psychoanalysis*. Ed. Tim Dean and Christopher Lane. Chicago: University of Chicago Press, 2001: 3–42.

Delgado, Richard and Jean Stefanic. *Critical Race Theory: An Introduction*. New York: New York University Press, 2017.

Deleuze, Gilles and Elias Sanbar. "The Indians of Palestine." Trans. Timothy S. Murphy. *Discourse* 20, 3 (1998): 25–29.

Derbyshire, Jonathan. "Interview with Slavoj Zizek." *New Statesman* (October 29, 2009). https://www.newstatesman.com/ideas/2009/10/today-interview-capitalism.

Derrida, Jacques. *Aporias*. Trans. Thomas Dutoit. Stanford: Stanford University Press, 1993.

Derrida, Jacques. "Autoimmunity: Real and Symbolic Suicides—A Dialogue with Jacques Derrida." In *Philosophy in a Time of Terror: Dialogues with Jürgen Habermas and Jacques Derrida*. Ed. Giovanna Borradori Chicago: University of Chicago Press, 2004: 85–136.

Derrida, Jacques. "A Europe of Hope." *Epoché* 10, 2 (2006): 407–12.

Derrida, Jacques. "'Eating Well,' or the Calculation of the Subject." Trans. Peter Connor and Avital Ronell. In *Points …: Interviews, 1974–1994*. Ed. Elisabeth Weber. Stanford: Stanford University Press, 1995: 255–87.

Derrida, Jacques. "Faith and Knowledge." In *Acts of Religion*. Ed. Gil Anidjar. New York: Routledge, 2002: 40–101.

Derrida, Jacques. *Negotiations: Interventions and Interviews 1971–2001*. Ed. and trans. Elizabeth Rottenberg. Stanford: Stanford University Press, 2002.

Derrida, Jacques. *Of Hospitality: Anne Dufourmantelle Invites Jacques Derrida to Respond*. Stanford: Stanford University Press, 2000.

Derrida, Jacques. "Racism's Last Word." Trans. Peggy Kamuf, *Critical Inquiry* 12, 1 (1985): 290–9.

Derrida, Jacques. *Rogues: Two Essays on Reason*. Trans. Pascale-Anne Brault and Michael Naas. Stanford: Stanford University Press, 2005.

Derrida, Jacques. "Some Statements and Truisms about Neologisms, Newisms, Postisms, Parasitisms, and Other Small Seismisms." In *The States of "Theory."* Ed. David Carroll. New York: Columbia University Press, 1989: 63–94.

Derrida, Jacques. "Violence and Metaphysics." *Writing and Difference*. Trans. Alan Bass. Chicago: University of Chicago Press, 1978: 31–63.

Dershowitz, Alan. "Black Lives Matter Must Rescind Anti-Israel Declaration." *Boston Globe* (August 12, 2016). https://www.bostonglobe.com/opinion/columns/2016/08/12/black-lives-matter-must-rescind-anti-israel-declaration/EHDYV3gNLwrTTwfp0JA8QN/story.html.

DiAngelo, Robin. *White Fragility: Why It's so Hard for White People to Talk about Racism*. Boston: Beacon Press, 2018.

Eisenstein, Paul and Todd McGowan. *Rupture: On the Emergence of the Political*. Evanston: Northwestern University Press, 2012.

Esposito, Roberto. *Terms of the Political: Community, Immunity, Biopolitics*. New York: Fordham University Press, 2013.

Fanon, Frantz. *Black Skin, White Masks*. Trans. Richard Philcox. New York: Grove Press, 2008.

Fanon, Frantz. *A Dying Colonialism*. Trans. Haakon Chevalier. New York: Grove Press, 1965.

Fanon, Frantz. *Toward the African Revolution*. Trans. Haakon Chevalier. New York: Grove Press, 1967.

Fanon, Frantz. *The Wretched of the Earth*. Trans. Richard Philcox. New York: Grove Press, 2004.

Fareld, Victoria. "*Ressentiment* as Moral Imperative: Jean Améry's Nietzschean Revaluation of Victim Morality." In *Re-thinking Ressentiment: On the Limits of Criticism and the Limits of its Critics*. Ed. Jeanne Riou and Mary Gallagher. Bielefeld: Transcript Verlag, 2016: 53–70.

Feldman, Keith. P. *A Shadow Over Palestine: The Imperial Life of Race in America*. Minneapolis: University of Minnesota Press, 2015.

Finkielkraut, Alain. "Interview: Simon Schama and Alain Finkielkraut Discuss a Perceived Resurgence of Anti-Semitism in the US and Europe." *NPR. All Things Considered* (May 13, 2004). http://www.npr.org/programs/atc/transcripts/2003/may/030513.finkielkraut.html.

Finkielkraut, Alain. *L'identité malheureuse*. Paris: Stock, 2013.

Fischbach, Michael R. *Black Power and Palestine: Transnational Countries of Color*. Stanford: Stanford University Press, 2018.

Fojas, Camilla. *Zombies, Migrants, and Queers: Race and Crisis Capitalism in Pop Culture*. Urbana: University of Illinois Press, 2017.

Freud, Sigmund. *Group Psychology and the Analysis of the Ego*. Trans. James Strachey. New York: Norton, 1959.

Freud, Sigmund. *The Interpretation of Dreams*, in *The Standard Edition of the Complete Psychological Works of Sigmund Freud*. Vol. 4. Ed. James Strachey. London: Hogwarth, 1953–1974.

Gandhi, M. K. *Hind Swaraj and Other Writings*. Ed. Anthony J. Parel. Cambridge: Cambridge University Press, 2009.

Garza, Alicia. "A Herstory of the #BlackLivesMatter Movement." *Feminist Wire* (October 7, 2014). https://thefeministwire.com/2014/10/blacklivesmatter-2.

Genova, Nicholas De. "The 'Migrant Crisis' as Racial Crisis: do *Black Lives Matter* in Europe." *Ethnic and Racial Studies* 41, 10 (2018): 1765–82.

Gill, Karl. "Oppression, Intersectionality and Privilege Theory." *Irish Marxist Review* 3, 9 (2014): 62–8.

Gilroy, Paul. *Against Race: Imagining Political Culture beyond the Color Line*. Cambridge: Harvard University Press, 2000.

Gilroy, Paul. *Darker than Blue: On the Moral Economies of Black Atlantic Culture*. Cambridge: Harvard University Press, 2010.

Giroux, Henry. "The Militarization of Racism and Neoliberal Violence." *Truthout* (August 18, 2014). https://truthout.org/articles/the-militarization-of-racism-and-neoliberal-violence/.

Giroux, Henry. *Stormy Weather: Katrina and the Politics of Disposability*. Boulder: Paradigm, 2006.

Goldberg, David Theo. *Are We All Postracial Yet?* Cambridge: Polity, 2015.

Goldberg, David Theo. *The Threat of Race: Reflections on Racial Neoliberalism*. Malden: Wiley-Blackwell, 2009.

Goldberg, David Theo. "Why 'Black Lives Matter' Because All Lives Don't Matter in America." *Huffington Post* (September 25, 2015). https://www.huffingtonpost.com/david-theo-goldberg/why-black-lives-matter_b_8191424.html.

Gooding-Williams, Robert. "Outlaw, Appiah, and Du Bois's 'The Conservation of Races.'" In *W. E. B. Du Bois: On Race and Culture*. Ed. Bernard R. Bell, Emily R. Grosholz, and James B. Stewart. New York: Routledge, 1996: 39–56.

Gordon, Neve. "The 'New Anti-Semitism.'" *London Review of Books* 40, 1 (January 4, 2018). https://www.lrb.co.uk/v40/n01/neve-gordon/the-new-anti-semitism.

Green, Emma. "Israel's New Law Inflames the Core Tension in Its Identity." *Atlantic* (July 21, 2018). https://www.theatlantic.com/international/archive/2018/07/israel-nation-state-law/565712/.

Greenblatt, Jonathan A. "ADL Statement on Black Lives Matter." *Jewish Week* (July 28, 2016). https://heartland.adl.org/news/adl-statement-on-black-lives-matter.

Haddad, Toufic. *Palestine Ltd.: Neoliberalism and Nationalism in the Occupied Territories*. London: I.B. Tauris, 2016.

Haider, Asad. *Mistaken Identity: Race and Class in the Age of Trump*. New York: Verso, 2018.

Hall, Stuart. "Gramsci's Relevance for the Study of Race and Ethnicity." *Journal of Communication Inquiry* 10, 5 (1986): 5–27.

Hallward, Peter. *Absolutely Postcolonial: Writing Between the Singular and the Specific*. New York: Palgrave, 2001.

Hanson, Jon and Kathleen Hanson. "The Blame Frame: Justifying (Racial) Injustice in America." *Harvard Civil Right—Civil Liberties Review* 41 (2006): 415–80.

Harrington, Thomas S. "Alan Dershowitz's 'Advice' to Black Lives Matter." *Counterpunch* (August 16, 2016). https://www.counterpunch.org/2016/08/16/alan-dershowitzs-advice-to-black-lives-matter/.

Harshaw, Tobin. "Obama's Cover Flap." *New York Times* (July 14, 2008). https://opinionator.blogs.nytimes.com/2008/07/14/obamas-cover-flap/.

Hartman, Saidiya V. *Lose Your Mother: A Journey along the Atlantic Slave Route*. New York: Farrar, Straus and Giroux, 2007.

Hartman, Saidiya V. *Scenes of Subjection: Terror, Slavery, and Self-Making in Nineteenth-Century America*. Oxford: Oxford University Press, 1997.

Hartman, Saidiya and Frank B. Wilderson III. "The Position of the Unthought." *Qui Parle* 13, 2 (2003): 183–201.

Harvey, David. *Seventeen Contradictions and the End of Capitalism*. New York: Oxford University Press, 2014.

Hassan, Zaha. "Still Waiting for a Palestinian Gandhi? S/he's Already Here." *Haaretz* (July 30, 2017). https://www.haaretz.com/opinion/still-waiting-for-a-palestinian-gandhi-s-he-s-already-here-1.5437153.

Hitchcock, Peter. "Revolutionary Violence: A Critique." *symplokē* 20, 1–2 (2012): 9–19.

Hook, Derek. *A Critical Psychology of the Postcolonial: The Mind of Apartheid*. New York: Routledge, 2012.

Irigaray, Luce. *This Sex Which is Not One*. Trans. Catherine Porter. Ithaca: Cornell University Press, 1985.

Jameson, Fredric. "First Impressions." *London Review of Books* 28, 17 (2016). www.lrb.co.uk/v28/n17/fredric-jameson/first-impressions.

Jameson, Fredric. *Postmodernism; Or, the Cultural Logic of Late Capitalism*. Durham: Duke University Press, 1991.

Jameson, Fredric. *Representing Capital: A Reading of Volume One.* New York: Verso, 2011.

Jameson, Fredric. "Third-World Literature in the Era of Multinational Capitalism." *Social Text* 15 (1986): 65–88.

Johnston, Adrian. "Nothing Is Not Always No-One: (A)voiding love." *Filozofski Vestnik* 26, 2 (2005): 67–81.

Johnson-Huston, Nikki. "The Culture of the Smug White Liberal." *Huffington Post Online* (August 17, 2016). https://www.huffingtonpost.com/nikki-johnsonhuston-esq/the-culture-of-the-smug-w_b_11537306.html.

Kamiya, Gary. "Rush Limbaugh Was Right." *Salon* (July 15, 2008). https://www.salon.com/2008/07/15/new_yorker_cartoon/.

Kant, Immanuel. "An Answer to the Question: What Is Enlightenment?" In *What Is Enlightenment? Eighteenth-Century Answers and Twentieth-Century Questions.* Ed. James Schmidt. Berkeley: University of California Press, 1996: 58–64.

Kapoor, Ilan. *Celebrity Humanitarianism: The Ideology of Global Charity.* New York: Routledge, 2013.

Kapoor, Ilan. "Žižek, Antagonism and Politics Now: Three Recent Controversies." *International Journal of Žižek Studies* 12, 1 (2018): 1–31.

Kelley, Robin D. G. "The U.S. v. Trayvon Martin: How the System Worked." *Huffington Post Online* (July 15, 2013). https://www.huffingtonpost.com/robin-d-g-kelley/nra-stand-your-ground-trayvon-martin_b_3599843.html.

Kelley, Robin D. G. "Yes, I Said, 'National Liberation.'" In *Letters to Palestine: Writers Respond to War and Occupation.* Ed. Vijay Prashad. New York: Verso, 2015: 139–53.

Kerwick, Jack. "Trayvon Martin: A Child, or a Thug Wannabe?" *New American* (July 15, 2013). https://www.thenewamerican.com/reviews/opinion/item/15986-trayvon-martin-a-child-or-a-thug-wannabe.

Khader, Jamil. "Class Struggle for the 21st Century: Racial Inequality, International Solidarity, and the New Apartheid Politics." *Journal of World-Systems Research* 23, 2 (2017): 474–98.

Khader, Jamil. "Concrete Universality and the End of Revolutionary Politics: A Žižekian Approach to Postcolonial Women's Writings." In *Everything You Always Wanted to Know about Literature but Were Afraid to Ask Žižek.* Ed. Russell Sbriglia. Durham: Duke University Press, 2017: 137–68.

Khader, Jamil. "The Living Dead in Palestine and the Failure of International Humanitarian Intervention." *Truthout* (November 8, 2015). https://truthout.org/articles/the-living-dead-in-palestine-and-the-failure-of-international-humanitarian-intervention/.

Khalek, Rania. "Black Activists Slam Israel Lobby Attack on Movement for Black Lives." *Electronic Intifada* (August 6, 2016). https://electronicintifada.net/blogs/rania-khalek/black-activists-slam-israel-lobby-attack-movement-black-lives.

Khan-Cullors, Patrisse and Asha Bandele. *When They Call You a Terrorist: A Black Lives Matter Memoir.* New York: St. Martin's Press, 2018.

Kidron, Peretz. *Refusenik!: Israel's Soldiers of Conscience.* New York: Zed Books, 2004.

Kimmel, Michael and Abby Ferber, eds. *Privilege: A Reader.* Boulder: Westview Press, 2010.

Kornbluh, Anna. "Romancing the Capital: Choice, Love, and Contradiction in *The Family Man* and *Memento*." In *Lacan and Contemporary Film*. Ed. Todd McGowan and Sheila Kunkle. New York: Other Press, 2004: 111–44.

Kriss, Sam. "Building Norway: A Critique of Slavoj Žižek." *Idiot Joy Showland* (September 11, 2015). https://samkriss.com/2015/09/11/building-norway-a-critique-of-slavoj-zizek/.

Lacan, Jacques. *Anxiety: The Seminar of Jacques Lacan. Book X*. Ed. Jacques-Alain Miller. Cambridge: Polity, 2014.

Lacan, Jacques. *On Feminine Sexuality, the Limits of Love and Knowledge, 1972–1973: Encore, the Seminar of Jacques Lacan, Book XX*. Trans. Bruce Fink. New York: Norton, 1998.

Lacan, Jacques. "The Signification of the Phallus." In *Écrits: The First Complete Edition in English*. Trans. Bruce Fink. New York: Norton, 2006: 575–84.

LaCapra, Dominick. *History and Its Limits: Human, Animal, Violence*. Ithaca: Cornell University Press, 2009.

Laclau, Ernesto. "Constructing Universality." In *Contingency, Hegemony, Universality*. Ed. Judith Butler, Ernesto Laclau, and Slavoj Žižek. New York: Verso, 2000: 281–307.

Landes, Richard and Benjamin Weinthal. "The Post-Self-Destructivism of Judith Butler." *Wall Street Journal* (September 9, 2012).

Lentin, Ronit. *Traces of Racial Exception: Racializing Israeli Settler Colonialism*. New York: Bloomsbury, 2018.

Levinas, Emmanuel. *Difficult Freedom: Essays on Judaism*. Trans. Seán Hand. Baltimore: Johns Hopkins University Press, 1990.

Levinas, Emmanuel. *Entre Nous: On Thinking-of-the Other*. Trans. Michael B. Smith and Barbara Harshav. New York: Columbia University Press, 1998.

Levinas, Emmanuel. *Ethics and Infinity: Conversations with Philippe Nemo*. Trans. Richard A. Cohen. Pittsburgh: Duquesne University Press, 1985.

Levinas, Emmanuel. "Ethics and Politics." In *The Levinas Reader*. Ed. Seán Hand. Oxford: Blackwell, 1989: 289–97.

Levinas, Emmanuel. "The *I* and the Totality." In *Entre Nous: Thinking of the Other*. Trans. Michael B. Smith and Barbara Harshav. New York: Columbia University Press, 1998: 13–38.

Levinas, Emmanuel. *Otherwise Than Being, or, Beyond Essence*. Trans. Alphonso Lingis. The Hague: Martinus Nijhoff, 1981.

Levinas, Emmanuel. *Totality and Infinity: An Essay on Exteriority*. Trans. Alphonso Lingis. Pittsburgh: Duquesne University Press, 1969.

Levinas, Emmanuel. "The Trace of the Other." In *Deconstruction in Context: Literature and Philosophy*. Ed. Mark C. Taylor. Trans. Alphonso Lingis. Chicago: University of Chicago Press, 1986: 345–69.

Levinas, Emmanuel. "Zionisms." In *The Levinas Reader*. Ed. Seán Hand. Oxford: Blackwell, 1989: 268–88.

Lévy, Bernard-Henri. *Left in Dark Times: A Stand Against the New Barbarism*. New York: Random House, 2008.

Loumansky, Amanda. "Israel and the Palestinians: The Challenge to Levinasian Ethics." *SCTIW Review: Journal of the Society for Contemporary Thought*

*of the Islamicate World* (February 21, 2019). https://sctiw.org/wp-content/
uploads/2019/02/175-Continental-Philosophy-and-the-Palestinian-Question-
Amanda-Loumansky.pdf.

Lynch, Michael P. "Fake News and the Internet Shell Game." *New York Times*
(November 28, 2016). https://www.nytimes.com/2016/11/28/opinion/fake-news-
and-the-internet-shell-game.html.

Makdisi, Saree. *Palestine Inside Out: An Everyday Occupation*. New York:
Norton, 2008.

Malaklou, M. Shadee. "DAPL and the Matter/ing of Black Life." *Feminist
Wire* (November 30, 2016). https://thefeministwire.com/2016/11/
dapl-mattering-black-life/.

Malcolm, X. "Message to the Grassroots" (1963). http://www.blackpast.
org/1963-malcolm-x-message-grassroots.

Marcuse, Herbert. "The End of Utopia." In *Marxism, Revolution, and Utopia:
Collected Papers*. Vol. 6. Ed. Douglas Kellner and Clayton Pierce. New York:
Routledge, 2014: 249–63.

Marcuse, Herbert. *Eros and Civilization: A Philosophical Inquiry into Freud*. Boston:
Beacon Press, 1955.

Marcuse, Herbert. *Five Lectures: Psychoanalysis, Politics and Utopia*. London: Allen
Lane, 1970.

Marcuse, Herbert. *One-Dimensional Man: Studies in the Ideology of Advanced
Industrial Society*. Boston: Beacon Press, 1964.

Marcuse, Herbert. A Revolution in Values." In *Towards a Critical Theory of
Society: Collected Papers*. Vol. 2. Ed. Douglas Kellner. New York: Routledge,
2014: 193–201.

Marx, Karl. *Capital: A Critique of Political Economy*. Vol. 1. Trans. Ben Fowkes.
New York: Penguin Books, 1976.

Marx, Karl. "Letters from the *Deutsch-Französische Jahrbucher*." In *Collected Works of
Marx and Engels*. Vol. 3. New York: International Publishers, 1975: 133–45.

Martel, James R. *The Misinterpellated Subject*. Durham: Duke University
Press, 2017.

Mason, Victoria and Richard Falk. "Assessing Nonviolence in the Palestinian Rights
Struggle." *State Crime Journal* 5, 1 (2016): 163–86.

Mbembe, Achille. "Conversation: Achille Mbembe and David Theo Goldberg on
*Critique of Black Reason*." *Theory, Culture, and Society* (July 3, 2018). https://
www.theoryculturesociety.org/conversation-achille-mbembe-and-david-theo-
goldberg-on-critique-of-black-reason/.

Mbembe, Achille. *Critique of Black Reason*. Trans. Laurent Dubois. Durham: Duke
University Press, 2017.

Mbembe, Achille. "Necropolitics." Trans. Libby Meintjes. *Public Culture* 15, 1
(2003): 11–40.

Mbembe, Achille. "Nicolas Sarkozy's Africa." Trans. Melissa Thackway. *Africultures*
(August 7, 2007). http://africultures.com/nicolas-sarkozys-africa-6816/.

Mbembe, Achille. "Raceless Futures in Critical Black Thought." *Archives of the
Nonracial* (June 30, 2014). https://www.youtube.com/watch?v=VkqmAi1yEpo.

McCann, Bryan J. "On Whose Ground? Racialized Violence and the Prerogative of 'Self-Defense' in the Trayvon Martin Case." *Western Journal of Communication* 78, 4 (2014): 480–99.

McIntosh, Peggy. "White Privilege and Male Privilege: A Personal Account of Coming to See Correspondences through Work in Women's Studies." In *Race, Class, and Gender.* Ed. Margaret L. Andersen and Patricia Hill Collins. Belmont: Wadsworth, 2001: 95–105.

Medina, José. "Varieties of Hermeneutical Injustice." In *The Routledge Handbook of Epistemic Injustice.* Ed. Ian James Kidd, José Medina and Gaile Pohlhaus. New York: Routledge, 2017: 41–52.

Mignolo, Walter D. *The Darker Side of Western Modernity: Global Futures, Decolonial Options.* Durham: Duke University Press, 2011.

Mignolo, Walter D. "The Decolonial Option and the Meaning of Identity in Politics." *Anales Nueva Época* 9, 10 (2007): 43–72.

Mignolo, Walter D. "Decolonizing the Nation-State: Zionism in the Colonial Horizon of Modernity." In *Deconstructing Zionism: A Critique of Political Metaphysics.* Ed. Gianni Vattimo and Michael Marder. New York: Bloomsbury, 2013: 57–74.

Mignolo, Walter D. "I Am Where I Think: Remapping the Order of Knowing." In *The Creolization of Theory.* Ed. Françoise Lionnet and Shu-mei Shi. Durham: Duke University Press, 2011: 159–92.

Mignolo, Walter D. *Local Histories/Global Designs: Coloniality, Subaltern Knowledges, and Border Thinking.* Princeton: Princeton University Press, 2000.

Mignolo, Walter D. "Yes, We Can: Non-European Thinkers and Philosophers" (February 19, 2013). http://www.aljazeera.com/indepth/opin ion/2013/02/20132672747320891.html.

Mills, Charles W. *Black Rights/White Wrongs: The Critique of Racial Liberalism.* Oxford: Oxford University Press, 2017.

Mills, Charles W. *The Racial Contract.* Ithaca: Cornell University Press, 1997.

Mishani, Dror and Aurelia Smotriez, "What Sort of Frenchmen are They? Interview with Alain Finkielkraut." *Haaretz* (November 17, 2005). https://www.haaretz.com/1.4882406.

Morgan, Michael L. *The Cambridge Introduction to Emmanuel Levinas.* Cambridge: Cambridge University Press, 2011.

Muñoz, José Esteban. *Disidentifications: Queers of Color and the Performance of Politics.* Minneapolis: University of Minnesota Press, 1999.

Nayman, Louis. "Whither Žižek?: On Zionism and Jews." *In These Times* (March 18, 2015). http://inthesetimes.com/article/17745/whither-zizek-on-zionism-and-jews.

Nesbitt, Nick. *Caribbean Critique: Antillean Critical Theory from Toussaint to Glissant.* Liverpool: Liverpool University Press, 2013.

Nietzsche, Friedrich. *On the Genealogy of Morals.* Trans. Walter Kaufmann. New York: Vintage, 1989.

Noble, Safiya Umoja. "Teaching Trayvon: Race, Media, and the Politics of Spectacle." *Black Scholar* 44, 1 (2014): 12–29.

Oliver, Kelly. *Carceral Humanitarianism: Logics of Refugee Detention.*
Minneapolis: University of Minnesota Press, 2017.

Pappé, Ilan. *The Ethnic Cleansing of Palestine.* Oxford: Oneworld, 2006.

Pappé, Ilan. "The Inevitable War on Terror: De-terrorising the Palestinians." In *States of War Since 9/11 Terrorism, Sovereignty and the War on Terror.* Ed. Alex Houen. New York: Routledge, 2014: 84–102.

Pappé, Ilan. "The Old and New Conservations." In Noam Chomsky and Ilan Pappé, *On Palestine.* Ed. Frank Barat. Chicago: Haymarket Books, 2015: 9–46.

Pappé, Ilan. *Ten Myths about Israel.* New York: Verso, 2017.

Pappé, Ilan. "Zionism as Colonialism: A Comparative View of Diluted Colonialism in Asia and Africa." *South Atlantic Quarterly* 107, 4 (2008): 611–33.

Patterson, Orlando. *Slavery and Social Death: A Comparative Study.* Cambridge: Harvard University Press, 1982.

Penney, James. "Passing into the Universal: Fanon, Sartre, and the Colonial Dialectic." *Paragraph* 27, 3 (2004): 49–67.

Puar, Jasbir. *The Right to Maim: Debility, Capacity, Disability.* Durham: Duke University Press, 2017.

Puar, Jasbir. *Terrorist Assemblages: Homonationalism in Queer Times.* Durham: Duke University Press, 2007.

Rabbani, Mouin. "Israel Mows the Lawn." *London Review of Books* (July 31, 2014). https://www.lrb.co.uk/v36/n15/mouin-rabbani/israel-mows-the-lawn.

Radhakrishnan, R. "Poststructuralist Politics: Towards a Theory of Coalition." In *Postmodernism/Jameson/Critique.* Washington: Maisonneuve Press, 1989: 301–32.

Ramdani, Nabila. "It's Not Surprising That Fuel Protests in Paris Turned Violent— The French Establishment Has Long Ignored Social Inequality." *Independent* (November 25, 2018). https://www.independent.co.uk/voices/paris-protests-fuel-tax-france-police-emmanuel-macron-yellow-vests-immigrants-a8650901.html.

Rancière, Jacques. *Disagreement: Politics and Philosophy.* Trans. J. Rose. Minneapolis: University of Minnesota Press, 1999.

Rancière, Jacques. *The Emancipated Spectator.* Trans. G. Elliott. New York, Verso, 2009.

Rancière, Jacques. *The Politics of Aesthetics: Distribution of the Sensible.* Trans. G. Rockhill. New York, Continuum, 2004.

Rankine, Claudia. *Citizen: An American Lyric.* Minneapolis: Graywolf, 2014.

Rasmussen, Eric Dean. "Liberation Hurts: An Interview with Slavoj Žižek." *Electronic Book Review* (2004). http://www.electronicbookreview.com/thread/endconstruction/desublimation.

Ravid, Barak, Avi Issacharoff and Jack Khoury. "Israel, Hamas Reach Gilad Shalit Prisoner Exchange Deal, Officials Say." *Haaretz* (October 11, 2011). http://www.haaretz.com/israel-news/israel-hamas-reach-gilad-shalit-prisoner-exchange-deal-officials-say-1.389404.

Rawls, John. *A Theory of Justice.* Cambridge: The Belknap Press of Harvard University Press, 1971.

Reul, Sabine and Thomas Deichmann. "The One Measure of True Love Is: You Can Insult the Other." *Spiked* (November 15, 2001). http://www.spiked-online.com/newsite/article/10816#.W0VMLxD3N54.

"Richard Spencer Tells Israelis They 'Should Respect' Him: 'I'm a White Zionist.'" *Haaretz* (August 16, 2017). https://www.haaretz.com/israel-news/richard-spencer-to-israelis-i-m-a-white-zionist-respect-me-1.5443480.

Riemer, Nick. "How to Justify a Crisis." *Jacobin* (October 5, 2015). https://www.jacobinmag.com/2015/10/refugee-crisis-europe-zizek-habermas-singer-greece-syria-academia/.

R. L. "Wanderings of the Slave: Black Life and Social Death." *Mute* (June 5, 2013). http://www.metamute.org/editorial/articles/wanderings-slave-black-life-and-social-death.

Robinson, Cedric J. *Black Marxism: The Making of the Black Radical Tradition.* Chapel Hill: University of North Carolina Press, 2000.

Robinson, Cedric and Elizabeth Robinson. "Ferguson, Gaza, Iraq: An Outline on the Official Narrative in 'Post-Racial' America." *Commonware* (September 4, 2013). https://www.commonware.org/index.php/cartografia/452-ferguson-gaza-iraq-outline.

Rose, Jacqueline. *The Question of Zion.* Princeton: Princeton University Press, 2005.

Rovner, Adam. *In the Shadow of Zion: Promised Lands before Israel.* New York: New York University Press, 2014.

Ryan, Josiah. "'This Was a Whitelash': Van Jones' Take on the Election Results." *CNN* (November 9, 2016). https://www.cnn.com/2016/11/09/politics/van-jones-results-disappointment-cnntv/index.html.

Said, Edward W. *Culture and Imperialism.* New York: Vintage, 1994.

Said, Edward W. "An Ideology of Difference." *Critical Inquiry* 12, 1 (1985): 38–58.

Said, Edward W. *The Politics of Dispossession: The Struggle for Palestinian Self-Determination 1969–1994.* New York: Vintage, 1994.

Said, Edward W. *The Question of Palestine.* New York: Vintage Books, 1992.

Said, Edward W. *Representations of the Intellectual.* New York: Vintage, 1996.

Said, Edward W. "My Right of Return." In *Power, Politics, and Culture: Interviews with Edward W. Said.* Ed. Gauri Viswanathan. New York: Vintage, 2001: 443–58.

Said, Edward W. *The World, the Text and the Critic.* Cambridge: Harvard University Press, 1983.

Salamanca, Omar Jabary, et al. Eds. "Past Is Present: Settler Colonialism in Palestine." *Settler Colonial Studies* 2, 1 (2012): 1–8.

Sartre, Jean-Paul, "Black Orpheus," in *What is Literature? And Other Essays.* Trans. John McCombie. Cambridge: Harvard University Press, 1988: 289–330.

Sartre, Jean-Paul, "Preface." In *The Wretched of the Earth.* Trans. Richard Philcox. New York: Grove Press, 2004. xliii–lxii.

Senghor, Léopold Sédar. "De la négritude." In *Liberté V: Le Dialogue des cultures.* Paris: Seuil, 1993: 14–26.

Sexton, Jared. *Amalgamation Schemes: Antiblackness and the Critique of Multiracialism.* Minneapolis: University of Minnesota Press, 2008.

Sexton, Jared. "People-of-Color-Blindness: Notes on the Afterlife of Slavery." *Social Text* 28, 2 103 (2010): 31–56.

Sexton, Jared. "Proprieties of Coalition: Blacks, Asians, and the Politics of Policing." *Critical Sociology* 36, 1 (2010): 87–108.

Sexton, Jared. "The Social Life of Social Death: On Afro-Pessimism and Black Optimism." *In Tensions* 5 (2011): 1–47.

Sexton, Jared. "Unbearable Blackness." *Cultural Critique* 90 (2015): 159–78.

Simek, Nicole. "The Criticism of Postcolonial Critique." In *Criticism after Critique: Aesthetics, Literature, and the Political.* Ed. Jeffrey R. Di Leo. New York: Palgrave, 2014: 113–26.

Singh, Nikhil Pal. "On Race, Violence, and 'So-Called Primitive Accumulation.'" In *Futures of Black Radicalism.* Ed. Gaye Theresa Johnson and Alex Lubin. New York: Verso, 2017: 39–58.

Skinner, Jordan. "Thought is the Courage of Hopelessness: An Interview with Philosopher Giorgio Agamben." Interview by Jordan Skinner. Verso Books (June 17, 2014). https://www.versobooks.com/blogs/1612-thought-is-the-courage-of-hopelessness-an-interview-with-philosopher-giorgio-agamben.

Smallwood, Stephanie. *Saltwater Slavery: A Middle Passage from Africa to American Diaspora.* Cambridge: Harvard University Press, 2007.

Smith, Andrea. "Unsettling the Privilege of Self-Reflexivity." In *Geographies of Privilege.* Ed. France Winddance Twine and Bradley Gardener. New York: Routledge, 2013: 263–79.

Soske, Jon and Sean Jacobs, eds. *Apartheid Israel: The Politics of an Analogy.* Chicago: Haymarket Books, 2015.

Speri, Alice. "Israel Security Forces Are Training American Cops Despite History of Rights Abuses." *Intercept* (September 15, 2017). https://theintercept.com/2017/09/15/police-israel-cops-training-adl-human-rights-abuses-dc-washington/.

Spillers, Hortense J. "Mama's Baby, Papa's Maybe: An American Grammar Book." *Diacritics* 17, 2 (1987): 64–81.

Spivak, Gayatri Chakravorty. *Critique of Postcolonial Reason: Toward a History of the Vanishing Present.* Cambridge: Harvard University Press, 1999.

Spivak, Gayatri Chakravorty. *The Post-Colonial Critic: Interviews, Strategies, Dialogues.* Ed. Sarah Harasym. New York: Routledge, 1990.

Stam, Robert and Ella Shohat, *Race in Translation: Culture Wars around the Postcolonial Atlantic.* New York: New York University Press, 2012.

Stangler, Cole. "What's Really Behind France's Yellow Vest Protest? It's Not Just about the Fuel Tax; It's about Anger at Ever-Increasing Burdens on the Working Class." *Nation* (December 7, 2018). https://www.thenation.com/article/france-yellow-vest-protest-macron/.

Strickland, Patrick. "Bombing of Gaza Children Gives Me 'Orgasm': Israelis Celebrate Slaughter on Facebook." *Electronic Intifada* (July 13, 2014). https://electronicintifada.net/blogs/patrick-strickland/bombing-gaza-children-gives-me-orgasm-israelis-celebrate-slaughter-facebook.

Szeman, Imre. "Who's Afraid of National Allegory? Jameson, Literary Criticism, Globalization." In *On Jameson: From Postmodernism to Globalism.* Ed. Caren Irr and Ian Buchanan. New York: State University of New York Press, 2006: 189–211.

Taguieff, Pierre-André. *Rising from the Muck: The New Anti-Semitism in Europe.* Trans. Patrick Camiller. Chicago: Ivan R. Dee, 2004.

Tally, Robert T. *Utopia in the Age of Globalization: Space, Representation, and the World-System*. New York: Palgrave Macmillan, 2013.

Tamari, Salim. "The Dubious Lure of Binationalism." *Journal of Palestine Studies* 30, 1 (2000): 83–87.

Tannous, Nadya Raja. "Palestinians Join Standing Rock Sioux to Protest Dakota Access Pipeline." *Mondoweiss* (October 24, 2016). http://mondoweiss. net/2016/10/palestinians-standing-pipeline/. Accessed September 26, 2018.

Taylor, Keeanga-Yamahtta. *From #BlackLivesMatter to Black Liberation*. Chicago: Haymarket Books, 2016.

Taylor, Paul A. *Žižek and the Media*. Cambridge: Polity, 2010.

Terkel, Amanda. "Black Lives Matter Disavows Democratic Party's Show of Support." *Huffington Post* (August 31, 2015). https://www.huffingtonpost.com/entry/ black-lives-matter-dnc_us_55e48104e4b0c818f6188cab.

Tobin, Jonathan S. "Democrats Reach a Tipping Point on Israel." *National Review* (May 18, 2018). https://www.nationalreview.com/2018/05/democrats-israel-tipping-point/. Accessed September 26, 2018.

Vattimo, Gianni and Michael Marder. "Introduction: 'If Not Now, When?'" In *Deconstructing Zionism: A Critique of Political Metaphysics*. Ed. Gianni Vattimo and Michael Marder. New York: Bloomsbury, 2013: ix–xvii.

Veracini, Lorenzo. *Israel and Settler Society*. London: Pluto Press, 2006.

Wacquant, Loïc. "From Slavery to Mass Incarceration: Rethinking the 'Race Question in the US." *New Left Review* 13 (2002): 41–60.

Warren, Calvin L. "Black Nihilism and the Politics of Hope." *CR: The New Centennial Review* 15, 1 (2015): 215–48.

Warren, Calvin L. "Black Time: Slavery, Metaphysics, and the Logic of Wellness." In *The Psychic Hold of Slavery: Legacies in American Expressive Culture*. Ed. Soyica Diggs Colbert, Robert J. Patterson, and Aida Levy-Hussen. New Brunswick: Rutgers University Press, 2016: 55–68.

Weheliye, Alexander G. *Habeas Viscus: Racializing Assemblages, Biopolitics, and Black Feminist Theories of the Human*. Durham: Duke University Press, 2014.

Wilderson, Frank B. III. "Afro-Pessimism and the End of Redemption." *Humanities Futures. Franklin Humanities Institute: Duke University* (October 20, 2015). https://humanitiesfutures.org/papers/afro-pessimism-end-redemption/.

Wilderson, Frank B. III. "The Black Liberation Army and the Paradox of Political Engagement." In *Postcoloniality-Decoloniality-Black Critique: Joints and Fissures*. Ed. Sabine Broeck and Carsten Junker. Frankfurt: Campus Verlag, 2014: 175–210.

Wilderson, Frank B. III. "Gramsci's Black Marx: Whither the Slave in Civil Society?" *Social Identities* 9, 2 (2003): 225–40.

Wilderson, Frank B. III. "Irreconcilable Anti-Blackness and Police Violence." *IMIXWHATILIKE!* (October 1, 2014). http://imixwhatilike.org/2014/10/01/frank wildersonandantiblackness-2/.

Wilderson, Frank B. III. "The Prison Slave as Hegemony's (Silent) Scandal." *Social Justice* 30, 2 (2003): 18–27.

Wilderson, Frank B. III. *Red, White, and Black: Cinema and the Structure of U.S. Antagonisms*. Durham: Duke University Press, 2010.

Wilderson, Frank B. III. "Reparations...Now." https://vimeo.com/73991006.

Wilderson, Frank B. III. "Wallowing in the Contradictions, Part 2 with Percy Howard" (July 14, 2010). https://percy3.wordpress.com/2010/07/14/ frank-wilderson-wallowing-in-the-contradictions-part-2/.

Wilderson, Frank B. III, Saidya Hartman, Steve Martinot, Jared Sexton, Hortenese J. Spillers. "Editors' Introduction." In *Afro-Pessimism: An Introduction*. Ed. Frank B. Wilderson III, Saidya Hartman, Steve Martinot, Jared Sexton, Hortenese J. Spillers. Minneapolis: Racked & Dispatched, 2017: 7–13.

Williams, Patricia J. "The Monsterization of Trayvon Martin." *Nation* (July 31, 2013). https://www.thenation.com/article/monsterization-trayvon-martin/.

Winnubst, Shannon. *Way Too Cool: Selling Out Race and Ethics*. New York: Columbian University Press, 2015.

Wolfe, Patrick. "Settler Colonialism and the Elimination of the Native." *Journal of Genocide Research* 8 (2006): 387–409.

Wulfhorst, Ellen, Daniel Wallis, Edward McAllister. "More than 400 Arrested as Ferguson Protests Spread to Other U.S. Cities." *Reuters* (November 25, 2014). https://www.reuters.com/article/us-usa-missouri-shooting/ more-than-400-arrested-as-ferguson-protests-spread-to-other-u-s-cities-idUSKCN0J80PR20141126.

Yancy, George. *Black Bodies, White Gazes: The Continuing Significance of Race in America*. Lanham: Rowman & Littlefield, 2008.

Yancy, George and Judith Butler. "What's Wrong with 'All Lives Matter'?" *New York Times* (January 12, 2015). http://opinionator.blogs.nytimes.com/2015/01/12/ whats-wrong-with-all-lives-matter/.

Yancy, George and Paul Gilroy. "What 'Black Lives' Means in Britain." *New York Times* (October 2015). https://opinionator.blogs.nytimes.com/2015/10/01/ paul-gilroy-what-black-means-in-britain/.

Yiftachel, Oren. "Call Apartheid in Israel by Its Name." *Haaretz* (February 11, 2016). https://www.haaretz.com/opinion/. premium-call-apartheid-in-israel-by-its-name-1.5402831.

Zalloua, Zahi. *Continental Philosophy and the Palestinian Question: Beyond the Jew and the Greek*. New York: Bloomsbury, 2017.

Zalloua, Zahi. *Theory's Autoimmunity: Skepticism, Literature, and Philosophy*. Evanston: Northwestern University Press, 2018.

Žižek, Slavoj. *Absolute Recoil: Towards a New Foundation of Dialectical Materialism*. New York: Verso, 2014.

Žižek, Slavoj. "Actual Politics." *Theory & Event* 14, 4 (2011).

Žižek, Slavoj. "Afterword: Lenin's Choice." In V. I. Lenin, *Revolution at the Gates: Selected Writings of Lenin from 1917*. Ed. Slavoj Žižek. New York: Verso, 2002: 165–336.

Žižek, Slavoj. "Afterword: With Defenders Like These, Who Needs Attackers?" In *The Truth of Žižek*. Ed. Paul Bowman and Richard Stamp. New York: Continuum, 2007: 197–255.

Žižek, Slavoj. *Against the Double Blackmail: Refugees, Terror and Other Troubles with the Neighbors*. London: Penguin Random House, 2016.

Žižek, Slavoj. "Anti-Semitism and Its Transformations." In *Deconstructing Zionism: A Critique of Political Metaphysics*. Ed. Gianni Vattimo and Michael Marder. New York: Bloomsbury, 2013: 1–13.

Žižek, Slavoj. "Are We in a War? Do We Have an Enemy?" *London Review of Books* 24, 10 (May 23, 2002). https://www.lrb.co.uk/v24/n10/slavoj-zizek/are-we-in-a-war-do-we-have-an-enemy.

Žižek, Slavoj. "The Audacity of Rhetoric." *In These Times* (September 2, 2008). http://inthesetimes.com/article/3862/the_audacity_of_rhetoric/.

Žižek, Slavoj. "Avatar: Return of the Natives." *New Statesman* (March 4, 2010). https://www.newstatesman.com/film/2010/03/avatar-reality-love-couple-sex.

Žižek, Slavoj. "Beyond Discourse Analysis." In *Interrogating the Real*. Ed. Butler Rex and Scott Stephens. London: Continuum, 2005: 271–84.

Žižek, Slavoj. "Class Struggle or Postmodernism? Yes, Please!" In *Contingency, Hegemony, Universality: Contemporary Dialogues on the Left*. Ed. Judith Butler, Ernesto Laclau, and Slavoj Žižek. New York: Verso, 2000: 90–135.

Žižek, Slavoj. "Confessions of an Unrepentant Leninist." *International Journal of Žižek Studies* (2008). http://www.lacan.com/zizbomarz.html.

Žižek, Slavoj. *The Courage of Hopelessness: Chronicles of a Year of Acting Dangerously*. New York: Allen Lane, 2017.

Žižek, Slavoj. "*Da Capo senza Fine*." In *Contingency, Hegemony, Universality: Contemporary Dialogues on the Left*. Ed. Judith Butler, Ernesto Laclau, and Slavoj Žižek. New York: Verso, 2000: 213–62.

Žižek, Slavoj. *In Defense of Lost Causes*. New York: Verso, 2008.

Žižek, Slavoj. *Demanding the Impossible*. Ed. Yong-June Park. Cambridge: Polity, 2013.

Žižek, Slavoj. *Did Somebody Say Totalitarian? Five Interventions in the (Mis)use of a Notion*. New York: Verso, 2001.

Žižek, Slavoj. *Disparities*. New York: Bloomsbury, 2016.

Žižek, Slavoj. "Disputations: Who Are You Calling Anti-Semitic?" *New Republic* (January 6, 2009). https://newrepublic.com/article/62376/disputations-who-are-you-calling-anti-semitic.

Žižek, Slavoj. "Divine Violence and Liberated Territories: SOFT TARGETS talks with Slavoj Žižek." *Soft Targets* (March 14, 2007). http://www.softtargetsjournal.com/web/zizek.php.

Žižek, Slavoj. "Divine Violence in Ferguson." *European* (March 9, 2015). https://www.theeuropean-magazine.com/slavoj-zizek/9774-slavoj-zizek-on-ferguson-and-violence.

Žižek, Slavoj. *Enjoy Your Symptom!: Jacques Lacan in Hollywood and Out*. New York: Routledge, 1992.

Žižek, Slavoj. "Entretien avec Slavoj Zizek—Le nouveau philosophe." *Le Nouvel Observateur* (November 11, 2004). http://www.lacan.com/nouvob.htm.

Žižek, Slavoj. *Event: Philosophy in Transit*. London: Penguin Books, 2014.

Žižek, Slavoj. "The Fear of Four Words: A Modest Plea for the Hegelian Reading of Christianity." In Slavoj Žižek and John Milbank, *The Monstrosity of Christ: Paradox or Dialectic?* Ed. Creston Davis. Cambridge: The MIT Press, 2009: 24–109.

Žižek, Slavoj. *First as Tragedy, Then as Farce*. New York: Verso, 2009.

Žižek, Slavoj. *For They Know Not What They Do*. New York: Verso, 1991.

Žižek, Slavoj. *The Fragile Absolute; or, Why Is the Christian Legacy Worth Fighting for?* New York: Verso, 2000.

Žižek, Slavoj. "Happiness? No, Thanks!" *The Philosophical Salon* (April 2, 2018). https://thephilosophicalsalon.com/happiness-no-thanks/.

Žižek, Slavoj. "Holding the Place." In *Contingency, Hegemony and Universality: Contemporary Dialogues on the Left.* Ed. Judith Butler, Ernesto Laclau, and Slavoj Žižek. New York: Verso, 2000: 308–29.

Žižek, Slavoj. "How to Begin from the Beginning." *New Left Review* 57 (2009): 43–55.

Žižek, Slavoj. *How to Read Lacan.* New York: Norton, 2006.

Žižek, Slavoj. "Human Rights and Its Discontents." Lecture at Bard College (November 15, 1999). http://www.lacan.com/zizek-human.htm.

Žižek, Slavoj. "A Leftist Plea for 'Eurocentrism.'" *Critical Inquiry* 24, 4 (1998): 988–1009.

Žižek, Slavoj. "Learn to Live Without Masters." *Naked Punch* (October 3, 2009). http://www.nakedpunch.com/articles/34.

Žižek, Slavoj. *Less than Nothing: Hegel and the Shadow of Dialectical Materialism.* New York: Verso, 2012.

Žižek, Slavoj. "Liberal Multiculturalism Masks an Old Barbarism with a Human Face." *Guardian* (October 3, 2010). https://www.theguardian.com/commentisfree/2010/oct/03/immigration-policy-roma-rightwing-europe.

Žižek, Slavoj. *Like a Thief in Broad Daylight: Power in the Era of Post-Humanity.* New York: Allen Lane, 2018.

Žižek, Slavoj. *Living in the End Times.* New York: Verso, 2010.

Žižek, Slavoj. *Looking Awry: An Introduction to Jacques Lacan through Popular Culture.* Cambridge: MIT Press, 1992.

Žižek, Slavoj. "Love Thy Neighbor? No, Thanks!" In *The Psychoanalysis of Race.* Ed. Christopher Lane. New York: Columbia University Press, 1998: 154–75.

Žižek, Slavoj. *The Metastases of Enjoyment: Six Essays on Women and Causality.* New York: Verso, 1994.

Žižek, Slavoj. "Migrants, Racists and the Left." *Spike Review* (May 2016). http://www.spiked-online.com/spiked-review/article/migrants-racists-and-the-left/18395#.W0jv1RD3N54.

Žižek, Slavoj. "Multiculturalism, or, the Cultural Logic of Multinational Capitalism." *New Left Review* 225 (1997): 28–51.

Žižek, Slavoj. "Multitude, Surplus, and Envy." *Rethinking Marxism* 19, 1 (2006): 46–58.

Žižek, Slavoj. "The Need to Traverse the Fantasy." *In These Times* (December 28, 2015). http://inthesetimes.com/article/18722/Slavoj-Zizek-on-Syria-refugees-Eurocentrism-Western-Values-Lacan-Islam.

Žižek, Slavoj. "Neighbors and Other Monsters." In *The Neighbor: Three Inquiries in Political Theology.* Ed. Slavoj Žižek, Eric L. Santner, and Kenneth Reinhard. Chicago: University of Chicago Press, 2006: 134–90.

Žižek, Slavoj. "Nobody Has to be Vile." *London Review of Books* 28, 7 (April 6, 2006). https://www.lrb.co.uk/v28/n07/slavoj-zizek/nobody-has-to-be-vile.

Žižek, Slavoj. "The Non-Existence of Norway." *London Review of Books* (September 9, 2015). https://www.lrb.co.uk/2015/09/09/slavoj-zizek/the-non-existence-of-norway.

Žižek, Slavoj. "Occupy Wall Street: What Is to be Done Next?" *Guardian* (April 24, 2012). https://www.theguardian.com/commentisfree/cifamerica/2012/apr/24/occupy-wall-street-what-is-to-be-done-next.

Žižek, Slavoj. "'OMG Some leftists Would Lynch Me for That'—Part I." *Doxa Journal* (November 16, 2017). http://doxajournal.ru/en/texts/zizek1.

Žižek, Slavoj. *On Belief*. New York: Routledge, 2001.

Žižek, Slavoj. *Organs without Bodies: On Deleuze and Consequences*. New York: Routledge, 2004.

Žižek, Slavoj. "The Palestinian Question: The Couple Symptom/Fetish." *Lacan.com* (2009). http://www.lacan.com/essays/?page_id=261.

Žižek, Slavoj. *The Parallax View*. Cambridge: MIT Press, 2006.

Žižek, Slavoj. "Philosophy, the 'Unknown Knowns' and the Public Use of Reason." *Topoi* 25, 1–2 (2006): 137–42.

Žižek, Slavoj. *The Plague of Fantasies*. New York: Verso, 1997.

Žižek, Slavoj. "'Pornography No Longer Has Any Charm'—Part II." *Doxa Journal* (January 19, 2018). http://doxajournal.ru/en/texts/zizek2.

Žižek, Slavoj. "Preface: Burning the Bridges." In *The Žižek Reader*. Ed. Elizabeth Wright and Edmond Wright. Oxford: Blackwell, 1999: vii–x.

Žižek, Slavoj. "Provocations: The 1968 Revolution and Our Own." *World Policy Journal* 35, 2 (2018): 124–29.

Žižek, Slavoj. *The Puppet and the Dwarf: The Perverse Core of Christianity*. Cambridge: MIT Press, 2003.

Žižek, Slavoj. "*Quasi Duo Fantasias*: A Straussian Reading of 'Black Panther.'" *Los Angeles Review of Books* (March 3, 2018). https://lareviewofbooks.org/article/quasi-duo-fantasias-straussian-reading-black-panther/#!

Žižek, Slavoj. "The Revolt of the Salaried Bourgeoisie." *London Review of Books* 34, 2 (January 26, 2012). https://www.lrb.co.uk/v34/n02/slavoj-zizek/the-revolt-of-the-salaried-bourgeoisie.

Žižek, Slavoj. *Revolution at the Gates: Selected Writings of Lenin from 1917*. New York: Verso, 2002.

Žižek, Slavoj. "Robespierre, or, the 'Divine Violence' of Terror." In Maximilien Robespierre, *Virtue and Terror*. Ed. Jean Ducange. Trans. John Howe. New York: Verso, 2007: vii–xxxix.

Žižek, Slavoj. "The Seeds of Imagination." In Fredric Jameson, *An American Utopia: Dual Power and the Universal Army*. Ed. Slavoj Žižek. New York: Verso, 2016: 267–308.

Žižek, Slavoj. "Shoplifters of the World Unite." *London Review of Books* (August 19, 2011). https://www.lrb.co.uk/2011/08/19/slavoj-zizek/shoplifters-of-the-world-unite.

Žižek, Slavoj. "Slavoj Žižek: The End Times." *Huck Magazine* (May 18, 2011). https://www.huckmag.com/perspectives/opinion-perspectives/slavoj-zizek/.

Žižek, Slavoj. "The Spectre of Ideology." In *Mapping Ideology*. Ed. Slavoj Žižek. New York: Verso, 1994: 1–25.

Žižek, Slavoj. "The Subject Supposed to Loot and Rape: Reality and Fantasy in New Orleans." *In These Times* (October 20, 2005). http://inthesetimes.com/article/2361.

Žižek, Slavoj. *The Sublime Object of Ideology*. New York: Verso, 1991.

Žižek, Slavoj. *Tarrying with the Negative: Kant, Hegel, and the Critique of Ideology*. Durham: Duke University Press, 1993.

Žižek, Slavoj. *The Ticklish Subject: The Absent Center of Political Ontology*. New York: Verso, 1999.

Žižek, Slavoj. "Today's Anti-Fascist Movement Will Do Nothing to Get Rid of Right-Wing Populism—It's Just Panicky Posturing." *Independent* (December 7, 2017). https://www.independent.co.uk/voices/antifa-populism-white-nationalism-populism-brexit-donald-trump-alt-right-racism-a8097376.html.

Žižek, Slavoj. *Trouble in Paradise: From the End of History to the End of Capitalism*. Brooklyn: Melville House, 2014.

Žižek, Slavoj. *The Universal Exception*. New York: Bloomsbury, 2014.

Žižek, Slavoj. *Violence: Six Sideways Reflections*. New York: Picador, 2008.

Žižek, Slavoj. *The Void of Incontinence: Economico-Philosophical Spandrels*. Cambridge: MIT Press, 2017.

Žižek, Slavoj. *Welcome to the Desert of the Real! Five Essays on September 11 and Related Dates*. New York: Verso, 2002.

Žižek, Slavoj. "Welcome to the Desert of the Real." *Lacanian Ink* 2 (2002). http://www.lacan.com/desertsymf.htm.

Žižek, Slavoj. "What does a Jew Want? On the Film *Local Angel*." In *What Does a Jew Want?: On Binationalism and Other Specters*. New York: Columbia University Press, 2011: 173–78.

Žižek, Slavoj. "Whither Zionism?" In *These Times* (March 2, 2015). http://inthesetimes.com/article/17702/slavoj_zizek_zionism.

Žižek, Slavoj. "Woman Is One of the Names-of-the-Father, or How Not to Misread Lacan's Formulas of Sexuation." *Lacanian Ink* 10 (1995). http://www.lacan.com/zizwoman.htm.

Žižek, Slavoj. "The Yellow Vest Protesters Revolting Against Centrism Mean Well—But Their Left Wing Populism Won't Change French Politics." *Independent* (December 17, 2018). https://www.independent.co.uk/voices/yellow-vest-protests-france-paris-gilets-jaunes-macron-fuel-tax-minimum-wage-populism-a8686586.html.

Žižek, Slavoj and Glyn Daly. *Conversations with Žižek*. Cambridge: Polity, 2004.

Žižek, Slavoj, Eric L. Santner, and Kenneth Reinhard. "Preface, 2013." In *The Neighbor: Three Inquiries in Political Theology, with a New Preface*. Chicago: University of Chicago Press, 2013: vii–ix.

# INDEX